TAX
REVOLT
1980

TAX REVOLT 1980

A How-To Guide

by Sheldon D. Engelmayer
and Robert J. Wagman

ARLINGTON HOUSE/PUBLISHERS
333 Post Road West, Westport, CT 06880

To Carol Ann—for her love
To Lisa—for then, for now, forever

Copyright © 1978 and 1980 by Multi-Media Enterprises, Ltd.

All rights reserved. No portion of this book may be reproduced
without permission from the publisher except by a reviewer who may
quote brief passages in connection with a review.

Manufactured in the United States of America

A different version of this book was published in 1978 by Dale
Books under the title *The Taxpayer's Guide to Effective Tax Revolt*

Library of Congress Cataloging in Publication Data

Engelmayer, Sheldon D
  Tax revolt 1980.

  Edition for 1978 published under title: The taxpayer's guide to
effective tax revolt.
    1. Taxation—United States. 2. Local Taxation—
United States. 3. Taxation, State. I. Wagman,
Robert J., joint author. II. Title.
HJ2381.E53 1980   336.2'05'0973   80-13535
ISBN 0-87000-469-7

Manufactured in the United States of America

9 8 7 6 5 4 3 2 1

CONTENTS

CONTENTS

ACKNOWLEDGMENTS

THE AUTHORS wish to thank the following people, without whom this book would not have been possible:

Jameson Campaigne and Lewis Uhler of the NTLC, and William Rickenbacker formerly of the NTLC, for rallying to our support and barraging us with helpful information.

Peggy Glance, for her work on the Proposition 13 chapter.

Alan Tigay, for his work on the Michigan chapter.

Yvonne Chicone of the ACU, for her just-in-the-nick-of-time research.

Ted Maass, for his patience, and Lucianne Goldberg, for her faith in us.

Karl Pflock for putting up with us, and Arlington House for putting the book out.

And finally, Vickie Bezanilla and Grover Norquist, both formerly of the NTU, for their many hours of work and invaluable assistance.

INTRODUCTION

WE REALLY do not know how to break this to you, but more than half the people in the United States are being supported wholly or in great part by tax dollars, according to a study done by North American Newspaper Alliance, a supplementary news service which, until economics forced it to suspend operations on February 29, 1980, spent a great deal of time over the last few years exposing wasteful government spending programs and misleading government statistics (which are used to spend even more of our hard-earned money).

The Census Bureau estimates that there currently are 218 million people in the United States. Using the most recent government figures (and conservative estimates where direct counts are not possible), 124 million people—56 percent of the population—are directly dependent upon tax dollars in one form or another for at least a great part of their income. This 124 million includes those who work for all levels of government and their dependents, those in the armed forces and their dependents, and those receiving various direct cash government aid payments and their dependents.

However, it does not include the millions who receive so-called in-kind payments (i.e., food stamps, Medicare, Medicaid, etc.). It also does not include the estimated 8 million workers whose jobs depend upon government contracts and their dependents; nor does it take into account those people whose livelihoods are based on government aid programs and their dependents (i.e., physicians for whom Medicare reimbursements are the primary source of income).

The largest portion of this tax-supported population consists of those receiving direct cash government aid or retirement benefits. These include those retirees receiving Social Security payments or payments from other tax-supported retirement systems—such as for the military, civil service or state and local systems, including those for teachers, widows and dependents receiving survivor benefits. These persons number over 30.3 million; perhaps another 5 million persons are their dependents.

Another group in the direct-payment category is the disabled, including the blind. This group numbers 9 million, with another 1.6 million as dependents. Closing out this category are those on public assistance programs of one form or another. This includes Aid to Families with Dependent Children and unemployment benefits, among others. This group numbers 26 million.

While it is easy to determine the number of persons on government payrolls or those receiving various kinds of tax-supported aid, it is much more difficult to determine the total number of persons directly dependent upon that aid. With the assistance of Census Bureau experts, NANA sought to make such a determination. In all cases, the estimates were conservative, census officials noted. And, while many persons are receiving aid, in some cases either the aid is not sufficient to provide total support or the recipient is not totally dependent upon that aid for his or her support.

Some sources NANA contacted argued that programs such as Social Security are not payments from tax dollars but insurance programs. But it is clear from the difficulties that the Social Security system is suffering that it is supported by the monthly amounts withheld from paychecks and from the employers' matching shares. Tax dollars are tax dollars by whatever name. And up to three times as much money will be coming out of our paychecks next year to help keep Social Security afloat.

The most clearly supported by tax dollars are those on government payrolls. According to the Department of Labor, there are currently more than 15 million government workers at all levels. By a conservative estimate, there are another 32.14 million people dependent upon those 15.2 million paychecks. And there are about 2.1 million military personnel on active duty. Again using conservative estimates, another 3 million are dependent upon those paychecks.

It must be noted, of course, that persons on the government payroll also pay taxes. Which means, in part, that they are paying taxes with tax money. But the point we are trying to make here is that our tax money is supporting more than half of the people in the United States—and that is a heck of a load for us to be carrying on our shoulders.

How did this all come about? Simply because we were not paying close attention to what the people we elected were doing with our money. And we never gave any consideration to what big-budget government programs, such as welfare or Social Security, actually meant to our pocketbooks. We stuck our heads in the sand and believed that it was the government that was paying for all this, completely oblivious to the fact that the only way government can pay for anything is by making us pay the government.

Sure, there is a great deal of good that government does. But there is also a great deal of harm. For example, a good argument can be made that those expensive transfer payments which are costing us a bundle are actually providing people with reasons *not* to work, but to sit home and live off of our money.

What good is a government program that rewards people for not working, and punishes those that do by ever-increasing taxes?

In 1968, taxes represented an amount equal to 18.5 percent of the Gross National Product. Today, that percentage has climbed above 20 percent. During that same period, the total average federal tax load on a middle-class family has gone up 110 percent.

By 1978, the average U.S. taxpayer paid $2,686 annually in taxes to government at all levels. This broke down to $1,754 to the federal government, $564 to state government and $368 to local units.

In fact, during the five years from 1973 to 1978, as inflation has pushed up every cost in sight, taxes led the parade. That's right—not food, not clothing, not shelter. Taxes! During those five years taxes jumped 83 percent. Fully one-third of the additional outlay required by the average family is made up in taxes.

The chart below graphically shows this. It represents an average family with a single wage earner:

	1973	1978
Income:	$18,201	$27,420
Expenses:		
Food	22.1%	21.2%
Clothing	8.0	6.4
Shelter	24.1	23.1
Taxes	20.5	24.9

The lion's share of income taxes is being paid by persons having incomes between $17,000 and $40,000. Once you pass that $17,000 barrier, you are in the top 50 percent of income earners in this country and *that top 50 percent pays fully 92 percent of all taxes,* according to recent studies by the Internal Revenue Service. (Many people with very large incomes pay less taxes than the rest of us, incidentally, because of the availability to them of shelters and loopholes).

A recent study by the Washington-based American Enterprise Institute, a conservatively oriented think tank, puts this frightening situation into better perspective. According to AEI's calculations, a family of four which made $8,500 in 1967 would now have to make $16,500 because of taxes and inflation just to have the same buying power. If that same family of four had earned $12,000 in 1967, it would today have to make $25,000 dollars just to keep pace.

Why? Because the tax rate for that 1967 $12,000 family has gone up 32 percent in the last ten years, from 13.6 percent to 16.8, while at the same time the effective tax rate for lower income groups has dropped (a family making

$4,500 in 1967 paid 8.3 percent in taxes; today, it would pay 6.4 percent).

State and local taxes also have risen precipitously. In the ten-year period, per capita state and local taxes increased 152 percent from an average of $290 a year to $730. In one year alone, 1976, state and local taxes amounted to a total of $156.8 billion—*up over 10 percent from the year before.*

According to a study by the Advisory Commission on Intergovernmental Relations, the average Californian who earned $22,000 in 1967 must now have an income of around $55,000 just to have kept pace with inflation. In 1967, he was paying effective state and local tax of 1.1 percent and federal tax of 20.4 percent. Today, he would be paying state and local taxes equal to 5.5 percent of his income and a federal tax of close to 22 percent.

And things are not going to get much better. A recent congressional study shows that just by the effect of inflation alone Americans paid $9 billion more in taxes in 1978, $11.5 billion more in 1979, and will pay $15 billion more in 1980, for a total of $35.5 billion in the last three years.

One of the results of this very rapid growth in recent years is that state treasuries are in many cases bursting at the seams. Many states raised tax rates during the recession of the early 1970s. When the recovery set in, they kept the high tax rates—or even raised them. Why? Because they suddenly found themselves taking in a lot more than they ever dreamed they could. It was easy money and they were not about to let go. This, naturally, make these states the ideal target of disgruntled taxpayers. Here is a list of those states with their 1978 budget surpluses (the figures are in millions of dollars unless otherwise noted):

Arizona	$ 5–30	New Hampshire	$ 1
Arkansas	37–40	New Jersey	147
California	5.2 (billion)	New Mexico	10
Colorado	60	New York	4
Connecticut	81	North Carolina	184
Delaware	14	North Dakota	130
Florida	175	Ohio	79
Illinois	30	Oklahoma	35
Indiana	100	Oregon	64
Iowa	100	Rhode Island	10
Kansas	142	Tennessee	61
Kentucky	65	Texas	3 (billion)
Louisiana	56	Utah	5
Maine	35	Vermont	7
Maryland	109	Virginia	56
Massachusetts	200	Washington	172
Mississippi	107	West Virginia	26

Missouri	100	Wisconsin	427
Montana	25	Wyoming	0.2
Nevada	63		

In very few of these cases are the surpluses earmarked for tax reduction. Rather, they are going to pay for expanded state programs.

As far as property taxes are concerned, over the ten-year period ending in 1976, they rose nationally an average of 111 percent. In total, they went up $266 for every man, woman and child in the United States. They hit taxpayers especially hard because they must be paid in a lump sum and there is no withholding.

Here are the property tax increases state by state (figures are actual dollars; figures in last column are in percent; Alaska has been excluded because the pipeline has invalidated these figures in the state):

	1966	1976	Increase
Alabama	$ 33	$ 57	73%
Arizona	138	282	104
Arkansas	49	101	106
California	198	415	110
Colorado	156	271	74
Connecticut	161	369	129
Delaware	65	130	100
Florida	98	191	95
Georgia	62	178	187
Hawaii	79	174	120
Idaho	113	190	68
Illinois	150	284	89
Indiana	140	226	61
Iowa	163	278	71
Kansas	148	274	85
Kentucky	52	105	102
Louisiana	53	90	70
Maine	125	297	138
Maryland	121	239	98
Massachusetts	190	431	127
Michigan	135	324	140
Minnesota	165	254	54
Mississippi	50	110	120
Missouri	97	195	101
Montana	162	350	116

Nebraska	178	319	79
Nevada	137	272	99
New Hampshire	152	348	129
New Jersey	186	446	140
New Mexico	60	103	72
New York	167	412	147
North Carolina	54	130	141
North Dakota	130	212	63
Ohio	126	224	78
Oklahoma	78	124	59
Oregon	142	333	135
Pennsylvania	88	176	100
Rhode Island	128	294	130
South Carolina	40	116	190
South Dakota	153	288	88
Tennessee	57	129	126
Texas	100	213	113
Utah	117	172	47
Vermont	116	308	166
Virginia	75	173	131
Washington	104	236	127
West Virginia	55	106	93
Wisconsin	153	289	89
Wyoming	170	352	107
District of Columbia	109	210	93

Is it any wonder, then, that the tax revolt hit with a vengeance in 1978? And the results so far have not been insignificant. According to a recent survey done by the National Conference of State Legislatures, many states reduced taxes in some form in 1979. Some of these reductions were brought about by direct voter mandate, others by pressure put on state legislatures. Still others, more token in nature, were initiated by the legislatures themselves in hopes of forestalling direct voter action.

The actions ranged from across-the-board property and income tax reductions, to state spending limitations, to the removal of certain items from either sales or property taxes (food and drugs in Nevada, sugar beet refining machinery in North Dakota, etc).

Specifically, according to the survey: 22 states reduced property taxes (some of the "cuts," however, amount only to small amounts of relief for specific groups such as the poor or elderly); 15 states either reduced sales taxes or exempted certain items from the sales tax; 18 states effectively reduced state income taxes either by an across-the-board reduction or an increase in the number or amount of deductions; 8 states introduced spending limitations that will result in lower future tax needs; and 12 other states reduced or eliminated other taxes or fees of various kinds.

Some states reduced taxes in several areas. The state-by-state breakdown of 1979 tax reductions follows:

Property Tax Cuts: Arkansas, Florida, Idaho, Iowa, Kansas, Kentucky, Maryland, Massachusetts, Minnesota, Missouri, Montana, Nevada, New Mexico, North Dakota, Ohio, Oregon, South Dakota, Tennessee, Utah, Washington, Wisconsin and Wyoming.

Sales Tax Reductions: Kansas, Kentucky, Maine, Maryland, Michigan, Minnesota, Mississippi, Nevada, New York, South Dakota, Tennessee, Virginia, Washington, West Virginia and Wisconsin.

Income Tax Reductions: Arizona, Colorado, Delaware, Indiana, Iowa, Kansas, Minnesota, Mississippi, Montana, New Mexico, New York, North Carolina, Oklahoma, Oregon, Rhode Island, Vermont, Virginia and Wisconsin.

Spending Limitations: Florida, Massachusetts, Montana, Nebraska, Oregon, Rhode Island, South Carolina and Utah.

Even with the tax cuts listed above, when all tax collections for 1979 are added up the total take in the 50 states will be about $1 billion higher than in 1978—and in 1978 they in turn were $1.3 billion higher than in 1977.

This is leading taxpayers in many states to demand that their state legislatures get on the tax revolt bandwagon. They believe that lower taxes do not mean a poorer standard of living for their states.

In this they are armed with a number of new studies. Typical is one by economists Robert Genetski and Young Chin of Chicago's Harris Bank, which shows that the rate of economic growth in states is inversely proportional to tax burden. Genetski and Chin examined all 50 states and found that those with the lowest tax burdens had the highest rates of economic growth. At the same time, in those states (such as New York) where the tax burden continues to grow there has been an actual decline in economic expansion.

So taxpayers are now starting to clamor for tax reductions as a way to actually stimulate new economic growth.

That is what this book is about—the tax revolt and how you can join in and do something about this drain on your pocketbook. We have attempted to keep the book as simple as possible and yet as complete as possible. The first section takes you on a step-by-step approach to a tax revolt campaign. The second section discusses the various kinds of tax revolts and then offers case studies of the various types, some successful, some not.

Following that is a section on what can be done on the federal level— because, when you come right down to it, whatever you save on the state and local level means added income that will be taxed on the federal level. And by far the biggest tax bite you face is the federal bite.

Finally, we discuss additional things you must know to stage an effective tax revolt and offer a brief look at the many national tax organizations that stand ready to help you in your fight. There is also an appendix section that gives you examples of various things discussed in the book itself. These could prove invaluable to you in your tax revolt.

One last word. We briefly discuss tax tradeoffs in this book, meaning what you will not be getting once you have cut down your "giving." But although our discussion is brief, the issue itself is anything but simple. Whatever tax revolt you choose to conduct, you must take into consideration these tradeoffs. If you do not, and those tradeoffs can be made to appear to the public as threats against it, then you will lose—no matter how good a campaign you conduct and how much money you spend.

Good luck.

SHELDON D. ENGELMAYER
ROBERT J. WAGMAN

New York
December 1979

HOW TO STAGE AN EFFECTIVE TAX REVOLT

CHAPTER 1.

TEN STEPS TO EFFECTIVE TAX REVOLT

A LL RIGHT. You have had it up to here with taxes and you want to join the tax revolt. You are sick and tired of spending nearly five months of every year just to pay off your various tax bills—especially when you discover that you are getting less and less in return for paying more and more with every passing year.

So what do you do first?

Take a deep breath, sit back and give some serious thought to the whole situation and what you want to do about it. For, to be brutally frank, despite recent publicity to the contrary, things are not as easy as saying, "Okay, gang, let's march on the capital and get those taxes cut."

Unfortunately, you can end up doing yourself more harm than good, waste a lot of people's valuable time and wind up accomplishing nothing. To begin with, your anger might be misdirected. Or your solution might result in higher taxes somewhere else. Or, worse still, you might know that you are angry but not know at what you are angry.

Consider this. When the people of the state of California, by an almost two-to-one margin, voted for a 57 percent, $7 billion cut in state property taxes, they cheered at the windfall that was now theirs.

But they were wrong. They indeed will pay less property tax, but they are going to have to pay more federal and state income taxes as a result. In fact, it is estimated that Californians will end up having to pay the federal government an additional $2.3 billion in income taxes as a result of the lower property taxes. And the state will most likely wind up with an additional $300 million in state income taxes.

That's not all. According to analysts for the state legislature, the $7 billion windfall to California homeowners will probably be a lot closer to $2.3 billion. The rest of the money to be saved belongs to the owners of rental property, the state's utilities and railroads and giant companies like Standard Oil Company of California and Lockheed Aircraft.

Quite obviously, "Prop 13" made a whole lot of noise—important noise, to be sure—but it did not really do much for the overburdened taxpayer. This does not mean that California's voters should not have approved the property tax cut, but it does illustrate the need to establish what it is you are revolting against, what results you expect to achieve and what are the best means to achieve these results.

Which brings us to—

STEP 1: LAYING THE GROUNDWORK

In Section II of this book, you will find a discussion of various types of taxes, including income, property, sales, school and even bond issues, since someone has to pay the interest and that someone is always you. Acquaint yourself with these taxes and what the purpose of each is.

After you have done that, sit down and put together a list of every tax you must pay. Then try to find out what percentage of each dollar in taxes you pay goes to each tax. Next, find out what each tax is used for. Also try to determine to whom you are paying each tax. Merely because the local tax assessor collects a tax does not mean that it is a local one. Water-use taxes, for example, might be collected at a local level but are actually levied by the state, with local tax officials serving as collecting agents only. Of course the opposite may be true: just because the state is collecting a tax, it may be levied by the county or by a local taxing body such as a school district or a water district. Don't be afraid to ask your tax department or local legislator for the information. They are working for you, after all. And don't be afraid to hound them until you get the information, either.

Now take all that information, analyze it and—

STEP 2: TALK TO YOUR FRIENDS

Let's face it—tax revolt is not a one-man show. If you have dreams of becoming another Howard Jarvis, just remember that Howard Jarvis alone did not make "Prop 13" a winner. For one thing, there was Paul Gann, the other man whose name is on "Prop 13" (it is known as the Jarvis-Gann amendment, after all). Then there are all those people who day after day, week after week, month after month, spent their spare time getting signatures on petitions, running off literature, handing out flyers, knocking on doors, planning strategy and bringing out the vote on election day.

So talk to a few of your friends. Go over the information you have gathered and ask them to join you in your revolt. As soon as you have enlisted the aid of at least four good people, you are ready for—

STEP 3: CHOOSING A TENTATIVE TARGET

Using the information you have gathered, discuss the various taxes with the group and tentatively decide which one you are going to go after. In doing so, keep the following in mind:

—Do you want to get rid of the whole tax, or only a part of it (like "Prop 13")? If only a part, how much do you want to cut off?

—What are the ramifications, if any? (See our comments on tax tradeoffs in Chapter 18.)

—Are you sure the public will support you? It is really just a waste of time if you choose as your target a tax which people do not mind paying or do not realize they are paying and, therefore, cannot get overly excited about. For example, Jarvis has figured out that there are as many as 116 taxes levied on a single loaf of bread. Can you really see yourself leading a campaign to "Stamp Out the 116 Bread Taxes!"—even if you could figure out what these are?

—Are there any other tax revolts brewing in your community, and what are the targets of those revolts? This is extremely important. If there are other revolts brewing whose targets are not the same as yours, then all the revolts are doomed to failure because you will be splitting votes and dividing energies. Discuss the other revolts among yourselves and decide whether to join in or whether to get the other revolters to see things your way. But do one or the other!

—Wouldn't you rather go fishing? Don't laugh, please, because this is a serious question. Once you start the tax revolt, you cannot back out until the last vote is counted—*and you have won.* Giving up in midstream or after one or two (or three or four) defeats is going to be a clear signal to the powers that be that your community really does not mind working from January through May just to pay its taxes. If that happens, then get ready to work through June or July, because the raid on your salary check will only get worse after that.

Just remember this: it took Howard Jarvis sixteen long years and any number of defeats to become an "overnight hero" on the morning of June 7, 1978. Either you are in the tax revolt for the distance, or stay out of it and let someone else carry the ball.

Before we go on to the next step, we would like to make one more important point. Once you have assembled your little group, which will become the nerve center of your tax revolt, please do not start by trying to decide who the chairperson will be. This is no time for democracy in the living room. You are literally in the fight of your life and the last thing you need is to be divided by something as ridiculous as who should be the leader of the group.

Quite obviously, it was your initiative that brought the group together, your research that assembled the necessary data and your idea to begin with. So you take command, at least until after the first campaign. Then you can hold elections.

There are now five of you and together you have chosen a target. Obviously, then, the next step must be deciding what to do about it, right?

Wrong!

If you choose a course of action at this stage of the game, rest assured that you are blowing yourself out of the water before you have even built the life raft.

Why? Well, to begin with, you may not have chosen the right target. This is no reflection on you and your friends, but the fact is that the target you have chosen may not be the one that will win you the most support. But it could be the one that will win you the most enemies. That is why it is a "tentative" target at this stage.

Don't delude yourself into believing that everybody wants to see spending limitations, tax cuts or balanced budgets. There really are people out there who are against such unheard-of things and they are going to fight you with every weapon at their command. And, believe us, those weapons can be considerable.

Who are these weirdos who want you to keep paying through the nose, you wonder? Bureaucrats, public employee unions, education associations and teacher's unions, welfare rights groups and anyone else who gets a piece of the pie you bake for the government between New Year's Day and Memorial Day.

They have been living off of your money for a long time now and they are not yet ready to concede that you may have a better use for your money than they have. They are entrenched, they are powerful, they are well organized and well financed—and they are going to do their level best to beat you deep into the ground.

Now, wait a minute, you say. Don't these people pay taxes, too? Aren't they faced with the same problems as I am? Don't they have the same obligations? Why shouldn't they support us?

Well, sir or madam, wake up. You are trying to be overly logical (any degree of logic, no matter how simple, is being overly logical when it comes to this crowd). If such a thought ever entered their minds, do you really think there would be a need for a tax revolt? As we pointed out in our introduction, just look at what's been going on these last few years:

—Federal income taxes jumped 125 pecent between 1967 and 1977.

—State and local income taxes jumped an outrageous 405 percent in the same period.

—Social Security taxes rose 220 percent between 1967 and 1977—and just wait until next January, when the biggest single tax increase in history greets your pay check as the Social Security tax climbs 30 percent over the 1977 level.

—Property taxes zoomed upward between 1967 and 1977 by 132 percent.

—Sales taxes climbed 199 percent in this period.

Who do you think has been getting this money, anyway? They are not about to help you take it away from them now. And you should not help them by going out in full battle dress to fight against the wrong target.

Another reason not to decide on a solution just yet is that you may choose the wrong solution, one that your opponents will be able to pick apart so badly that you may wish you had gone fishing after all.

If choosing a solution is not the next step, maybe organizing is? Organizing what? You are still uncertain of your target, you do not have any solution. How long can you hold on to people's interest if you yourself don't know yet what's happening?

Take it slow and easy. Things are going to get rough enough as time goes on as your campaign builds momentum. And by that time, you and your group are going to have to be experts. And that is—

STEP 4: SETTING UP THE CRUCIAL COMMITTEES

There are five committees that you must have if your group is to function efficiently:

1. Finance. As we said a while ago, the opposition is probably well heeled and it may be prepared to pour a lot of money into defeating any action you take. So you are going to have to spend as much as possible in an effort to win. You are also going to need money with which to operate. If you do not think you can get that kind of money, forget the whole thing right now. You are lost before you start.

If you do think you can get the money, then appoint one of your number, preferably someone who has had experience raising funds, the finance director. Later on in this section, we will offer some tips on how to raise the money.

2. Research. The only way to win is to know what you are talking about. And the only way you are going to know what you are talking about is by diligent, cumbersome and absolutely essential research. You personally started the research process in Step 1. Now appoint someone to head the research committee and have that person start digging for the answers to the following:

    a. the real personal income in your state
    b. what percent of this income goes to pay for federal, state and local taxes
    c. the growth of state and local expenditures over a given period (five, ten, or twenty years should do)
    d. the growth of the percentage of personal income taken in taxes during the period chosen
    e. the percentage growth of all levels of taxation during this period
    f. a cost-of-living analysis for this period

g. the growth of the number of state programs and agencies during this period

h. the growth in the cost of these programs and agencies

i. the overall growth of the government workforce during this period

j. the growth of the payroll costs of all levels of government during this period

k. the growth of fringe benefits to public employees during this period

l. the amount of state and local debt, *and the amount of interest paid on that debt*

m. the growth of that debt *and interest* over the chosen period

n. the number and size of state and local taxes other than income taxes

o. the current size of social welfare programs at the state and local levels and the growth of those programs over the chosen period

p. the amount of per capita taxes paid and the estimated state and local taxes paid by an average family of four

q. the average property tax in your state and local area

r. a breakdown of state expenditures, department by department

s. the amount of capital construction undertaken by your state and local government, and the exact nature of the projects undertaken

t. a comparison between the estimated cost of each project when first proposed and the final, actual cost

u. the method used in floating state and local bond issues and the amount of bond indebtedness outstanding

v. a compilation of the tax voting record of individual state and local legislators

w. a list of all influential individuals and groups in your community (and state, if this is a statewide campaign), with addresses and, whenever possible, phone numbers

x. registered voter lists for all parties and independents in your campaign area (at least three copies)

y. a community services survey (We'll discuss this in Section III.)

z. anything else you think you ought to know

3. Publicity. The very last thing you want to do is run a secret campaign. Later on in this section we offer some guidance on the ways and means of publicity. The best kind of person for this task is someone who has had some journalism, advertising or public relations experience. And be prepared to hire some professional help too. You are going to need it.

4. Membership. Whoever heads this committee is not going to have much to do for a while, but he or she should start plotting a membership drive and should assist in the specific recruitment mentioned below.

5. Legal. Why a legal committee? For a number of very good reasons which will be discussed on the next few pages. Quite obviously, the best person to head this committee is a lawyer.

Now that you have appointed your committee directors, all of you must get out and recruit some other people to staff the committees. Five good, hard-working people per committee should be enough. Together with the five of you, who will now function as an executive committee, that will mean your organization has already grown to thirty people—and you haven't even started your membership drive! If you keep this up, and if your five committees do good jobs with their initial tasks, just think how impressive, knowledgeable and professional your tax revolt is going to look by the time you do start signing up members and soliciting contributors.

One last thing. Before the meeting breaks up, choose a name for your group and a mailing address and be sure to let the local post office know about it. As soon as possible, order some telephones, too.

Now, back to the question: Why a legal committee? Why must it be set up immediately and why must it begin functioning just as fast?

There are several very good reasons for this.

Let's face it. You are probably new to the political game. You do not know the ropes as well as the opposition does and now is not the time for trial-and-error tactics. Once you actually get started on promoting your solution to the targeted tax, you are going to have to be legally letter-perfect and, if your solution involves voter approval, you are going to have to know the ins and outs of your state or local election laws.

Because the other side is just waiting to rip you apart—one way or another.

That's why you need a legal committee, and that's why, if at all possible, you should get a lawyer to head it and other lawyers or paralegals to staff it.

As soon as the committee is formed, it should start with the following tasks:

1. Preparing Legal Guidelines. The first thing that must be determined is the manner by which your geographical campaign area allows for citizen input. Yours may be a state which allows voter initiatives, referendums or both. Or quite possibly your state has a completely different system. Then again, yours may be a lobbying effort. Since your whole campaign is going to be based on what you are able to do, you are going to need this information up front. (There is a discussion of the various methods in Section II.)

Once the means have been determined, the legal committee must write up easy-to-understand guidelines based on the particular law or laws your campaign falls under.

Election law, for example, varies from state to state and locality to locality. But the basics of what that law has to say are the same. It will tell you the only proper way to prepare your petitions (in some areas, it will even insist on a certain color paper). It will tell you the size of each petition, how many signatures to a page, what other information besides signatures are required for each person signing, who may sign, who may collect the signatures, how and when the signatures may be collected, when the signatures must be filed with the proper governmental authority and how to file those signatures (how they should be bound, numbered, etc.). It will also describe the manner in which the petition must be worded (although, obviously, it will leave up to you the task of wording the special amendment).

Sure, this sounds like a whole lot of nonsensical bureaucratic requirements to have to meet—but do not for one moment believe that just because 100,000 people (or whatever number) signed your petition, anyone will be obligated to take it seriously. It does not work that way.

We have seen too many instances where even carefully prepared political petitions have been tossed out on the most minor and absurd technicalities. In New York City, for example, the Board of Elections has ruled signatures on petitions invalid because the signers put their titles before their names ("There is no one registered by the name of 'Dr.' Harvey Healthful"), or because the signers did or did not use middle initials (having registered in the opposite way) or because they appreviated "street" or "avenue." We've seen Democratic candidates lose their chance to get on the ballot in New York City because their petitions were white (the law says they must be green), and Republicans suffer the same fate because they used green (instead of white).

It might sound stupid, dumb, ridiculous and absurd to you—and, in most cases, it probably is—but it is the law and you are just going to have to live with it. And make no mistake about it, the opposition is going to look for every infringement of the law in an effort to knock you out of the ring before the bell sounds for Round Two. If it can do it because people on your petitions live on Main St. instead of Main Street, it will do just that.

Lobbying, too, is usually covered by various laws. You may have to register your organization; in some cases, even certain individuals within your organization may have to be registered. You may be required to file periodic forms detailing your activities during a given period, detailed financial statements, lists of contributors, etc.

So have the legal committee draw up those easily understood guidelines. And, if you are headed for the ballot box, make sure those guidelines also include information on legal campaign procedure, poll-watching procedures, etc.

2. Preparing Legally Letter-Perfect Alternative Solutions. Before you and your four other committee directors tackle the problem of a solution to the targeted tax, have the legal committee explore various alternative solutions and how they should be handled under law.

A poorly worded or legally imperfect petition, referendum or initiative will be torn apart by the opposition line for line and word for word until there is nothing left of it and you will lose. Or, if you are as lucky as Howard Jarvis, you will win and then have to worry whether the courts will have enough guts to stick to the law despite "the will of the people" (you will be surprised to find that there are judges who, faced with possible loss of some of their perquisites, will be able to muster up significant courage to throw you and your victory out of court).

Jarvis's Proposition 13 may yet turn out to be a prime example of a legal nightmare come to life. According to the California state constitution, say the still very active opponents of Jarvis-Gann, an initiative may contain only one subject. "Prop 13," at least on its face, has two subjects, they say: the property tax cut and the requirement of a two-thirds vote in the state legislature for the passage of any new taxes. As if that were not bad enough, say these post-election opponents, Proposition 13 also rolls back state property taxes to their 1976 levels, except when the property is new or has changed ownership. This, they charge, violates the Fourteenth Amendment to the Constitution, which provides for "equal protection" under the law. There's more. According to "Prop 13," counties are to collect the new property tax and then distribute it "according to law"—but no such law exists. In fact, one of Governor Brown's legal aides told reporters, "I have identified sixteen provisions of the state constitution that are impossible to reconcile with Proposition 13."

The reason for this legal mess is that Howard Jarvis, folk hero though he may be, likes to be a one-man show, despite the citizen's army he needed to help him carry on his fight. He brags about the fact that he personally wrote every word of the eight paragraphs that may very well keep the California courts busy for a long time to come.

You cannot afford to make the same kinds of mistakes because you will not stand a chance on D-Day. Proposition 13 was headed for defeat at the polls because the opposition was having a field day with its imperfections. Then Los Angeles County tax assessor Alexander Pope, for political reasons, sent out the new tax assessments weeks earlier than was legally necessary. Some of those assessments were more than triple the previous tax and California newspapers went to town.

But you are not going to be so lucky. So you must make absolutely certain that whatever you and your organization propose will meet every legal test that can be thrown at it.

3. Preparing Fund-Raising Guidelines. Your state or local law may prescribe the proper means for raising funds. The legal committee must draw up easily understood guidelines based on these laws.

4. Setting Up a Legal Entity. Your state or local law may require that you register your organization with the proper governmental authority. Or it may require that you incorporate in order to raise funds (which is a good idea, in any case). This is another job for the legal committee.

Once the legal committee has set up its various alternative solutions, make certain that they are circulated to all the members of the executive committee at least a week in advance of the meeting you will call to make that decision.

It is to be hoped that the research committee will have come up with enough facts and figures by this time that this information can also be forwarded to the executive committee along with the legal committee's report. If research has not completed its initial work, then hold off until its report is ready. You are going to need all this information and everyone should be given enough time to digest it.

Whatever you do, do not start rushing things. Remember, the product of haste is mistake—and that is just what the opposition will be hoping for.

Once the reports from the legal and research committees have been completed and in the hands of the various executive committee members *for at least a week,* then you are ready for—

STEP 5: MAKING THE FINAL DECISIONS

Call a meeting of the executive committee. The purpose of this meeting is twofold:

1. To decide whether your original target was the right one. This is where you begin to use material from the research committee. Discuss it among yourselves, evaluate it, weigh the pros and cons and then take a vote on it. If there is still any doubt lingering about the target, ask the research director to gather whatever additional information may be required to remove that doubt. Do so *even if you have narrowly voted in favor of the target tax* (in other words, by a three-two vote). If there is no such doubt, then go on to the second part of the meeting.

One word of caution. You may be running the show, and we did say this is no time for democracy in the living room, but you are going to need everyone in that living room to be dedicated and committed to the fight ahead. You cannot afford to be heavy-handed and dictatorial by trying to force your own opinions on the rest of the executive committee. And you do not want to break up long-standing friendships, either. So, let everyone have his or her say; do not put anyone down, and give serious consideration to all objections.

2. To decide on a solution. Once you have chosen a target tax that you all can live with, it is time to choose the solution. If the target tax is the same one you already chose, then take up the legal committee's report. If not, then do not hesitate to send the legal committee back to the law books to come up with solutions to the new target. Do not start worrying about having wasted the committee's time with the first set of solutions. Believe us, it was a valuable learning experience. And remember to allow the executive committee members at least a week to digest the new legal committee report before the next meeting.

Now that the target tax and a solution have been chosen, ask the research director to identify the legislators who would most likely support your efforts. (We use the term *legislator* generically. It can refer to any lawmaker at any level of government, from freeholder, school board member of councilperson all the way up to a member of the House of Representatives or the Senate.) Make every effort to select several legislators, making certain that they represent more than one political party and more than one political philosophy. Try not to seek support from only Republicans or only Democrats, from only conservatives or only liberals. If you limit yourself to only one party or philosophy, you will be giving the opposition a valuable piece of ammunition to use against you. (Admittedly, most liberals are very liberal with your money and may not be too receptive to your revolt. But there are some liberals and many middle-of-the-roaders who will be glad to help. It is your job to seek them out.)

With your list of prospective legislative supporters in hand, proceed to—

STEP 6: GOING PUBLIC

There are two phases to this operation: (1) lining up your legislative support, and (2) letting the media know about it.

The first phase is of paramount importance. Getting two or three legislators on your side right at the beginning gives you a greater legitimacy. And if your solution is legislative rather than voter oriented, then you may be doomed without such support.

Ask the various legislators on your list for an appointment. Do not send more than two of you to each meeting. There may be safety in numbers, but you do not want to scare off prospective supporters. At each meeting, set forth your case, using the material provided by the research committee. Then explain the careful work that went into choosing the target and the solution. Finally, ask the legislator for suggestions and help.

Do not expect an answer at this meeting, and make certain that each legislator you meet with understands this. Tell each one that you are not interested in a pat on the back, a friendly handshake and a smile. Impress upon him or her the seriousness of your effort and the need for the full support he or she can give to that effort. Review his or her legislative record to show why you are asking for that support.

If the individual legislator then suggests that he or she will be glad to help you *if you agree to have your organization support his or her reelection bid,* say thanks but no thanks. You have more than enough trouble fighting for your solution without getting involved in partisan politics. And your opponents will jump all over you if you do, even though they *always* play partisan politics. Explain, also, that your organization is broad based, cutting across party and philosophical lines, and that *you do not want to turn off any of your members or workers by endorsing a candidate they may not approve.*

Then point out to the legislator the benefits of supporting your effort. Tell the legislator that, while your organization cannot endorse any candidate, that does not mean that a candidate who supports the organization gets nothing in return. The fact that the candidate or legislator is a part of your effort can be played up in his or her campaign literature and in a variety of ways.

Once you have won over two or three legislators, ask them if they will agree to attend a joint press conference with your organization. Then set up a mutually agreeable time.

Now the publicity committee comes into play. As you enter the second phase of Step 6, have that committee prepare a press kit which includes the following:

1. A press release on the formation of your group. This release should include the names of the executive committee members, a list of those legislators supporting you, your target tax and your solution. In the appendix section, we offer a model press release you may want to follow.

2. An announcement of your press conference. This should include the time and place, who will be attending (with the focus on the legislators), what will be discussed and the name of the publicity director (along with address and telephone number). There is a sample in the appendix.

3. Biographical sketches on executive committee members. These should not be more than one page in length for each member and should be limited to pertinent facts—birth date, marriage, education, employment, clubs, etc. A sample biography is included in the appendix. If possible, include photographs of each executive committee member.

Have the publicity committee send out copies of all these items to every newspaper (weekly, as well as daily), radio and television station covering your geographical campaign area. Copies to newspapers should go to the editor, managing editor and city editor; mailings to radio and television stations should go to the news director and the assignment desk.

Two days before the press conference, the publicity director should contact one person at each newspaper, radio and television station and ask whether anyone will be covering the press conference. The odds are that someone will be covering, but that is not the real reason for the phone call. The actual purpose is to establish contact with the media. So be very friendly and courteous. If someone does not want to speak to you because he or she is "on deadline," when the workload is the heaviest, ask when a good time to call would be and hang up. At no time should you be pushy. You do not want to get the media angry with you.

When the publicity director finally does get through to the proper person and it is established whether someone will be covering the press conference for that newspaper or broadcasting station, try to take it one step further. Ask the editor or news director if he or she could meet with representatives of your organization for an informal discussion of your goals. If such a meeting can be arranged, follow the discussion pattern used to woo the legislators.

Several days before the press conference, call your executive committee together and go into training. A press conference means people will be asking questions and expecting answers from you. Take all the research used to make your decision regarding the target tax and the solution, and learn it inside and out, backwards and forwards. Have each member of the executive committee become an expert in a given area of the research. Finally, have dry runs or rehearsals. Throw questions at each other; and make certain they are tough questions, too, because those are the kind the media will ask.

At the press conference itself, have the publicity director briefly introduce the various people gathered in front. They should include the legislators and the executive committee members and no one else! You should be introduced last.

After you are introduced, make a brief opening statement, no more than three minutes. Write it down beforehand, time it, and study it well. Do not attempt to memorize it, however; you are liable to forget parts of it when the cameras are rolling. Then invite the legislators to come forward and say a few words (do this in a mutually agreed-on sequence). Finally, open the floor to questions.

When the press conference is over, take another one of those long, deep breaths. You have just fired the first shot in your tax revolt—and there is no turning back.

One final word of advice about the press conference: resist all temptations to turn it into a political rally. Try to keep the various legislators' aides from handing out campaign literature, buttons, balloons, etc. And do not "pack" the house with friends who will be primed to cheer your every word and boo every mention of the hateful tax. Save that for your public rallies.

The press conference is over and, if handled right, you have gotten some very good—and very free—publicity. If you are lucky, your opposition has already begun to rant and rave about the maniacal course you have chosen, which means more free and not really negative publicity (although it sure sounds like it).

But you are still only a group of thirty people, and you are going to need a whole lot more. You also are going to need a lot of money (you have probably already spent a couple of hundred dollars), which leads us to—

STEP 7: GATHERING TROOPS AND CASH

There are two committees involved here: membership and finance. And they are going to need the help of the publicity committee, too.

But before they get started, your executive committee is going to have to make another all-important decision: *how much to charge for membership.*

That's right, dues. This fight is not a free one by any means, as we have already pointed out. It requires money and dues is one way of raising that money.

Before making that decision, however, some data needs to be collected:

—What are the advertising linage rates of every newspaper in your geographical campaign area, weeklies as well as dailies? The publicity director should handle this task. The advertising departments of each newspaper will be glad to supply him or her with that information. Rates might differ depending on the size of the ad that runs, the frequency, whether it is straight text or requires artwork, photographs, etc. Also, try to determine which section or page of the newspaper is best for your purposes. It is a question of where your audience is. You may be tempted to put the ad on page 3, but your audience spends less time on that page and more time doing the crossword puzzle on page 38.

—What will the cost be for radio and television advertising? In most cases, the amount varies depending on time of day, which program, etc. Also, stations tend to offer discounts of varying degrees depending on frequency of commercials aired, in much the same way as newspapers do. This information, which also should be obtained by the publicity director, can be gotten easily by contacting the various station advertising departments or their representative.

—When is the best time to advertise on television and radio? Which programs will bring the most audience attention at the lowest possible cost? This, too, is the task of the publicity director. He or she would be well advised to seek the help of a local advertising agency. You are going to need professional help anyway, to draw up the advertisements and commercial spots. Or ask station managers to the latest ratings sheets (yes, there are ratings for radio, too). Do not be afraid to ask; the stations want your money and they will be only too glad to cooperate.

When it is time to make a choice, do not necessarily go with a prime-time show. Here, too, you must consider who your audience is and try to determine which shows it is watching (that should be a part of the ratings, by the way;

if it is not, ask for a demographic breakdown). "60 Minutes," for example, may be doing very nicely in your area at 7 P.M. on Sunday night, but it is not attracting the people you want. They may be watching the lower-rated "Best of Groucho" reruns at 11:30 P.M. on Saturday night, so you would be getting more for your money with the lower-rated show. Or the hard rock stations may be raking in the radio ratings, but the people you want to reach are tuned in to the mellow sound.

You are probably going to be struggling for cash all the way up to the very last minute of your campaign (and very often beyond that point), so be careful in making decisions regarding the spending of whatever money you do have. If you can afford television and radio early on, fine; if you cannot, then save them for the final days.

—How much will an advertising agency cost? You are going to need professional help and now is the time to line it up.

—What will be the printing costs you will incur? This is another job for publicity. Contact a number of printers to determine what the rates would be for the printing up of petitions, circulars, brochures, posters, membership forms, etc. And try to get a printer to donate a portion of the printing needed. After all, he or she is paying taxes, too.

—What will be the mailing costs and telephone charges? Obviously, the people to talk to are at the post office and the telephone company.

—Are you going to have to pay any rent or utility bills? If so, how much do you estimate for each? Let finance handle this one.

—What other operating costs do you foresee and what is the estimate? Again, let finance come up with a figure.

Once all this information is in hand, let the publicity director prepare a report on advertising and promotion expenses, including a recommendation regarding which advertising agency to hire. With that in hand, let the finance director integrate the information with what he or she has come up with and prepare a proposed operating budget. That budget should be circulated among the various executive committee members *at least a week in advance* of the meeting at which the budget will be adopted and what to charge for dues decided. (All of this, by the way, can be done while the legal committee is doing its work, and the amount of dues can be decided upon at the same time you make final a target and choose a solution.)

After the budget has been decided upon, let the finance director solicit some contributions to help pay for initial printing and other needs. And do not be ashamed to have the rest of the executive committee help out. Raising money is not an easy task. (Reminder: there is a chapter on fund raising at the end of this section.)

Once the dues are decided—and whatever you do, do not make them so high that no one would join—let the publicity committee prepare some initial brochures or flyers and let membership draw up an appropriate form to go with this literature. Even before the literature is drawn up, however, and even before the membership forms are ready, you can start by collecting dues from the thirty original members and from anyone else who in the interim has asked to join.

Once the literature is ready, set the membership committee loose on the rest of the community.

The kind of literature you create will depend on the kind of campaign you are running, what your objectives are, etc. We offer several samples in the appendix section. You might be able to adapt those, or you may want to do your own thing. There is no way we can advise you on what is best for you. But there are a couple of points we can make:

1. Be as clear and concise as possible; no one likes to read long-winded campaign flyers, no matter what the campaign.

2. Try to be as visually appealing as possible in your literature; the more eye-catching a piece is, the more likely that it will be read.

3. Make certain that your case against the target tax is as graphically explained as possible and that your solution is also well explained; if a chart or a bar graph can be used, use one.

4. In early pieces, do not waste time by defending your position against what the opposition might say. Wait for the opposition to attack; do not help it by revealing what you think are the weak points in your arguments.

5. In later pieces, if you must address yourself to opposition arguments, go on the offensive; do not defend your side, attack theirs.

This last point needs some explaining. Naturally, you are going to be called upon to defend your position; that is to be expected. But there are ways of defending a position that appear to the general public as weakness and even wrong-mindedness on your part. That is especially true when your defense is merely an answer, no matter how strongly and brilliantly formed, to the charges that have been leveled against you or your solution.

Then there are ways of defending a position that makes the public think you know what you are talking about and the opposition does not.

Here is an example. You are trying to roll back a school-tax increase of, say, 2 percent. The local education association charges that such a rollback would force some schools to close, many teachers to be fired and classroom size to double. The quality of education, it says, will be diminished in your area. Local governmental authorities back up the claims.

The wrong way to answer this charge would be to merely negate what the education association says:

"There is absolutely no need for schools to close or teachers to be fired. That fact of the matter is that the 2 percent rollback will only amount to $100,000, and that could be made up by some much-needed economizing on the part of the school board itself."

True, that lays it on the line—but it does not do much to dispel the fear that the professional educators know better than you do what kind of money is needed to run the schools. Contrast that answer with this one:

"We expect the education association to come up with such nonsense. Look what they have to protect. In the last five years, the school tax has increased by 10 percent, but the teaching staff has increased by almost 30 percent. And what have we gotten for it? According to the latest statistics, our children are learning less while we keep paying more.

"There are 12 percent more functional illiterates graduating from our community high schools today than there were five years ago. We're not saying that; the state education department is.

"Fifteen percent fewer students graduating from our high schools are able to do the simplest arithmetic. Again, that is the state education department talking.

"There are 23 percent fewer scholarships awarded in our community, and college enrollment from our high schools has dropped by 8 percent in the last year alone.

"And all this with more teachers than five years ago—almost 30 percent more.

"What the education association is afraid of is that the rollback will force the school board to institute teacher accountability. That means that our teachers will be allowed to continue teaching for only as long as our children continue to learn.

"And that is what the teachers—with their two-month paid vacations in the summer and another month throughout the year, not to mention a generous pension system, health plan and a whole lot of other fringe benefits—do not want: *to be held accountable for what our children learn and do not learn.*

"As for the rollback, it will only amount to $100,000, and the school board can certainly find a few expensive and unnecessary extras to get rid of—like catered dinners after every weekly board meeting (they can 'brown bag' it like the rest of us do, or they can go home and eat); paid-for junkets to 'examine' school districts in warmer or more exotic climes; and that catered Christmas party they throw for their friends each year (not to mention the ever-growing school board staff).

"If the school board and the education association want more money from us, let them show us they deserve it—by seeing to it that our children learn for a change!"

We violated for own "be clear and concise" rule in presenting our answer, but only to prove a point: that in our answer, it is the education association and the school board that come up looking bad. They are the ones who must now defend their positions, and they will not be able to do so effectively because you have the goods on them.

Sure, the second answer says the same thing as the first answer when you get right down to it; that the school board can make up the lost income by trimming the fat. But look at the way it was presented: by showing what a crummy job was being done in educating your children; how the schools in your area were graduating students who are dumber and dumber with each passing year, while the educational establishment is growing fatter and fatter.

One word of warning: you can play with the facts, but do not make them up or misuse them in such an outrageous way that your whole campaign will be exposed. If you followed all the steps required in making a decision regarding a target tax, then you should be armed with enough real facts and figures to shoot holes in your opponents' arguments. *There is no need to rely on make believe.*

The finance committee is out collecting money; it will continue to do so until that money is no longer needed (and that could be well after your tax revolt has officially ended).

The publicity committee continues to crank out the necessary press releases, position papers and campaign literature, and works with the advertising agency. It will do so up until the very last minute of the campaign.

The membership committee, meanwhile, will keep on adding new members day by day. New members, after all, are votes you can count on (if the ballot box is where your solution lies) or bodies that legislators can count (if your solution is a lobbying effort). New members also mean more money to use in your campaign. And more workers, too.

The research committee will keep on digging up new facts to use in your campaign, and to help expose the opposition's arguments for what they are, from your organization's point of view.

And the legal committee will go right on working on all the little nuisances the opposition will throw at you (such as challenges to petition for referendums and initiatives on various grounds) while making certain that your campaign continues to function within the law.

So what's left to do?

A whole lot, believe us. There are petitions that need signatures, citizens who need to be canvassed and convinced, envelopes that need to be stuffed, literature that needs to be handed out, more legislators to see things your way, civic leaders to join the bandwagon, street-corner rallies to be held and telephone calls to be made.

All of that will require an army of volunteers and that army, if your membership drive is an effective one, is right at your fingertips. It is made up of all those people who put their cash where your mouth is and who thus have a vested interest in your effort. It is now time to call your first big meeting.

Before you do so, however, have your executive committee decide on the dates, times and places of *the first three meetings*. This is suggested by the National Taxpayer's Union and it makes a lot of sense. By the time your first membership meeting is called to order, you have already set up a well-oiled and efficient-looking organization. You know what you want and you know how to get it. You have already proven that yours is a serious effort backed by some very important people, including several lawmakers. Your opposition has probably already attacked you at least once, which means that it is at least somewhat worried that you might succeed.

So you do not want to blow this great image by standing in front of a lot of strangers, who have either given you their money or are considering it, and say, "Does anybody here have any idea when we should meet again. Is the 14th okay? Oh, sorry Harry. Forgot it was your bowling night. What about the 15th? No. Mabel already said she can't make it then because of an important business meeting. How about . . . ?"

On and on it will go, and out and out will go your much-needed citizen's army. That's why you should plan at least three dates in advance and select times and places for them. If at all possible, move the meeting places around, too. *Show the people out there that you are interested in holding meetings where it is convenient for them, not just for you.*

Now let the publicity committee send out a mailing to all present members and any prospective ones suggested by the membership committee. The two committees, obviously, should be working together on this.

Also, put up posters in various locations announcing the first meeting. If possible, buy some advertising space and radio and television commercials announcing the meeting. And ask the radio and television stations to include an announcement of the meeting as part of their "community bulletin board" or "calendar of events." Such announcements are part of a broadcaster's public service requirement, and therefore should be free.

Make some telephone calls to a few civic leaders and ask them to come to the meeting, too. You might offer two or three of the most important ones honorary cochairperson titles. That usually does the trick. (This is why we prefer to call the executive committee members "directors." You do not want too many "chairpersons" around.)

Also, make certain that a copy of the first meeting's agenda is included in all of the mailings, and on the flyers and posters. When the meeting is finally underway, stick to that agenda and do not let anyone (especially the opposition, which almost certainly will be there) succeed in turning it into a verbal free-for-all. Remember, you have gone to great lengths to put a professional, highly organized polish on your campaign and you do not want that image tarnished in any way. If you can do this, you will not only impress your supporters and would-be supporters, but you will scare the opposition. And then, maybe *it* will make the mistakes (but do not count on that; they have real professionals at their beck and call).

Three days before the meeting, have the publicity committee notify the media, but only if you are reasonably certain of a good turnout. If you are not reasonably certain, and you invite the media anyway, you are going to look very foolish in the morning. By the same token, if you are not certain of a reasonably good turnout and you do not invite the media, do not attempt to keep them out if they show up regardless. Put on your best smile and keep saying over and over again how you got more people than you ever expected.

The agenda for the first meeting should look something like this:

1. Introductory remarks
2. Introduction of officers, civic leaders and legislators
3. A brief discussion of why you chose your target tax and your solution, followed by a question-and-answer session
4. Brief speeches by the legislators
5. Announcement of the next two meetings

Keep the introductory remarks short and to the point. Thank the people for having come to the meeting, tell them that the fight is their fight and that you hope they will help out. Try to keep it all under five minutes.

Then introduce the officers, civic leaders and legislators. Do not make flowery introductions; they are boring to listen to and they do not impress anyone. Especially keep it simple when introducing the legislators. Waxing eloquent about them will only sound as if you are campaigning for them or supporting them, and this, remember, you do not want to do.

Next, call on the director of your legal committee to give a brief discussion on the planning that went into selecting a target tax and a solution, why it is important that you succeed in your tax revolt and how you intend to go about it. Setting a time limit on this is difficult, but he or she should try and keep it under ten minutes if at all possible (and it usually is). Don't let the question-and-answer session that follows run over fifteen minutes, either. People may start getting restless, and the opposition may be trying to question you out of existence.

Now call upon the legislators to say a few words. But make certain that they understand that it is only a few words. Let them know, with everyone listening, that the audience came to the meeting to show its support, not to listen to too many speeches. But do it in a nice way.

Finally, ask anyone who has not yet joined to fill out a membership form, thank everyone for coming, announce the time and place for the second meeting and send them home.

The purpose of the second meeting is to enlist more campaign workers. Divide the group up into five smaller ones, corresponding to your five committees. Invite all those in the audience who wish to help out in the campaign to see one of the five executive committee members, depending on just what kind of work each individual wants to do. Have the five executive committee members scattered around the room so that one group will not be stepping all over the toes of another.

But wait a minute, you say. We're missing a sixth committee—the campaign committee. Don't we need a campaign committee to run a campaign?

You are right, of course. Every campaign has to have a campaign committee and your campaign is no different. But you already have such a committee— the executive committee.

Think about it for a minute. Legal is handling the petitioning and will be handling the canvassing; finance is raising the money; publicity is preparing the literature, planning the rallies and generally doing its thing, as are membership and research. Why load up your campaign with a whole lot of extra committees (we can think of at least five more right off the bat) whose functions will only overlap those of the committees you already have? We are not trying to build an empire here; *we are trying to lower taxes through citizen action.*

So divide the second meeting up among the five committees; people who want to carry petitions should go to legal; if they want to make telephone calls or stuff envelopes, then they have their choice of publicity or membership; if they think they can raise money, finance is the right place; and if they know their way around a library, direct them to research.

Now, let each committee director take down the names, addresses and telephone numbers of the people who volunteer. Next to their names, have them list what job each individual would like to do and what times that person is available.

Allow enough time for everyone to sign up. That includes giving the people a chance to find out what work is available. Then, thank everyone for coming, thank them in advance for their help, announce the time and place of the third meeting and wish them all a good night. (The agenda for the third meeting is up to you, and it will depend on coming events in your campaign.)

If you have handled the meetings well, a good many of these people actually will show up to help when called. They might even bring along some friends.

There is one thing, however, that must be done within a day or two of that second meeting if you really want the best results (or any results at all): the follow-up. Make absolutely certain that each committee director contacts everyone who signed up for his or her committee as soon as possible to thank them and to try and set up a work schedule with them. There is a lot of hard work ahead and no more time to waste. You have gone public with your campaign and now that public is watching closely to see if you are really serious or just on an ego trip.

The opposition is watching, too. It may not have shown itself just yet, but it is there.

Your campaign is now in full gear. All that is left now is to work hard toward your objective, making certain that every committee is doing the job expected of it. And then there is D-Day (for decision), but that is the subject of Step 10. Right now, we are only concerned with—

STEP 8: THE CAMPAIGN

We have tried to keep this section as simple as possible while at the same time trying to be as complete as possible. It probably seems as though we have been leading you by the hand as we would a child. And we have been—because you are a child in the political wilderness in the sense that most likely you have never been involved in a real campaign effort before.

Naturally, it has all been leading up to this moment, when the campaign begins in earnest.

So this is one hell of a time to have to tell you that from here on in you are flying solo. Unfortunately, however, we must do so at this point. For every campaign will be different. It all depends on your objective, the kind of system under which you are operating (initiative, referendum, lobbying, etc.), how much money and how many people you have, the shape and substance of your opposition and the time you have to accomplish your goal. There is just no way to write guidelines to fit every situation and every need.

What we can do is provide you with some basic tips on running an effective campaign (Step 8), working through the final days (Step 9), and what to do on D-Day itself (Step 10). And in Section II, we provide you with some tax revolt case histories—some successful, some not; some that are nearing the end of the road and some that have been there before and are trying again.

But that is all we can do. After that, you are on your own. But do not start worrying, though; if you have a hard-working core of people dedicated to the cause, you should do quite well even without professional guidance. Just keep your mind open to suggestions and make all decisions methodically and with great care.

Almost every campaign is going to involve the gathering of signatures on petitions, which is a task for the legal committee to handle. (Note: Some of what follows may not apply to lobbying efforts; additional guidelines for such efforts can be found further on in this step)

The first thing to do is make absolutely certain those easy-to-read guidelines we discussed earlier really are easy to read—and understand. No legal gobbledygook allowed. The best way to insure this is to "test market" the guidelines. Let copies of the guidelines be distributed among the other executive committee members and a few friends and relatives. Let everyone study them and then state their opinions. If you find that some matters must be clarified or simplified, have the legal committee do that work.

One word of caution here. Do not insist that changes be made merely because one person said that a change is needed. Make changes only when a consensus is had on each change. And do not start worrying about T-crossings and I-dottings. The guidelines are not meant to win a Pulitzer prize for literature; they are meant to simplify complicated rules and regulations and to explain to people who may have never carried petitions before how it is done. If the guidelines meet those two objectives, they are perfect. *Only when they do not do so should changes be made.*

Here are some tips on collecting those signatures:

1. Remember those voter registration lists the research committee was assigned to get back in Step 4? Well, have research take those lists and break them down into geographical areas (such as election districts, wards, blocks, etc.). In most cases that should be easy, because the lists are already prepared that way. Now let the lists be turned over to the legal committee (with copies for the membership committee and the publicity committee).

2. About a week before you start petitioning, let legal call a meeting of all those people who are going to carry the petitions and divide them up among the various geographical areas. Then the teams should transfer each name on the list onto an individual index card, along with the address and, if you want, party affiliation. If the petitions have a legal purpose, such as putting a referendum on the ballot, make certain the name on the index card is written exactly as it appears on the voter registration list. If there are no abbreviations, do not abbreviate any part of the name.

3. The night before petitioning begins, let the group reassemble for final instructions. At that time, the head of the legal committee should hand out a schedule for each team to follow. That schedule should show when particular sectors of each team's petitioning area are to be completed. The reason for this is simple: If you tell someone a particular job must be finished by a certain date, then it is likely to be finished by that date or soon thereafter. If you just tell that person to do the job but do not set a deadline, then you are running the risk of not having that job done in time.

4. Do not set signature goals for each team, but do set them for the overall effort. If a team runs into particular trouble in its area, it will become disheartened, probably feel inadequate and quit if it cannot meet its quota. By the same token, you have a quota to fill. So the best thing to do when a team runs into trouble in one area is to work harder in more productive areas. As for your quota, that will depend on the reasons for collecting those signatures. If it is for a lobbying effort and you want the signatures as added pressure, set your goal at around a third of the registered voters in your

geographical campaign area. If it involves placing a referendum or initiative on the ballot, then triple the amount of signatures that are required by law. That way, even if the opposition succeeds in eliminating 50 to 60 percent of your signatures because of various nitpicking technicalities, you still will have more than enough signatures to qualify. (Then again, if the opposition can prove that a lesser amount of signatures, say 20 to 30 percent, were fraudulently obtained or are forgeries, all of your petitions will be invalidated; so be very careful.)

5. Let each team divide itself up into subteams with each subteam being given a particular sector to cover. During the daylight hours, it is all right for one person to cover a given area. Always send two people per area at night. And never send a man alone. This is not sexist; it is a fact that people will open their doors more readily for a woman than a man.

6. Each time a person is approached, try to be as brief as possible. Do not waste too much valuable time at every stop. If the person wants more information before signing, leave some literature and tell that person that someone else will contact him or her to see if any more information is needed. If the person is willing to give you his or her phone number, put that down on the index card. And make certain that you put a notation on the voter registration list that this is someone who must be contacted by publicity. Also make certain that publicity gets those names within twenty-four hours of the initial contact. Remember, half this game is trying to convince the public that you are a well-oiled operation and therefore are going to win. Everybody loves a winner. Try that person again a week later. If he or she still will not sign, cross that name off of the voter registration list and write "no" on the index card.

7. When a person signs the petition, indicate this on the index card with a "yes" and on the registration list with a checkmark. Make certain that membership and finance get the names of all people who signed within twenty-four hours. Those people should be contacted as soon as possible thereafter. People who sign your petition are prime candidates for membership and some may even be willing to donate some extra money to the cause. (We will explain more about the index cards later on.)

8. If a person refuses to sign the petition "because I never sign anything" but promises to support you nonetheless, indicate on the index card that this person is a "possible." Then cross the name off the registration list. Do not go back for that signature at a later date because the individual may feel harassed.

9. If a person refuses to sign the petition and shows hostility to the cause, cross that name off of the registration list and indicate on the index card that this person is a "no."

10. If the law permits it, place card tables at shopping centers and other

strategic locations so that signatures can be gathered on the street. And make certain that each team is notified—that day, if possible—who from their areas signed the street petitions. You do not want to ask people to sign something they have already signed. At best, it makes you look poorly organized; at worst, unethical.

11. If your petitions have a legal purpose, then the law will provide a starting date for the collection of petition signatures. Make certain that your teams start gathering petitions on that date, not a day later—and definitely not a day earlier. The latter is fraud; the former is wasted time. That same law will probably set a time for ending signature gathering and for filing. *Set your last day at least a week ahead of the date the law has set.* You are going to need that time to prepare those petitions properly for filing.

12. For those petitions with a legal purpose, once all the signatures are in, the legal committee has to go over each one very carefully. Does the name match up exactly as it appears on the registration list? Are the addresses listed properly next to each name (or below, if that is the way the petition was required by law to be designed)? Are the dates properly noted? (If the law specifies that the month must be spelled out and the year written in full, then only April 18, 1979, will do; not 4/18/79.) Are the dates in proper order? (If the 19th comes before the 18th on a particular sheet, you have a problem.) Do any dates signify signature gathering before the legal starting date? Do titles (such as "Dr.") appear before names? Is a name or address smudged? Did anyone sign the petition with a pen that skipped and then try to re-sign right over it? Whatever problem is found with a signature, that signature should be crossed off in the legally prescribed manner. Many localities, for example, require that a single line be placed from one end of the line to the other, right down the middle of the signature and address, and that the petition gatherer's initials be placed on one or both sides. Another thing to check for, if the law requires it, is whether the petition gatherer signed the bottom of each petition and filled in all other data required. Also, be certain that each petition gatherer was eligible to be one in the first place. Most, if not all, localities require registered voters only; some specify registered voters living in the area where the signatures were gathered. If any signatures were collected by someone not eligible to do so, throw those petitions away. *Do not have someone who did not collect those signatures sign them.* If the opposition finds out (and it often does), you will be charged with fraud.

13. After the petitions have been gone over in this manner, they must be bound according to the requirements of the law. If no such requirements exist and there is nothing in the law that prohibits it, bind the petitions anyway. It looks a whole lot neater. (If there are no such regulations and you are permitted to bind the petitions, try to do so by geographical area.)

14. If a date has been set by law for the filing of petitions, make certain that those petitions are filed on time and in the manner prescribed by law.

15. Make copies of each petition for those petitions with a legal purpose. These copies will come in handy when the opposition begins to challenge the signatures.

Do not think the opposition will not challenge those signatures. It will. It will also charge you with fraud and all sorts of nasty deeds. Do not worry, though. If you have done a thorough job and have not intentionally violated any law, your petitions are safe.

Before going on to other aspects of the campaign, we would like to add these two hints for petitions with a legal purpose:

1. Make certain that petition gatherers carry enough pens and that there is enough ink in them. Preferably, a new pen should be used each day and certainly when it looks like the one in use is drying out. Also, if possible, arm each petition gatherer (or each pair) with a clipboard to make it easier for people to sign.

2. In checking over the petitions before filing, look to see if any petitions appear to have been forged. The opposition does play dirty sometimes and it may send you some "volunteers" whose job it will be to deliberately create fraudulent petitions in an effort to invalidate all of the signatures collected. If you have the slightest suspicion about a particular petition, throw it out.

Now to the campaign itself. Remember those index cards? They tell you at a glance who signed the petition and is a "yes" (and thus is someone who will probably vote your way or be of some other service to you), who is a "possible" and who is a "no." Put each group of cards in separate shoeboxes or files.

Make certain that those people who signed the petitions are contacted again at least once before D-Day. The "possibles" should be contacted at least twice. If at any time a person shows hostility, put his or her card in the "no" box. If that person looks like a "yes" by the end of the second visit or phone call, put that card in the box with those who signed the petitions. If that person is still uncertain, leave the card in the "possible" box.

If you are planning on holding street rallies, here are some guidelines to follow:

1. If the law requires a permit, get a permit.

2. If the law requires a flag, get a flag. If it does not require a flag, get one anyway.

3. If the law permits bullhorns but not loudspeakers, do not use loudspeakers.

4. Never hold a street rally in a strictly residential neighborhood.

5. Do not hold any rallies too early in the morning or too late in the evening.

6. Make certain that enough people are on hand to distribute literature and membership applications.

7. Do not attempt to "pass the hat" at street rallies; it looks terrible.

Another good technique is the coffee klatch. Try to get as many of these informal living-room meetings as possible.

As we stated earlier, always stay on the offensive even when you are defending your position; but never misstate the facts.

Every time a prominent citizen or a legislator joins your ranks, let the media know about it.

Try not to have cars outfitted with loudspeakers roaming the streets blasting away with your message. A lot of people will tell you that this is the best way to get your message across to the most people at one time. Baloney! All you do is annoy people who are trying to have a quiet meal, read a newspaper, watch some television or hold a pleasant conversation. Or worse, that person may be trying to get some sleep (someone who works nights, for example). If you annoy people too much, they will remember your message on D-Day, but they will not support you. It is not worth alienating people.

Whatever you do, make certain that it is within the law. That segment of the opposition known as "the government" will be out to harass you into oblivion. Any time you break a local law, rest assured that a policeman will be right there to give you a summons. If a rally permit says the north side of the street between 3:00 P.M. and 3:30 P.M. on the 14th, do not be on the south side, do not stay later than 3:30 P.M. and make sure it *is* the 14th. If a particular size flag is required, do not have a smaller one (a bigger one is probably okay). Do not park on the wrong side of the street. Do not do anything that will give "them" a chance to harass you.

There are two further points that are so obvious that we hesitate to make them:

1. Make certain that all your petition gatherers, street campaigners, door-to-door canvassers and anyone else who comes into contact with the public is dressed neatly and makes a generally pleasant appearance (in other words, do not let anyone who looks like a slob go out and deal with the public).

2. Instruct these people never to argue with anyone, not to be abrasive or rude, especially if there is a crowd gathered around. You cannot afford to turn anyone off.

Well, that's it. You've come to the final days. And you are probably wondering why we spent so much time in this chapter on petition gathering and so little on the rest of the campaign. For one thing, you probably need those petitions if there is going to be a campaign at all; without them, you cannot qualify for the ballot, or you will have little with which to pressure legislators. And whether the ballot box is where you are headed or it is a lobbying effort, petitions are the best way to identify your supporters early on.

We would like to stress again that this chapter only contains general information and helpful hints regarding your campaign. You are the only one who can supply the specifics for your particular situation. If you can afford it, get some professional help. If you cannot, but you plan carefully and well, it still should be smooth sailing.

To those of you who are engaged in a lobbying effort only, many of the things we have discussed in this step will be of little use to you—coffee klatches, street rallies and all the other trappings of an election campaign. But fear not, for we have not forgotten you.

1. Once your petitions are completed and bound, deliver them in person to the legislator from each district where signatures were collected (which is why it is a good idea to separate them in this way). It is probably more effective to do this than to hand all the petitions to only one legislator. Getting petitions from the home district always sends chills up a legislator's spine.

2. Try to set up meetings with as many legislators as possible and send a two- or three-person delegation to each meeting. Certainly try and meet with every legislator whose voting record indicates possible support (gathering data on voting records was a task assigned to research).

3. Ask the people who signed your petitions to write letters to several legislators, including their own, urging the action you are seeking. Although form letters are okay, suggest that each individual compose his or her own letter. But make certain you supply them with sufficient data to do so intelligently.

4. Plan a mass rally at the front of the building where the legislators meet (city hall, school board headquarters, state capital, etc.). Be certain to secure the necessary permits.

5. Mount a door-to-door and/or a street-rally campaign in the home districts of those legislators who refuse to support you. Just campaign for your position and against the legislator's intransigence. If the legislator is involved in a reelection effort, avoid at all costs attempting to link yourself with his or her opponent. End the campaign in any district where the legislator decides to see things your way after all.

We are going to put this very bluntly: all the work you and your organization have done will have been totally wasted if you are ill prepared for the last week of your campaign. The months and months of planning, knocking on doors, telephone calls, signature gathering—all of it can be lost by poor planning in these last seven days.

In the following two steps, we will outline some of the things you must do in that final week. Much of what you must do, of course, depends entirely on your individual campaign. But what follows are the basics, thus, we come to —

STEP 9: PLANNING THE LAST WEEK OF THE CAMPAIGN

To begin with, this is not something you can put off until the last minute. Your battle plan must be structured and refined *at least two months in advance,* and possibly three. Every one of your key staff members and all of your executive committee members must know *in detail* what their tasks will be in this crucial period. What was true of the campaign itself is just as true here—you cannot afford to make any mistakes. The only difference from the rest of the campaign is that now you have no time to recover.

Sure, there are going to be a whole lot of things popping up that you have not been able to foresee. There is no way you can prepare for every contingency, but that does not mean you should not try to do so.

The best way to go about this is to have all of your executive committee members, after meeting with their staffs, prepare detailed reports on what they see as their role in the final week. Then, circulate those reports among the various executive committee members for comments, refinements, suggestions, etc.

Once that is done, call a meeting of the whole committee and carefully go over each assignment. Eliminate overlapping assignments (we do not want people stepping over each other, after all). Finally, draw up a game plan for that final week.

At the meeting, make certain that everyone spends as much time as possible considering various contingency situations and how they should be handled. For example, the opposition may get some friends in the legislature to offer an alternative program "in the coming weeks," but the election is next week, or the legislative proposal you have been lobbying for comes up for a vote next week. Obviously, this is a smokescreen intended to siphon off some of your support for the "more moderate and reasonable approach." Such a tactic could be devastating unless you are well prepared for it.

Do not make your final game plan at that meeting. Let the executive committee members have some reasonable time to think about it after the meeting, and to discuss it with their staffers. Let them devote still more thought to possible roadblocks and situations that can crop up. Once that is done, make the plan final and make certain that copies go to all executive committee members and their key staffers.

Warning: Do not leave this material lying around or give it to someone you are not sure of. The opposition could conceivably have placed spies in your operation and this kind of information is just what it needs to make a mess of your campaign at the last minute. We are not being paranoid about it; we are just giving you a basic fact of political life.

All of your key people should be well rehearsed in what they must do and what the other parts of your operation will be doing. Do not worry about boring them with the same thing over and over again. There is no better way of insuring a smooth-running campaign in those hectic final days than by going over the plan again and again.

What follows are some basic guidelines to be used in the campaign's final week, given on a committee-by-committee basis.

Membership. Just because the campaign is entering its final stage does not mean that there are no new workers to sign up. Remember, every new member means four very basic things to your campaign—a possible worker, needed money, a committed supporter and a person who might be able to bring in more members and win over more supporters.

Have the membership committee working full time on this task down to the very last minute. As often as possible throughout this week, make certain the names of new members, their addresses and telephone numbers are circulated among the other committees. Index cards on each new member should be filled out and filed in the "yes" box with the petition signer's name.

Finance. Here is another committee whose work never seems to end, and this one may have to keep functioning long after the campaign is over if you have unpaid bills. Whenever someone denotes money to the campaign, make certain that an index card is filled out on the individual and placed in the "yes" box (provided that person is eligible to vote, if your campaign is an electoral effort).

Research. Probably the only thing this committee will need to do in the last week is come up with facts to counter any last-minute effort on the part of the opposition to set up a smokescreen solution. Much of this work will probably have been completed long ago, and everyone should be well versed enough in the data to counter any such effort with ease and authority. If so, reassign most of the research committee staff to other areas of the campaign where they will be of more use.

This, incidentally, holds true in all other campaign areas. Do not keep people assigned to tasks that are no longer operative and do not assign more people to a task than are actually necessary. There are plenty of things these people can be doing that are more productive.

Publicity. Whatever type of advertising and broadcasting effort you have put on until now is nothing compared to the final days. People should not be able to open up any newspaper in your geographical campaign area in this final week without finding one or two stories about your effort. Nor should they go through an entire newspaper without finding one or two advertisements pushing your cause. The same holds true for television and radio news and their commercial time, if you can afford it.

Of course, you have control over the amount of advertising and commercials that will appear in the final week. But how, you ask, can you control the news?

You cannot. But you can stage media events designed to give you favorable coverage. This might include a mass rally held at a strategic area (such as the steps of the state capitol, if your fight is statewide), a symbolic burning of forms for the target tax, debates with opponents (the best kind—and the hardest to get—are "empty chair" debates, where your opponent does not show up although a spokesman for the opposition camp was invited; but do not attempt to rig this because it will only blow up in your face) and even a march on the opposition headquarters to let it know that you have just begun to fight.

Whatever media event is staged, however, make certain that it is well planned and the media is given enough advance warning to cover it properly. Do not decide on the spur of the moment to "do something" and expect the media to be there en masse.

Another important thing to do here is seek to impress upon the newspaper editors and their counterparts at the radio and television stations (news director, editorial director, station manager, editorial vice president, etc.) the need for your solution. Try to win them over as best you can. Meet with them as often as they will allow. If you do win their support, urge them to do editorials supporting the cause in the final days and, if possible, to assign some reporters to do feature stories on the battle, the problem or any other relevant topic.

Most important, however, is that you must use tact and care. Do not sound like you are trying to do their jobs for them. If they show a coolness to your effort, do not resort to threats. Do not ever threaten the media because it will come back to haunt you on D-Day.

As for advertising and commercials, we again urge you to let a professional ad agency handle these. But if you do go it alone, make certain that all have been carefully planned. Each should state a portion of your case as graphically as possible. Do not attempt to tell the whole story in a single advertisement or in a 30- or 60-second commercial. It cannot be done.

Also, try to write the copy for both the advertisements and the commercials so that they will cover some of those smokescreen efforts put on by the opposition. Very often, this material has to be readied and submitted well in advance, when your opposition has not even begun to use all of the tricks it has planned.

This is one of the reasons for the contingency plans—to have a better handle on what can be thrown at you in these final days. Naturally, you cannot assume a particular tactic will be used against you and thus write your copy to fit that tactic; you would end up looking silly if the tactic were not used. But you can drive home the point that the opposition has been around for a lot longer than your organization, and nothing is ever done to cut taxes, only to raise them. You can hit home how time and again the politicians tell us how much they hate to see us poor, overburdened taxpayers getting the shaft and how, if elected, they will help lighten the load—but never do. This is the kind of approach that could prove most effective against anything the opposition dreams up to throw at you. Above all, however, play up the fact that your solution won't create havoc by forcing school closings, layoffs, curtailment of essential services and all the other scare tactics so often used to kill a tax revolt.

About three weeks prior to the final week, have publicity and research get together and go over everything the opposition has said to that point, every alternative it has proposed and every charge it has leveled: Then let publicity draw up some new literature to be used in the final week. It should not be defensive. We must stress again that you should always be on the offense. But it should effectively counter the opposition arguments.

If you have something really "hot" to disclose that could turn voters to your side in droves, save it for the last day. Then have a press conference to reveal it and have flyers out on the streets all day long.

This kind of information does not include the fact that the head of the opposition has a mistress or some such foible that is really not anyone's business, since it would make you look like a gutter player and throw the sympathy votes to the other side.

But it does include whether the opposition leadership (particularly legislators) paid their fair share of taxes, if such could be determined; information regarding an upcoming but as yet undisclosed increase in the target tax (as in California's case, where it was learned that some property owners were about to get hit with a new tax bill three times the size of the last one); information regarding misuse of tax money; or information relating to a new massive "giveaway" of public funds that the taxpayers might not be in favor of but for which they will be forced to foot the bill anyway.

Also, make certain that publicity has at least two mailings during this final week, one at the beginning of it and the other in time for the last day.

Legal. This committee handled your petition gathering. Its staff was then used for the door-to-door canvassing and it has been serving as the nerve center of the day-to-day campaign, with very little legal work since the petitions were out of the way.

Now it must get back to legal work. Whatever type of campaign you are running—even a lobbying one—involves rules and regulations set forth in local law. Those must be followed to the letter, and it is up to legal to do so. If financial statements must be filed, legal must make certain that the finance committee has all its records in order and that the paperwork is done on time. If lobbying groups and their representatives must be registered, legal must make certain that all the requirements of these laws have been met. The opposition will like nothing better than to have you hauled into court two days before D-Day for some foolish oversight that it intends to blow out of all proportion.

If your campaign is headed for the ballot box, legal must devise easy-to-read election-day guidelines for poll watchers, assistant poll watchers, and anyone else allowed at the polls; canvassing guidelines (if certain types of canvassing activity is prohibited) and general campaign guidelines. (If you ended up using sound trucks, the law may prohibit their use on election day or at least limit their use; you are not allowed to campaign within a certain distance from the polling places; you probably cannot wear campaign buttons or other paraphernalia inside the polls; etc.)

Most important are the guidelines for poll watchers and their assistants. Not only should these guidelines detail *as simply as possible* what the poll watcher must do and how according to law he or she must do it, but it must detail the kinds of things that are prohibited by law that may be done by the other side.

For example, the law may allow two election inspectors—one from each main political party—to go into a booth to assist a voter requesting such assistance. If there are only four feet under the curtain instead of six, a complaint should be filed. Whatever happens at the polls must happen *by the book.* If you let "them" take shortcuts or break rules it will probably work against you, because "they" are in no way working for you, although it is your money that is used to pay their salaries. Election inspectors, public employees though they may be, are actually local party functionaries who do their leaders' bidding and protect the establishment; no matter how friendly they are, *they are not your friends.*

At the same time, legal must continue its campaign tasks. This includes making one last effort to convince the people whose names are in the "possible" file to come over to your side. Anyone who still wavers in this last week should be placed in the "no" box. All who have been convinced go into the "yes" box. If possible, all the "yes" people should be visited or telephoned at least once in this week to remind them of what is expected of them on D-Day (a vote, a presence at a rally in front of the appropriate legislature, a telephone call, depending on what your campaign is leading up to). Once again, if an individual sounds more like a maybe or a no, remove that name from the "yes" box.

On the night before D-Day, the "yes" box should be broken down by polling places in the case of an electoral effort, and by some form of workable logistic formula in the case of a lobbying effort.

You are now ready for D-Day. It is finally here. The day you and your dedicated, hard-working team have been working toward from the very beginning. You have come to—

STEP 10: MAKING IT ALL HAPPEN

Whether yours is a ballot-box drive or a lobbying campaign, D-Day is divided into two parts: the night before, and the day itself.

The night before is simple and relevant to both types of effort. Gather everyone around for a meeting, explain what their responsibilities are, hand out the necessary guidelines, answer their questions, go over their responsibilities one more time, give them a pep talk and send them home for a good night's rest. Tomorrow will be the longest day of the year.

If yours is a lobbying effort, there is very little that we can tell you at this point. Just make sure that whatever you are going to be doing follows the applicable laws to the letter.

If yours is a ballot-box campaign, here are some things that must be done on D-Day itself:

1. Provide a list of the "yes" voters for each polling place to the poll watcher and his or her assistant, if the law allows for one. Then, as each person on the list comes in to vote, let that person's name be crossed off the list. If possible, let the list be typed on multiple-copy paper. Also, have each poll watcher maintain a "complaint sheet" on which he or she can list voting irregularities that crop up, with as much detail as possible for each incident.

2. Throughout various times during the day, starting at around 10:30 A.M. or 11:00 A.M., send a campaign staffer responsible for a given election district or ward to the various polling places in that area to collect copies of the "yes" list. Attempts should then be made to contact all those who have not yet voted, to remind them of the need to vote. Keep attempting to contact all the "yes" people until the polls close.

3. If any "yes" needs assistance on that day, try to provide it. Maybe the person is elderly and would like a ride to the polling place; maybe a mother needs someone to watch the children while she goes to vote. Whatever the need, try to meet it, because each time you cannot, a vote in your favor is lost.

4. Within the limits of the law, carry on your campaign as if it were any other day. Keep knocking on doors, except of those people classified as "no" in previous efforts; we do not want to remind them to vote. Keep making telephone calls and, if allowed, holding little street-corner rallies. Have literature handed out at shopping centers and other strategic locations. Do whatever you can to bring out the vote.

5. Avoid fights as much as possible. A typical opposition tactic in any kind

of election is to goad your side into shouting matches and fistfights at polling places, to let the people see just what kind of irresponsible animals your side is really made up of.

6. Set up "flying squads" to shoot from one poll to another, solving problems or just holding hands. If possible, these squads should be mobile and equipped with two-way communications with your headquarters so that they can be moved from one trouble spot to another quickly. Also, try to man these squads with at least one member of the legal committee, preferably a lawyer.

7. Have someone stationed at the local board of elections, election commission or courthouse (depending on how these things are handled in your area) to file formal protests whenever called for during the day. And make certain the media are notified each time such a protest is filed. And have a lawyer on hand to obtain court orders, if necessary, at a moment's notice. If possible, have the necessary legal papers drawn up in advance, leaving the actual details blank, to be filled in as needed.

8. Make certain that you and the other members of the executive committee spend time at each polling place, shaking hands, thanking people and lending moral support to your poll watchers. Only do so within the limits of the law.

9. If the law allows, have all your campaign people wear a particular identifying sign on their lapels or dresses. This could be a plain white button, a safety pin, even a particular flower. The idea is that each person entering a polling place should be able to readily identify another campaign worker without breaking the law by wearing something that can be construed as a "campaign" item (such as a button bearing your campaign slogan). Keep this a top secret until the polls open, so the opposition does not have time to copy what you are doing and send in "ringers" to gum up the works.

10. If poll watchers are not allowed any assistants, make certain that a system is devised whereby poll watchers can be periodically relieved. You do not want these people becoming so tired and bored that they start making mistakes in the final hours of D-Day.

When the polls close and the poll watchers return with the results, have each one debriefed by a member of the legal committee. Each one then hands in the "complaint sheets" and explains them, if necessary. You may need this in the event of a request for a recount or an action to set the election aside.

That's right. After all this, the painful fact is you may lose on election day. The opposition was better organized from the start, was a lot better off financially and probably had a firm grip on the electoral machinery. You were fighting an uphill battle all the way and round one has gone to the other side.

Most tax revolts take time to build. Most suffer one defeat after another until the day victory is finally achieved. What you have spent the last few months doing makes you better prepared for the next time. Instead of starting at Step 1, go back to Step 8 and keep the campaign alive until the next time.

In the event that you win, uncork the champagne. If you lose, put on an upbeat front for the media. You never really expected to win the first time around, anyway. And to tell the truth, you are amazed at the amount of support you did get at the polls. Why, your count showed that only 23 percent of the registered voters were on your side this first time around, and you actually got 34 percent. That's not a loss; that's a landslide.

The media probably will not buy it, but your supporters will, and they are the ones you will need to keep going.

After all legal remedies have been tried—getting a recount or moving to set aside the election because of fraud and irregularities at the polling places in close races—sit down with your executive committee and key staffers and try to determine where you went wrong, where your weak spots were, why the voters did not respond to your appeals. The media will help you in this. Newspapers and broadcasting stations will be filled with analyses of what happened and why.

Take all of this information in, digest it and set about correcting it for the next round. The main thing is to learn from your losses and to build on them, not to become disheartened and give up. We never said it was going to be easy, only that it could be done—if you are willing to stay in the fight for the duration.

And remember: if you do drop out, and your tax revolt dies as a result, you are sending a signal that taxes are not high enough just yet and that the people will not mind letting go of some more of their hard-earned cash. Under no circumstances must you let that happen. If you do not believe that you and your organization's leaders can tough it out after a defeat or two, do not get involved in the first place.

If this sounds like we are trying to scare you, that is exactly what we are trying to do. We will say it again: this is not the kind of thing ego trips are made of; this is as serious a business as you might ever be involved in. So be prepared to lose, and be sure you can take it, bounce back and start all over again.

Now, in case you are wondering why, if D-Day is over, Section I is not, it is because we have some unfinished business.

CHAPTER 2

UNFINISHED BUSINESS: TIPS ON FUND RAISING

W E ARE going to repeat ourselves, but here is another painful fact that must sink in: no matter how well-organized your campaign, no matter how many signatures on your petitions, no matter how many people come up to you and pledge their support, you are going to need money to operate. *And the more money you have, the better the chance of beating the opposition and carrying the day.*

Okay, so how do we go about raising funds, you ask. Well, to begin with, you start collecting some funds from yourself and the four friends whom you have enlisted as your executive committee. And when the five of you have added that additional twenty-five needed for the initial staffing of the committees you have set up, you will collect money from them, too.

Your fund-raising effort will be headed by the finance director and the people who staff that committee. They will raise money in two ways: individual solicitation and mass appeals.

Individual solicitation involves such things as knocking on doors of well-heeled friends, local businesspeople and civic leaders. When you line up your initial legislative support, you might do well to ask the individual legislators to suggest some of his or her contributors for you to put the bite on; after all, if those people donated to that legislator, it is probably because they agree with that individual's politics and would thus be interested in furthering your effort as well.

By far the most lucrative fund-raising areas are collection of dues (Step 7), public meetings (Step 7) and, potentially the richest vein of all, the people who sign your petitions (Step 8). These have been discussed earlier in this section.

As your organization begins to grow and develop its financial base, you might want to consider the second phase of fund raising: mass appeals. This usually involves advertising campaigns asking for money and the inclusion of an appeal for funds with all your handouts and other literature. A coupon on the bottom of the advertisements and literature should do the trick.

Naturally, anyone who does send in a donation should be sent a thank-you letter and then should be contacted to see if he or she is willing to do some work, recommend others who may wish to donate or simply be there when you need someone (at the polls to vote, at your mass rallies, etc.). Also, an index card on each donor should be made up and filed in the "yes" box, and that name added to the finance committee's donor list in case you need to go back for more funds.

As soon as you have sufficient money on hand, you should consider a direct-mail fund-raising campaign. The two essential elements of a successful campaign of this sort are the "mailing package" and the ability of your organization to "target" the most likely potential donors.

Both are exceedingly important. No matter how good a fund-raising letter you write, it will do no good if it is sent to the wrong people; and no matter how well-targeted a direct-mail campaign is, if it is poorly organized and poorly written, it also will fail.

As far as identifying the most likely potential donors—"targeting," as it is called—there are, of course, those signed petitions, which provide a pool of crime, potential donors. Another source of potential ready cash can be found in the people and organizations which stand to benefit from your effort. For example, if you are battling for a Proposition 13-type amendment cutting back property taxes, then your target donors would include homeowners and home-owner organizations. If tax limitation is your thing, there may already be similar groups in your state waging the same kind of campaign and they most likely would share their donor lists with you.

One way to be reasonably certain that a particular list will be successful is to do a test mailing. Select 10 percent of the names on that list at random. If the rate of return indicates that the list will provide more money than the cost of the mailing, then go ahead. But if the rate of return indicates that you will spend more money than you will take in, forget that list. You have not targeted properly and you must rethink who it is you are aiming at in your appeal.

But what if the test mailing indicates that all you can expect is to break even, just get back only as much money as the mailing cost you in the first place. Does that make the mailing a mere waste of time?

No way. It means that you will be able to get your message across to all those people on that list, and it probably will not cost you an extra dime out of your campaign coffer. And that does make it worthwhile to proceed with the full mailing.

Now, about that "mailing package." That is the single most important factor in any direct-mail campaign and it is made up of three parts: the actual letter, the return envelope and the outside envelope.

First, let us examine the letter. To begin with, it must be kept short and to the point. Sure, it can take you three or four pages to tell your story, but keep it down to only one page. If more explanation is required, include an appropriate piece of campaign literature. The longer the letter, the shorter the list of people who will actually read it.

Set up a one-on-one situation. You are writing to the recipient, and only that recipient. At least, that is the way the letter should read. The best way to accomplish this is by using automatic typewriters, which you can rent. If the cost of such typewriters is prohibitive, then you will have to use a mass-produced letter. In that case, strive to make that letter as personal as possible. Professional fund raisers suggest that you should scratch the organizational "we" for the more personal "I"—as in "I would like to ask you for help," rather than "we would." And try to include as many "you" pronouns as possible. When you are finished with the first draft of your letter, add up the "I" and the "we"; if the "we" outnumbers the "I", scrap the letter and try again. More important, if the "we" and/or "I" count exceeds the "you," then definitely scrap the letter. It will sound too much like an ego trip.

Your letter must grab the reader's attention right away. If the first couple of lines bore him or her, then none of the other lines will be read. The letter must explain the goals of your organization, why your group needs the money, how the person reading the letter will benefit if your cause is successful, and how the donated money will be put to use.

Do not be ashamed of asking for money in the letter. Too many people try to beat around the bush and never come straight out and say they need money. If you do not ask for money, you will not get money. It is as simple as that. And if you show the potential donor how he or she stands to save money in the end because of what you are trying to do, then you really have nothing to be ashamed of anyway. So ask!

The appeal letter should be on the organization's letterhead, printed in black ink on white or off-white paper, and should be signed by an individual or by a facsimile signature *in an ink of a different color than the letter itself.*

Even if you can afford a slick-looking direct-mail package, avoid the temptation. No one wants to give money to an organization that looks as if it really has no need for money, and a slick mailer smells of money. You might also think of a good postscript to put on your letter. It adds another personal touch, say the professional fund raisers.

The next important item in the mail package is the return envelope. You must have such an envelope in your mail package. Do not rely on the potential donor's using one of his or her envelopes, because it will never happen. Also, a well-designed return envelope should include a brief form on the inside flap which the donor is asked to fill in. This form provides useful information for your campaign, such as whether the donor is willing to work on the campaign or has organizational ties that could prove helpful to your effort.

The third item, and no less important, is the outside envelope. If that envelope looks like the rest of the junk mail an individual is pestered by, then that envelope will share the same fate: tossed unopened into the trash can. The key to a successful envelope, say the experts, is to keep it neat and discrete, making it appear like a personal letter to the addressee. If possible, individually type the name and address of the recipient onto the envelope. (If you must use labels, make them look as much like personally typed as possible.) And try to use stamps on the envelope rather than a postage meter. People are less likely to throw away unopened a letter with a stamp on it.

Here again, you must follow up on any donations. First, send a thank-you letter. Then, if the person indicates a willingness to work, have the appropriate executive committee member contact the individual. Put the person's name in the "yes" box if that is appropriate in your case (if yours is a ballot-box effort and the donor is eligible to vote).

In addition, you might want to include a form in your thank-you letter asking the donor to suggest other names of potential donors or campaign workers.

If you have an organization newsletter, all new contributors should be added to the mailing list. Let finance put those names on its list of possible future donors. Those people might be willing to put up some more money in the later stages of your campaign, especially if they see how effective you are as an organization.

Finally, in regard to direct mail, KRC Associates of New York has prepared the following list of the "Ten Fatal Mistakes" in writing fund-raising appeals:

1. Ignore the difference between a known contributor and a cold prospect; send both the same piece of copy.

2. Don't bother to determine or appeal to the reader's basic motivations for giving money to your organization.

3. Assume that the reasons for supporting your work are as self-evident to the prospect as they are to you.

4. Use the pronoun "we" in your message more often than the pronoun "you."

5. Write long, discursive letters, because you won't accept the discipline of writing short, concise ones.

6. Make your message hard to read by using paragraphs of eight lines or more.

7. Use elaborate and expensive artwork, preferably in four colors.

8. Don't bother to tell the prospect exactly what a gift of a given size will accomplish.

9. Don't specifically ask for a gift at the close of your message.

10. Don't express your gratitude for the check you ask the prospect to send you.

Warning: These are the things *you should not do.* Be careful to avoid these mistakes. Otherwise, you will be throwing money down the drain and, worse still, probably turning off people to your effort.

There are two excellent publications that are available to you on the subject of fund raising: *A Citizen's Guide to Direct Mail Fund-Raising* by David Grubb and David Zwick, available for $4.50 from Ralph Nader's Public Citizen, PO Box 19404, Washington, DC 20036; and KRC's *Portfolio of Fund-Raising Letters* by Richard Crohn and Mitchell Keller (or any of their five other books on the subject), from KRC Development Associates, 212 Elm Street, New Canaan, CT 06840.

Well, that's it. Now you really are on your own. We suggest you read the sections that follow carefully because they provide useful information that you will need to know. Most important, we provide case histories of various types of campaigns which demonstrate how the techniques outlined in this section were put to use.

SECTION II:

CASE HISTORIES

CHAPTER 3

THE CALIFORNIA EXPERIENCE: THE PASSAGE OF PROPOSITION 13 AND HOW IT IS WORKING

T HE MOST publicized tax revolt to date occurred in California in the form of the Jarvis-Gann initiative, popularly known simply as Proposition 13, which called for a drastic across-the-board property-tax cut.

Judging from all the publicity that followed its passage, it looks as if the campaign for "Prop 13" was born overnight and that Jarvis and his citizen army were able to steamroller their way to victory on the shoulders of a grass-roots movement buoyed by a lot of angry homeowners. But it is just not so. The taxpayers' victory in California was the result of a long and methodical drive that culminated in a multimillion-dollar media campaign that was as slickly produced and as lavish as any political campaign seen in California in many years. In fact, although Proposition 13 seems to have risen out of nowhere to victory, a long and frustrating history preceded its moment of national glory.

The Watson initiative, so-called because its primary sponsor was Los Angeles County assessor Philip E. Watson, found its way on to the November 1968 general election ballot. More than half a million people signed petitions to qualify it.

Watson described property taxes as "the most vicious and confiscatory taxes we have." His initiative, officially known as Proposition 9, called for a property-tax limit of 1 percent of market value on levies for property-related services provided by counties and cities.

In addition, it also demanded a phaseout of 20 percent a year on taxes for education and welfare. In other words, schools and welfare would no longer be supported by property taxes.

Opponents, calling Watson's plan "fiscal idiocy," scrambled to place an alternate choice on the ballot. Governor Ronald Reagan's and the legislature's Proposition 1-A offered homeowners a $750 exemption on the assessed valuation of their homes, amounting to about a $70 cash refund for the average taxpayer.

Californians chose to approve Proposition 1-A and $261 million in tax relief. Proposition 9 lost by a two-to-one margin.

Watson blamed his defeat on a lack of campaign funds. Backers of Proposition 1-A reportedly spent nearly $1 million to promote their side. But others blamed Proposition 9's unpopularity on the threat it posed to the schools, a touchy issue voters were unwilling to tamper with.

Again in 1972, Watson, still Los Angeles County assessor, sponsored another property tax initiative which appeared on the November ballot as Proposition 14.

This plan would have limited the property tax to $7 per $100 of assessed valuation. It also would have shifted the total cost of welfare administration and more than half the cost of education to the state. The resultant $1.5 billion in reduced property-tax revenues would be made up, Watson told the media, by "closing loopholes for insurance companies and banks, increasing the corporate tax 44 percent, imposing a 7 percent oil-severance tax, adding 2¢ to the state sales tax and increasing taxes on cigarettes and hard liquor by 10¢ a pack."

Opponents quickly raised $3 million to persuade voters that lower property taxes would be replaced by higher income and consumer taxes.

Property owners were convinced and voted Proposition 14 down, looking ever-expectantly toward Sacramento to fulfill its long-standing promise of a viable tax-relief plan. Property values and taxes continued to rise at an alarming rate, with homeowners groaning under the increasing weight.

One who groaned louder and more consistently than most people was a vociferous conservative political activist named Howard Jarvis. A successful manufacturer until he retired in 1962, Jarvis had long been battling for lower taxes from within the Republican Party. In addition to myriad county-level posts, he was Midwest campaign manager for Dwight Eisenhower in 1952 and 1956, and Western states manager for Richard Nixon in 1960. He ran for elective office three times (California state senator, Board of Equalization member and Los Angeles mayor), and three times he lost.

Jarvis's pet issue for most of the last sixteen years has been property taxes. As a paid director for the lobbyist group known as Apartment Association of Los Angeles, Inc., he was well aware of the alarming rise in California property taxes.

Jarvis composed initiatives for fourteen years but met with disappointment until 1976, when the Los Angeles County tax assessor's office sent out new property valuations to thousands of shocked homeowners. Taxes for some rose as much as 200 percent!

A stunned Malibu Canyon retiree who had lived in the same modest two-bedroom dwelling for twenty-five years had his yearly tax bill shoot from $800 to $2,300. A Palos Verdes engineer and his wife faced a $4,325 levy—up $2,100 —on a home they'd purchased for $80,000 three years earlier. The reassessed valuation: $162,000.

Many fixed-income couples as well as younger people with growing families were threatened with the prospect of selling out because of their inability to pay Caesar what Caesar thought was necessary.

Jarvis's United Organization of Taxpayers worked with renewed enthusiasm, circulating petitions to put a tax-reform initiative on the ballot. And this time he heard the unmistakable rumblings of a bona-fide grass-roots movement gaining speed.

One young volunteer alone gathered 4,000 signatures in three days simply by setting up a table in front of a large discount department store in Los Angeles. In San Fernando Valley, where the drive apparently gained its most dramatic momentum, neighborhoods banded together. They elected block captains who designated supermarket people, department-store people and workers who approached taxpayers standing in line at the assessor's office.

Literature was churned out, homes were donated as distribution centers. But only about half of Los Angeles County property had been reassessed, and the more affluent area at that. Those taxpayers were mad, but the rest were complacent. (It should be noted that the 9 million residents of Los Angeles County, by far the largest of California's fifty-eight counties, represent approximately 40 percent of the state's population and that the Southern California population far outnumbers Northern California dwellers.)

Consequently, the July 2, 1976, petition reached its deadline date 10,000 signatures short. Not discouraged, Jarvis and his band of trusty volunteers submitted a new petition and started all over again to gather names. This effort also failed, but by a mere 1,200 signatures.

That was in March 1977. Two months later, a coalition of state taxpayer organizations filed a new joint tax-limitation amendment.

Jarvis's United Organization of Taxpayers had joined with Northern California real estate salesman Paul Gann's group, the People's Advocate. The coalition proposed that property taxes be limited to 1 percent of assessed market value, that market-value appraisals be increased no more than 2 percent a year and that a two-thirds vote of the legislature be required to raise property taxes. But they needed almost half a million certified signatures by December 2, 1977, in order to qualify for the June 1978 ballot.

The flames of the Jarvis-Gann initiative were immediately fanned by another big batch of assessor's revaluations with attached eye-popping tax rates. The complacent half of Los Angeles County had been hit with the same salvos as their neighbors had in prior months.

To add insult to levy injuries, lawmakers in Sacramento had failed to agree on Governor Jerry Brown's tax-reform program before recessing in September. Brown told newsmen, "Quite frankly, I'm getting somewhat frustrated myself at the slow pace of property-tax relief."

"Right away, we could tell we were on the winning team this time," says

Glen Waldman, a Jarvis strategist. "People were calling in wanting to know how they could help and where they could send contributions. We had to do very little soliciting."

The Philip Watson campaign for his half-million tax reform signatures had cost $2 million. Jarvis-Gann campaign costs totaled $28,000 because volunteers were so plentiful and hard-working. Signatures from every county in the state appeared on the petition, even to the extent that Paul Gann braved four feet of snow in the upper reaches of Northern California to sign thirty-six people.

A total of 1.2 million certified taxpayer signatures were presented, more than double the number required (768,000 from Los Angeles County alone).

"Even after we knew our name count was way over the 499,000 required," reports Waldman, "we kept pushing as though we were still struggling so that legislators and opinion makers would realize the impact. Besides the 1.2 million we filed, more than one hundred thousand names came to us after the deadline."

By late December 1977, those doubters who had dismissed the Jarvis-Gann camp as a bunch of radical kooks suddenly began to take notice. Politicians skirted the issue, not sure yet which stand would best reflect the feelings of their constituents.

The measure easily qualified for the ballot and was dubbed Proposition 13. Jarvis was overjoyed. "Thirteen is an unlucky number for the legislature. I love it. They did us a favor, really."

A full-blown tax revolt was in progress. A Southern California printer offered to negotiate a good price on paper for the purpose of running off 150,000 bumper stickers. He donated his time and machinery to reproduce such hard-hitters as "Save the American Dream—Vote Yes on 13" and "Hell Yes on 13!" Another printer donated lawn signs reading "Limit Government Spending—Vote Yes on 13!" Pens, pencils, buttons and tons of literature were also provided by supporters. Some people even sported Howard Jarvis watches, featuring the grinning tax revolter wielding a pair of scissors to property taxes over the inscription "Jarvis Saves."

The media followed Jarvis everywhere, recognizing him from other political skirmishes and delighting in the colorful copy his expletive-sprinkled speeches provided. From cocktail parties at posh Beverly Hills watering holes to barrio family recreation centers to San Francisco fern bars, citizens were increasingly debating the advantages and disadvantages of "Prop 13." And for the first time in recent history, a light appeared to be blinking at the end of the taxpayer tunnel.

The California legislature began to get nervous as Proposition 13, despite early forecasts to the contrary, steadily won voter confidence. Warned Jarvis, "A politician who doesn't come out for this can't win the Republican nomination for governor. And if he waffles, he probably can't win either."

True enough, politicians running for election or reelection gained or lost popularity in relation to their stand on Jarvis-Gann. Clearly, an alternate had to be devised, however hastily.

Proposition 8, authored by Senator Peter H. Behr, a San Rafael Republican, and approved by the legislature, proposed a 30 percent cut on all owner-occupied homes and an increase in income tax credit for renters from $37 to $75. No commercial property tax relief was included.

If politicians wrung their palms in anxiety over which side to support, other groups stampeded to jump on the Jarvis-Gann bandwagon: the California Chambers of Commerce (made up of approximately eight thousand small businessmen), the California Farm Bureau ("We think our only salvation is to support Proposition 13"), commercial and industrial owners, Republicans in general, senior citizens and, of course, homeowners.

Economist Milton Friedman, writing in *Newsweek,* defended the initiative, citing the California state government's $3 billion surplus which would offset the $7 billion in lost revenue should Proposition 13 pass. "The remaining $4 billion is roughly 10 percent of the state and local spending now projected for the next fiscal year. Is there a taxpayer in California (even if he is a government employee) who can maintain with a straight face that there is not 10 percent fat that can be cut from government spending without reduction of essential services?"

Opposition forces dug in for the duration. Superintendent of Schools William Johnston predicted "a chaotic disruption of our educational program which could bring permanent damage to children and young people in our community." The school board launched a massive public information campaign and local elementary school students brought home propaganda given to them by teachers and principals.

Big business gathered monies against Jarvis-Gann, arguing that what business might win in short-term gains they would lose in the long run through offsetting corporate taxes.

Intense opposition plans were set into motion by public employee unions. Los Angeles District Attorney John Van de Kamp called Proposition 13 "a gift-wrapped time bomb" and "fiscal suicide," forecasting a frightening impact on law enforcement as policemen, firemen and prosecutors would have to be cut from the payroll.

Governor Brown, certain of the Democratic gubernatorial nomination in the June 6, 1978 primary, dubbed the Jarvis-Gann measure "a temporary mirage that in a few months will blow up in everybody's face" and urged tax-relief—seeking voters to opt for Proposition 8.

As the smart money leaned more and more heavily toward a Proposition 13 victory, the Orange County advertising firm of Butcher and Forde approached Howard Jarvis with a highly sophisticated presentation. With only three months until the election, Jarvis was at this point a one-man show, making speeches all day and talking on radio shows at night, sometimes putting in as much as eighty-six hours a week.

Rather than try to unite all the various tax-reform organizations under a single scheme, the firm decided it would be more expeditious to trust its own professionalism.

"We decided to raise funds by direct-mail appeals," ways Stuart Mollrick, a consultant at Butcher and Forde, "and use the contributions to buy radio and television time exclusively. It was tough because of the tight timing. We had to read our test mailing results quickly and act on them fast. The whole operation was computerized."

Over 2.5 million pieces were mailed to every conceivable property owner whose demographics fit the purpose. Potential donor names were bought with consideration given to income level, property valuation, political affiliation and other factors Butcher and Forde is reluctant to divulge.

Apartment owners, holders of commercial and industrial land, farmers and individual homeowners received a personally addressed mailer. By marrying county assessor tapes with the voter file, the advertising firm was able to compute approximate tax increases for each household. Therefore, attached to an appeal letter from Jarvis was a card that read "Pay this amount in additional 1978 property taxes if Proposition 13 is defeated $1,000."

Also included in the package was a simple chart comparing pre-13 tax bills with projected, much lower post-13 levies, as well as an editorial from former Republican Governor Ronald Reagan. Variations of this mailer were produced for specific types of taxpayers.

The campaign was so successful that $1.2 million was raised from 3 percent of the total number of people mailed.

"Persuading contributors isn't the same as persuading voters," says Mollrick, "but for every three persons who donated as a result of the direct-mail appeal, six read it and decided to vote for 'Prop' 13."

Prime-time television and radio spots were scheduled to the tune of $625,-000.

"The opposition bought a lot of daytime TV because polls showed that women comprised a good percentage of the undecideds," explains Mollrick. "We considered tax relief as more of a family decision and one that has traditionally been influenced by the male, so we bought time when husband and wife could be together and discuss it toward a mutual decision."

The radio spots featured Ronald Reagan; Dr. Richard Ferraro, an education expert; former Los Angeles police chief and gubernatorial candidate Ed Davis, who calmed fears of mass law-enforcement layoffs; and Milton Friedman.

Five thirty-second television commercials stressed two main points: that passage of Proposition 13 would cut property taxes by two-thirds and control high-spending politicians.

The first spot featured Jarvis (in a calmer, more conversational mood than is his normal manner) telling the average homeowner that he *can* do something about his high taxes by voting yes on 13.

The second spot featured the Nobel prize-winning Friedman making his first commercial ever (and vowing later never to make another). He told voters not to believe the scare tactics of the opposition but to vote for economy in government. Friedman helped enormously to reach opinion makers and to dispel the notion that Proposition 13 was a radical issue.

The third spot showed a jet taking off for the glamorous capitals of the world with the announcer noting wryly that the taxpayers are handed the bill for these junkets.

"The timing was right on that one because many families in the spring try to figure out if they can afford a vacation," explains Mollrick, who wrote and produced the spots. "We were telling them that politicians were making dummies out of them."

The fourth commercial summarized briefly and succinctly Proposition 13 and showed how Proposition 8 failed in every instance to affect real reform.

The fifth showed a toy jack-in-the-box. A laconic, mocking announcer told viewers that the politicians had a surprise for them. Jack popped up with a big smile holding a 100-percent increase in property assessments. "Surprise!" laughed the announcer.

But with all of this slick media campaigning, the opposition was beginning to get through to the voters. What had started out early in the year as a runaway victory began looking like a close call. Three weeks before the June 6 election, the polls showed Jarvis-Gann in a tailspin.

It was at that point that Los Angeles County tax assessor Alexander Pope, himself on the June 6 ballot, mailed out *six weeks ahead of schedule* some of the new assessments that were to take effect in July, some of which called for a tripling of property taxes. The media played the story in screaming headlines and blaring broadcasts. The anti-13 tide began to turn.

Now it remained for the voters to make the final decision. And they did, in record numbers, as "Prop 13" won by a two-to-one margin.

A true tax revolt had succeeded. Politicians and government officials had to sit up straight and take heed. By the next morning, Governor Brown was sounding like Proposition 13 had been his idea all along.

To those who charged that Jarvis's marvelous campaign had simply been a matter of timing, he retorted, "If you put a fish hook in the pond and leave it there for fifteen years, something's bound to bite."

As for tax assessor Pope, we are not certain about what he had hoped to accomplish by mailing out those assessments ahead of schedule, but what he did accomplish was to put Jarvis-Gann into California's law books.

Proposition 13, however, has not exactly lived up to all its expectations. It has been on the books for over a year, and even its most ardent supporters admit its results have been mixed at best.

To begin with, government spending has not decreased much. When the amendment went into effect last June 1, it was assumed that many tax-spending units in California would be forced to radically reduce their outlays. The amendment, after all, cut property tax by 57 percent and, therefore, it was only natural to assume that spending would have to be reduced.

But thanks to the distribution of almost $5 billion of a $6.6 billion state surplus and the imposition of a variety of "service fees," the annual spending by the state, its 58 counties, 417 cities, 1,046 school districts and 4,710 special taxing districts will actually *increase* by about 5 percent this fiscal year. Few if any taxing bodies have cut their budgets by more than a modest 5 to 10 percent.

The massive public-employ layoffs predicted before the vote never came. Only about 20,000 workers have been let go, many of them from the lowest paying jobs. And almost half now have been rehired, according to one estimate. One study shows that over two-thirds of the state's school districts actually have more money to spend this fiscal year than last. In addition, public works and construction projects are going forward full steam, almost as if Prop 13 never happened.

Many communities have radically increased their fees and license collections and, in many situations, imposed fees for previously free services. Communities now charge for trash collection and are paying for police traffic details by tripling parking meter fees.

In sports-minded Berkeley, the city's parks department did not lay off its tennis pros and close many off the city's tax-supported tennis courts. Instead, it imposed a $5 per hour court fee. Court usage has not dropped off at all, and now, with the court fees, Berkeley has more money to spend on tennis than it did before last July 1.

In Marin County, officials decided not to cut the library budget. Library users now must pay fees for library cards and to rent some books previously available free. The library's annual budget has actually grown slightly as a result.

In the Los Angeles County community of Ingelwood, a "fire protection fee" has been imposed on all small commercial enterprises within the city. The fees must be paid if these businesses want fire protection and, by the same measure, if they want fire insurance.

Before Prop 13, the average small business in the city was paying about $1,500 in property taxes. That has been cut to about $800. As we write this, however, fire protection bills of about $800 went out to these businesses. So this year they will pay the city about $100 more than if Prop 13 had lost.

This movement of shifting the burden for services directly to those who utilize them has even moved into the schools. In the first summer after Prop 13 passed, most California public elementary and secondary schools dropped their summer programs. But last summer, the second under Prop 13 funding limitations, most of the summer programs were back. How? By charging the students tuition. In some cases the schools themselves charged the tuition themselves, an average of $110 for a five-week course. In other cases school districts handed over the running of the programs to private, profit-making firms that leased facilities from the school districts and charged fees for programs.

This has led to several lawsuits by parents and teachers' unions claiming the charging of tuition violates state law and the state constitution. The school boards who are offering the programs are arguing that the programs are extra and that scholarship funds are available for the truly needy.

Some observers believe that if the school districts are upheld they may begin charging fees during the regular school year for "special" programs that have traditionally been free.

While governmental spending has not abated, neither has a windfall come to the state's hard-pressed middle class. When Howard Jarvis was campaigning for his amendment, he made it sound like the $7 billion less in taxes would wind up in the pockets of those hard-pressed wage earners. It hasn't happened.

About $4 billion of the tax cut goes to the business community, with companies like Southern Pacific Land Company saving $19 million a year, Bank of America, $13 million, and Atlantic-Richfield, $14 million. Of this amount, $3 billion goes to out-of-state companies and is completely lost to California. Add to this the additional $2.5 billion in federal taxes Californians must pay because of lowered property tax deductions and the actual gain to the hard-pressed middle class has been reduced to $1 billion.

Business, for its part, is not passing all of the savings onto their customers. One which is doing so is Pacific Telephone. It has announced a rate cut based on the millions it is saving in taxes. If the new rate structure is approved, residential customers will get a mere 25-cent-a-month reduction.

One effect predicted by opponents of Prop 13 has taken place apparently: shifting more of the tax burden from corporations to private citizens. State officials say that, because of Prop 13's provisions, the homeowner's share of state property tax, as compared to business' share, has sharply risen. For example, Los Angeles County Assessor Pope says total property assessments for the county this year will be $154 billion, up some 12 percent from last year. Prop 13 limits increases in assessments to 2 percent a year until the property changes hands; then it can be reassessed to bring it in line with changing market values.

Last year, 300,000 parcels of property changed hands in Los Angeles County. The greatest number of these were residential properties. This led to a reassessment of those properties, resulting in the overall 12 percent increase. It also resulted in the homeowners' share of the total property tax bill rising from 64 percent of the total in 1978 to 72 percent in 1979, while business' share dropped to 28 percent from 36 percent.

As Pope put it, "This eight percent shift is substantial. While our studies show the rate of the shift will slow over the next couple of years, we are estimating that by 1981, homeowners will be shouldering eighty percent of the property tax burden. I was against Prop 13 for reasons such as these, but now we have to live with it. But we must make some changes in it to make sure business pays its fair share of property tax."

Undoubtedly, some of the sting was taken out of Prop 13 by two court victories won by state employees suing to invalidate portions of the new law. In one decision, the California Supreme Court unanimously struck down a post–Prop 13 law which applied a statewide freeze on government pay increases, including those previously bargained for and thus covered under contracts existing at the time the Jarvis-Gann initiative passed. At the same time, the court struck down an accompanying law which tied receipt by local governments of state surplus "bail-out" money to a pledge not to give wage increases. The court ruled that the two laws violated both federal and state constitutional provisions against the impairment of contracts, as well as the specific home-rule provisions of California's state constitution. As a result, some one million state, county and municipal workers received retroactive pay increases totalling nearly $1 billion. Most local governments had escrowed the money while awaiting the court decision.

All this has led two conservative economists to conclude, in separate studies, that perhaps Proposition 13–type tax-cutting is not an effective method of tax revolt. In one major academic study on the effects of Prop 13, Ohio State University economist William Oakland says the measure merely shifts the tax burden, but saves the taxpayers little. Oakland's study was done for the private, Columbus-based Academy for Contemporary Problems. The study's central finding: Proposition 13 merely "shifts the emphasis from the property tax to the income tax." Other findings: Oakland concluded that, because of the size of California's budget surplus, the state most likely would have cut income taxes during the last legislative session. Prop 13 not only killed that income tax cut, but actually caused a slight increase so as to minimize the decline in the level of tax revenues.

One side effect noted by Oakland is a shift in the control of education from local school boards to the state. Before Prop 13, 52 percent of the schools' income was derived from local sources. Today, only 28 percent is, with the balance being made up in state funds. And, as the purse strings have shifted to state hands so has the control.

One area not hurt very much by Prop 13, Oakland found, is the very area which everyone said would be affected: public-sector employment. The number of people employed by California governmental units was supposed to have plummeted. Actually, it declined only by 2.8 percent compared to the previous year. Even after the state's large surplus runs out, Oakland said, the total loss of government jobs should be no more than four percent.

The second major Prop 13 study was conducted by Prof. Donald Hagman of the University of California. Hagman believes that traditional conservative economic principles are not "well served" by such meat-axe approaches to tax reform. As Hagman put it in his study, "Conservatives believe that waste and inefficiency in government must be controlled. Proposition 13, however, does not do this. In fact, it is shifting the emphasis toward greater government regulation and this could end up costing the taxpayer even more."

Prop 13 is aimed at the property tax, which is the main source of funds for most local units of government. These, Prof. Hagman found, are usually the best run, most efficient and most responsive units of government. They are simply the wrong units to attack, he said. Hagman suggests that conservatives should aim at those taxes—income, sales, corporate, etc.—which fuel the larger, more wasteful and least responsive units of government.

The general perception on the part of California voters that Prop 13 is not having its advertised results led to the passage last November of Proposition 4, known as the "Spirit of 13" initiative, and the placing on the June 1980 primary ballot of a Howard Jarvis–sponsored measure to cut personal income taxes in half. Prop 4, which is now law, was authored by Paul Gann, who split with Jarvis after the passage of Prop 13. It is a measure designed to close many of the loopholes that politicians have found in Prop 13. The new proposition, called by many "Jarvis II," is simply designed to force government and politicians to live on less.

The main thing that Prop 4 does is limit state and local spending to the previous year's level execpt for adjustments due to population growth and inflation. The measure also stipulates that at any time a surplus occurs, either statewide or in a local taxing district, the money must be returned to the taxpayers within two years.

Prop 4 easily passed, by a margin of more than 3 to 1. "Jarvis II" also is expected to pass.

CHAPTER 4.

THE MICHIGAN EXPERIENCE: A CASE OF TRY, TRY AGAIN

W ITH ALL the publicity that followed passage of California's Proposition 13, many people have gotten the idea that tax revolt is simply a matter of hard work, lots of money and good organization.

True, all these things are most important to any tax revolt. But having a well-organized, well-financed, hard-working taxpayer movement does not necessarily insure success. Of course, as the number of tax revolts around the nation increases and people thus become aware of the importance of these revolts, the job does become a little easier. But there are no guarantees.

We said it before and we must say it again now: *you stand a fair chance of losing your first time at bat.* The important fact to remember is that losing once, twice, even three times does not mean your cause is hopeless and you must give up the fight. It simply means that you must correct any mistakes you made in the losing effort and go for that long ball the next time around.

There are many cases where taxpayer organizations have experienced frustrating defeats. Some groups, such as in Indiana (we will examine that situation in the next chapter), have been so discouraged by defeat that they have simply dropped by the wayside. But others, such as Michigan's Taxpayers United for Tax Limitation, have stuck with it through several disheartening defeats until they won their fight, a victory which eluded them for five long years.

Let us look at the Michigan example. We think it is enough to give anyone the courage to face the possible defeats that lurk in the distance. Because from those defeats, Taxpayers United built itself up to the point where victory was achieved.

Taxpayers United got its start in 1974. Its founder, William Shaker, had been exposed to the idea of tax limitation for the first time two years earlier when his employer, Dow Chemical Company, sent him to California. There he was to observe the fledgling tax-limitation movement which had begun. He also came into contact with members of Governor Reagan's Tax Limitation Task Force, including Sacramento attorney Lew Uhler, who today heads the National Tax Limitation Committee.

In 1974, Shaker decided to put to use what he had learned in California. Taxpayers United was born. Using a nucleus of just a few friends and acquaintances, Shaker put together an organization of some 5,000 volunteers. But despite months of work, they were only able to get 100,000 signatures on their petitions. While this sounds like a respectable number—in some states it would be far more than enough to qualify a measure—in Michigan it was far short of the number necessary to put their proposal before the voters.

But the group was not discouraged. It immediately regrouped and began working toward putting the issue on the 1976 ballot. All during 1974 Shaker and a few key members of Taxpayers United kept the idea of tax limitation before the public in a variety of ways: by testifying before the legislature in hearings scheduled by a friendly state senator, by public appearances, through contacts with the media and by two large public rallies.

The core of the organization was kept intact and plans were readied to begin anew the petitioning process for the 1976 general election. Late in 1975, the organization began contacting the 5,000 or so volunteers who had worked for them in 1974. Those who were still willing to work were asked to come back and to recruit additional volunteers.

Thus, when 1976 began and using the 100,000 signatures from 1974 as a starting point, the group began circulating new petitions containing the same amendment. This time, Taxpayers United gathered the requisite number of signatures and qualified the amendment for the ballot.

Things began to fall into place. Everything seemed to be going Taxpayer United's way. Opinion polls taken only two weeks before the November election showed the amendment clearly in front and predictions were that it would win by a narrow margin.

But then political reality reared its head. The opposition was well-organized and well-heeled, and had been waiting for the right time to mount its counterattack. Led by the state's politicians and by the Michigan State Education Association, it began a furious media blitz.

The blitz against Proposal C was very similar to the anti-Proposition 13 campaign in California. There were dire predictions of what would happen if the initiative passed—police and firemen would be laid off, mental health services would be cut back, hospitals would close, the civil service pension system would face a crisis.

Taxpayers United tried to combat the charges. It tried desperately to show that these were simply scare tactics and that none of the dire predictions would come to pass if the comparatively mild Proposal C were approved on election day.

But it was too late. When all the votes were counted, the tax-limitation amendment had been defeated at the polls by a margin of 57 percent to 43 percent.

Not enough signatures in 1974. Outflanked in 1976. Such defeats could easily have destroyed Taxpayers United, but it did not. Well before anyone outside of California had ever heard of Howard Jarvis, Taxpayers United regrouped again and began preparing for its third and best shot at enacting a tax-limitation amendment in Michigan.

Once source of new help were people who began to realize that they had been suckered by the dire predictions of the politicians about what would happen if the amendment passed. One such person was Bill Hanson, a labor-relations manager for Massey-Ferguson who had bought the opposition claims and voted against Proposal C. Today, Hanson is executive director of Taxpayers United.

"It raised my dander that I'd been suckered in by the untruths over Proposal C," he now says.

With this influx of new blood, Taxpayers United got to work one more time. It hired its first full-time paid staff, including Hanson. It tapped Richard Headlee, a one-time aide to former Michigan governor George Romney and currently president of the Alexander Hamilton National Life Insurance Company, to be its president.

Headlee, in turn, put together a bipartisan board, trying to move the organization away from its image as a right-wing conservative group which Headlee believed had hurt it in 1976. He tried to balance the board almost equally between identifiable Republicans and Democrats. Arguing that "the fireman, policemen and teachers next door are not going to have to pay the price while we try to resolve the excesses of thirty years," he beat back a move by conservatives within the organization to put forth a more drastic tax-cutting proposal. The organization reworded the proposed amendment to remove certain minor points which opponents had seized upon in the final days before the 1976 election.

Ironically, considering the focus of current tax revolt efforts, the 1976 measure had said nothing about property taxes. That provision was added to the revised 1978 proposal, however.

More important, the '76 initiative would have imposed an arbitrary limit on state taxes. This was changed to what Headlee considered a more responsible alternative. In its earlier incarnation, the proposal put forth by Taxpayers United had been considered recklessly rightwing, but in the era of Jarvis-style rollbacks, the Michigan group's amendment is now considered mild. Instead of an absolute limit, the revised initiative allows taxes to grow—but only if the state economy grows too.

The central provision of the amendment would limit all future state and local taxes to their current proportion of the state's aggregate personal income, 9.7 percent. This would mean that, with the rate frozen, the only way for the taxing bodies to take in additional income would be for the state's economy to expand and personal income to go up. It also means that in those years when the economy contracts and personal income declines, the taxing bodies will also have to do with less income because they will not have the ability to increase the tax rates.

As for property taxes, the Michigan initiative allows them to rise only as fast as the rate of inflation. If property values rise faster than the inflation rate, property-tax rates would be rolled back so that the actual tax increase was no higher than the inflation rate.

Another feature of the Michigan proposal is a refund of taxes that exceed the revenue limit by more than 1 percent, with excesses of less than 1 percent put into the state's budget-stabilization (or "rainy-day") fund. Taxes could be increased to meet an emergency, but only with the approval of the governor and two-thirds of the legislature, and only for one fiscal year.

Also under the proposal, the state will have to provide the full funding for any new local program that it mandates. It would also have to maintain such existing mandated local programs as school aid and highways at the current level of state subsidy. Voter approval would be required whenever local governments wanted to use bond issues to finance current operating costs.

Taxpayers United said that its amendment is a modest, responsible, legitimate form of tax revolt. The organization is quick to point out that Michigan's state and local tax burden is by no means excessive. In fact, Michigan's per capita state and local taxes, $679 in 1974, were only slightly above the national average and far below New York's $952 and California's $762.

With the revised proposal in hand, the organization set out for its third try to convince the voters of Michigan to constitutionally limit their taxes. The revamped Taxpayers United organization remained small at the top, with only five full-time paid workers (Headlee was unpaid).

Taxpayers United divided the state into fifteen regions; the headquarters staff, in Southfield, chose regional chairpeople located in each of the fifteen regions. These chairpeople, working with local service organizations such as the Jaycees and local Chambers of Commerce, recruited approximately 300 community coordinators whose job it was to recruit and supervise an estimated 15,000 people who circulated petitions and who worked at getting out the vote on election day.

While these regional coordinators had some autonomy, it was mainly in the area of personnel selection. All advertising was done out of headquarters; all statements were released through one publicity coordinator; and most important, all funds were raised by the headquarters staff.

Fund raising was extremely important to Taxpayers United, as a look at their spending indicates. The organization estimates that it spent $750,000 on getting the proposal on the ballot and then voted on by the people. Of this huge amount, almost four-fifths, or about $600,000, was spent on media alone and almost all of this in the final eight weeks before election day.

In the year Taxpayers United was reorganizing and passing its petitions aimed at the 1978 election, it only spent, according to its records, $77,000. Most of this amount was spent to pay the salaries of headquarters clerical personnel and outside consultants, including public relations counsel and fund-raising counsel.

At the same time, it established a nonprofit foundation which raised about the same amount of money. This was used for research and to pay the salaries of key professional personnel who were then "loaned" to Taxpayers United. Once the initiative qualified for the ballot, however, this personnel could no longer be paid by the foundation because the purpose of the organization had changed from educational to political in the eyes of the law and a nonprofit educational foundation (contributions to which are tax deductible) could no longer "lend" people.

Much of the organization's fund raising early in the year had been conditional. Donors would give money when and if the initiative qualified for the ballot. With the petitions turned in and the initiative qualified, this money began to come in and formed the base for the expensive media campaign to come.

Because Michigan's taxes are not very high, Taxpayers United could not go to the voters screaming "We're paying too much." It just would not wash. So it decided that the best way to convince the voters to back the proposal was to compare the tax situation in Michigan today with the situation ten years ago. Citing official state figures, it argued that in the last ten years personal income in the state had increased 130 percent while state and local taxes had gone up 250 percent. In the same period, the state's population grew by 6.75 percent—to just over 9.1 million—while the number of state employees increased by over 50 percent.

Then the organization won a significant psychological victory when it convinced the state's major media outlets to start thinking about the reporting the situation in the same terms. Reporting a fairly typical case, the *Detroit News* presented the story of Lee and Julia Alagine, who bought their home in Livonia, a Detroit suburb, in 1947, when their annual tax on the property was $87.40. Over the next thirty years, as the Alagines approached retirement, inflation cut their old-age nest egg in half, while rising property values boosted their annual property tax to $996.37.

The Alagine's story was not that unusual. What was unusual was the source of some of their strongest support: tax assessor Ronald Madiras, now Livonia's chairman of Taxpayers United.

"I'm scared to death of what's happened in the last year and a half,"

Madiras said. "Assessments keep going up and up. When an assessor comes up and says the house you bought ten years ago for $19,000 is worth $50,000 today, people ought to be happy. But they want to throw me out because they know it means their taxes are going up. If we put a limit on taxes, maybe they'll let me march in the Memorial Day parade again."

But even with the revamped organization and the reworked proposal, and with the kind of facts that should shake up any taxpayer, as June came the volunteers for the struggling, twice-defeated tax-limitation group couldn't give away tickets to their slide presentation on tax reform. Then, on June 7, the day after two-thirds of California's voters approved the massive cut in their property taxes, nearly every politician in Michigan seemed to be calling up to find out when the next slide show was.

Taxpayers United got the lion's share of the Michigan fallout from Proposition 13, even though its proposed amendment to the state constitution was far more moderate—closer to California's defeated Proposition 8—and despite the activity of a more extreme Michigan group with a proposal similar to Jarvis's and with Jarvis's support.

It is difficult to say whether Taxpayers United would have been able to get its proposal on the November ballot without Jarvis-Gann. On June 6, the group had only 200,000 of the 266,000 signatures required. In the week after the passage of "Prop 13," it collected 60,000 names; on June 30, ten days before the filing deadline, Taxpayers United filed petitions with 410,000 names at the state capital in Lansing.

Even before Proposal C was assured of a place on the ballot, it wasn't hurting for prominent support. It had an early endorsement from Milton Friedman and from Paul McCracken, the former chairman of the President's Council of Economic Advisers, currently on the faculty of the University of Michigan.

Hanson says his group has had virtually no support from big Michigan companies such as the auto manufacturers, but support from middle-sized and small businesses has been substantial. The Jaycees, Michigan Retailers Association and Michigan Chamber of Commerce all supported Taxpayers United, as did a number of suburban-Detroit and small-town newspapers.

As in 1976, the main opposition still comes from the Michigan Education Association and the League of Women Voters. Union organizations also have been active against the proposed amendment, but Hanson says a lot of the rank and file support it.

The day after Proposition 13 passed, State Senator Patrick McCollough, a candidate for the Democratic nomination for governor, introduced a resolution in the legislature to put Taxpayers United on the November ballot even if it did not get enough signatures. Other gubernatorial candidates endorsed the group's proposal and the incumbent Republican Governor William Milliken, said he was considering supporting it because the plan was "carefully, skillfully and responsibly drawn." Even Detroit's Mayor Coleman Young, who had scored the tax-limitation movement for what he said were elements of racism, acknowledged a difference between Taxpayers United and Jarvis.

In the three weeks between Jarvis's victory and the day Headlee took his first batch of petitions to Lansing, the plan of Taxpayers United had been transformed from a maybe proposition to one the state couldn't refuse.

At least, that was what Headlee and his supporters believed. In the last few days before the election, however, opponents seized on a relatively minor provision of the proposal, which required that all bond issues be approved by the voters before they could go on sale. This, opponents charged, would slow down the pace of the state's renewal efforts, such as the one which was rebuilding downtown Detroit.

It almost worked, too. Unfortunately for the opposition, however, it had come up with the argument too late to completely turn the tide. But the vote was close nonetheless. When it was all over, the Taxpayers United amendment passed by a narrow 1,188,274 to 1,124,146.

(Part of the reason for the narrow vote, incidentally, was the presence on the Michigan ballot of two other tax initiatives—a Jarvis-backed Proposition 13–type property tax cut and a school voucher proposal. As we indicated in our step-by-step approach to tax revolts earlier in this book, the best chance citizen groups have to change the system is through unity, not divisiveness. Every effort must be made to put one good measure before the voters, not two or three proposals competing against each other.)

Looking back over the years of effort, the failures and now the victory, Headlee could find some advice for those organizations just beginning their own tax revolt:

"Avoid being slapped with a label. Be an all-things-to-all-people kind of movement because that's what tax limitation should be. Know the details of the situation in which you find yourself"—in other words, don't get carried away with a Jarvis-style proposal if you don't have to—"and find your area of support. You can build from there."

To which we add this reminder: if at first you don't succeed, try, try again. Because eventually you will come out on top.

CHAPTER 5.

THE INDIANA EXPERIENCE: LOBBYING AGAINST GREAT ODDS

N OT EVERY tax revolt results in whopping cuts and national publicity, nor does every one involve massive outlays of funds for media campaigns. But that does not make these victories any less important than the much-publicized Proposition 13 effort.

Any victory, large or small, involves men and women who have worked tireless hours to bring them off. Moreover, even the smallest victories provide people with the incentive to push on to greater things, because they show how a few people can organize and win out over entrenched interests who are better organized and better financed.

This is important to understand. Not everyone reading this book needs to start a campaign to cut taxes, because their taxes may not be excessive in the first place. But they might need to start one to keep those taxes from climbing out of control.

Most important, however, are these two points: not every campaign ends up at the ballot box; ....ny campaigns are lobbying efforts. And once you have won your fight, you must remain on guard, because "they" are still waiting to turn your victory into disheartening defeat.

Such a fight took place in Indiana, where the main issue was not cutting taxes, but simply holding the line in the face of mounting pressure by vested interest groups who thought the state treasury was the local tree on which free money grew. We believe it is a classic example of citizens' collectively stomping down on a lighted match before the curtains catch fire and the whole building burns down. It is also a prime example of a lobbying campaign.

The story began twelve years ago, in the summer of 1968, when virtually every important pressure group in Indiana got together to plot a raid on the state treasury. The list of participants was awesome: teachers, retailers, manu-facturers, truckers, electricity and petroleum interests, Chambers of Com-merce, auto dealers, the farm bureau. Many large corporations joined in: United States Steel, Aluminum Corporation of America (Alcoa), Radio Cor-poration of America (RCA), Inland Steel, General Electric, American Oil,

Ford Motor Company, among others. And (talking about strange bedfellows) big labor was also represented by the AFL-CIO and United Auto Workers. Indiana University, a state institution, and the Indiana Commission on State Tax and Financing Policy, a state agency, also took part.

These powerful organizations (later known collectively and derogatorily as the "Spending Lobby") sent their representatives to a series of three hush-hush "tax retreats" to work out a common position. Farmers wanted property-tax relief; business wanted relief from inventory taxes; labor had a stake in the "more spending" philosophy; and the rest, notably the teachers, were after pay raises or government contracts.

The plan they agreed on was an across-the-board increase in state taxes, dividing the new revenues between more general spending (most of it for education) and subsidies to local government for the purpose of property-tax relief. Unless tax rates were raised at once, they argued, the state would go broke. State services would have to be severely curtailed. Schools would be closed. Chaos would spread across the land.

The Spending Lobby was determined to get property-tax relief no matter what it cost the taxpayer. One month before the legislature opened its 1971 session, lawmakers were polled to determine where they stood. The result: they favored the increased-tax proposal by a margin of four to one, which is understandable, considering the awesome power wielded by the Spending Lobby. It looked as if the tax increases would pass in a breeze.

But a new organization suddenly popped up out of nowhere. Calling itself the Taxpayers' Lobby of Indiana, Inc., it had been quietly organized two months before the state's General Assembly was to convene. Unlike other lobbies, it was not asking for any favors or handouts from the state; it was out to block the proposed tax hikes and, if possible, to get some tax reductions too.

Behind the organization were several concerned citizens who were simply fed up with paying more and more money for taxes each year. Two young men took instant command of the new organization: Dr. Herman W. Andre, a young chemical-firm executive and former professor at Purdue (with a Ph.D. in nuclear chemistry) agreed to serve as TLI's chairperson and public spokesperson, and Timothy J. Wheeler, an editor and writer, was retained to prepare TLI's tax material and public releases.

A number of sympathetic businesspeople from around the state served on the board of directors. The group filed as a not-for-profit corporation and publicly surfaced on January 6, 1971.

TLI registered two lobbyists for the upcoming legislative session, two men pitted against the 211 previously registered lobbyists who were working for the various pressure groups which would reap the benefits of the massive tax increase. There were more than one hundred of "them" for each of the two TLI lobbyists.

But as it turned out, that was about an even match.

Before it completed the first month of its existence, TLI had launched a petition drive, undertaken a major study of the Indiana tax structure and was out buttonholing businesspeople to finance a few fund-raising newspaper advertisements.

TLI's petition read simply: "As taxpaying citizens of Indiana, we are opposed to any new taxes or tax increases. We call on our representatives to economize and cut unneeded spending to permit general tax reduction for Indiana."

In those early days, the only people passing out the petitions were a few hundred citizens whose interest had been sparked by news stories on the TLI campaign. But the organization knew its only real hope of success was to create a chain-letter effect, and it did.

When a fully signed petition came in, TLI added the names to its mailing list. Each signer was sent blank petitions and tax material. TLI also sent out fund requests. Soon, it had enough money in its coffers to take out additional small fund-raising advertisements in the state's newspapers.

The advertisement stated the issue simply: *Do you want another tax increase?* ( ) *Yes* ( ) *No.* It then repeated TLI's petition word for word, with room for a pair of signatures, and it asked for donations "to help spread the word and knock out a tax increase."

First a few, then a few hundred, and finally a few thousand replies began to pour in. TLI finally had a way to finance its efforts and the stop-the-treasury-raid movement was in full gear.

The organization got valuable assistance from Governor Edgar Whitcomb, who had first been elected in 1968 on a platform of a tight budget and, believe it or not, was trying to live up to his campaign promises. The governor had previously helped defeat a small tax increase and now he was going all-out to stop the new increase.

Whitcomb and his staff mounted their own campaign. Members of the administration began traveling around the state, taking their case directly to the taxpayers and refuting the Spending Lobby's arguments.

With the aid of a massive publicity campaign orchestrated by TLI, everyone in the state started calling the tax increase plan "Super Tax." As the legislative session began, TLI's efforts were starting to bear fruit. The petition campaign resulted in more than 50,000 signatures, which represented thousands of people who were willing to work against the tax increase.

TLI decided to stage a rally in the corridors of the state capitol itself. At the March rally, dubbed the "Giant Citizens' Anti-Tax Rally," more than 1,000 persons jammed the State House rotunda and let their representatives know exactly what they thought of the proposed tax increase. The resultant newspaper coverage portrayed infuriated taxpayers storming the Assembly's chambers, while the legislators cringed on the floor out of sight.

By now, the pro-tax legislators had reason to worry. To the rescue came the

Indiana Farm Bureau, which mounted a counterrally. But it was a hasty and generally ineffective gathering. In fact, when the Farm Bureau bused many of its members to the capital, TLI workers were there to hand out leaflets to the farmers as they got off their chartered buses.

The final vote on Super Tax came in April. The House passed it as expected, but by a surprisingly small margin. The Senate waited until the very last day the bill could constitutionally be considered—and voted it down.

But late that night, minutes before its mandate expired and after opponents of the tax measure had left the capitol to celebrate their victory, the Senate voted to reconsider, and passed Super Tax. All of it.

In the face of this apparent defeat, TLI simply went back to work. Its members realized that there was little time for gloom. Governor Whitcomb agreed to veto the measure and he had to make his veto stick, for the legislature could override it with a simple majority vote.

TLI had only four days (including a weekend) to prepare for the veto battle that would be as hard, if not harder, than the month-long battle against the original vote. It was up to the Taxpayers' Lobby to convince thousands of citizens to deluge their legislators with protests from their home districts. Volunteer workers stayed on the phone hour after hour to spread the word. Mail started piling up on Assembly desks.

Governor Whitcomb played his last trump: He used his veto message to urge taxpayers to write their representatives.

The mail flooded in.

Pro-tax legislators reported afterwards that their mail was running 200 and 300 to 1 against them. They had little choice but to abandon their stand and heed the wishes of their constituents.

The vote in the House was close, but the veto was sustained. This time, Super Tax was really dead. Months of effort by the Taxpayers' Lobby had paid off at the last moment.

In 1972, under a new law, the Indiana General Assembly met for the first time ever in an off year. Predictably, another tax fight developed, but it was only a pale copy of the 1971 battle. The spenders had no new arguments, no new ideas, no new supporters.

The Spending Lobby managed to herd a "New Super Tax" through the House, but the Senate wanted no part of another tax-increase battle. It even voted down a small cigarette tax hike requested by the governor. The Taxpayers' Lobby used a postcard campaign and full-page ads to help nail down the lid.

A year after its success, TLI executive director Timothy Wheeler was telling the story of his organization to anyone who would listen. He was fond of pointing out that in 1973 state taxes in Indiana took a smaller portion of a citizen's income than in any other state. And he loved telling the story of TLI's success to show what a few dedicated citizens could do if they worked hard enough.

If this were a fairy tale, we could say that TLI, and everyone concerned, especially the taxpayers of Indiana, lived happily ever after. But this is the real world of power politics, and reality came to Indiana in 1974.

Dr. Otis Bowen, who as speaker of the Assembly had led the fight for Super Tax, was elected governor. With the push for "tax reform" being led from the governor's mansion, the inevitable happened: the tax passed despite all of TLI's efforts to keep it from happening.

In fact, faced with this defeat, TLI just faded out of existence.

In 1978, Wheeler said of the exercise, "I'm glad we did it despite the fact that eventually they were able to buy enough legislators to get the tax measure through. TLI has not been active since we lost the fight, but several of us are thinking that the climate is now ripe for some real tax reform in Indiana. We have been talking and I would not be surprised to see TLI reborn again."

It hasn't been reborn, but many of TLI's former members, joined by latter-day converts to its brand of tax revolt, did continue the pressure through 1978 and 1979. The result: the state legislature rolled back some of the higher taxes enacted in Indiana in recent years.

Reluctantly, Governor Bowen signed into law a measure which provided a 15 percent tax credit on personal income taxes filed in 1980. The credit is estimated to be worth $96.1 million to the state's taxpayers. Also, the income tax rate in 1980 drops from 2.0 percent to 1.9 percent, cutting the state's tax revenues by $16.1 million in 1980 and an additional $36.8 million in 1981.

TLI may have been out of business by then, but the subsequent tax cuts would not have been made without the groundwork of the erstwhile tax revolt group.

CHAPTER 6.

THE TENNESSEE EXPERIENCE: A MATTER OF GREAT CARE

T HE FIRST victory in the tax revolt of 1978 did not come with the passage of Proposition 13 in California. The first victory came about on March 17, 1978, when the voters of Tennessee approved a constitutional amendment limiting the amount the state can spend in any one year.

The March vote was the culmination of four years of hard work by a citizens' group. Even more important, however, it was a victory for one man, who first had the idea of a constitutionally mandated spending limit and whose singlehanded effort brought it about. The March vote was a personal victory for Republican State Representative David Copeland and, to many people, it showed what effect a single individual can have if he or she is sufficiently dedicated to a cause. We include the Tennessee case in this section for another reason, however: it is a prime example of the care that must be taken in choosing a solution.

Copeland is a businessman who has been in the state legislature since 1968. Almost from the beginning of his legislative career, he was recognized as an expert on the subject of state finances. Because he often led the fight against spending measures, he was branded a "conservative nut" by many of the state's largest newspapers. Despite this, he was able to lead a legislative fight to mandate a cap on state spending, only to see it vetoed by the Democratic governor as "unworkable."

But this did not deter him; he continued as the legislature's biggest foe of increased state spending because, he says "Everytime we managed to take a million out of the state budget, the lobbyists were at work and got another million stuck back in somewhere else." Still no success.

Then fate, as it were, played right into Copeland's hands. In 1974, Tennessee faced a major crisis. Its constitution mandated the maximum amount the state could pay in interest on borrowed funds, but the money market was in a bad situation and interest rates had risen above the mandated level. The state was having great difficulty borrowing the money it needed to meet its short-term obligations; as a result, a constitutional convention was being suggested to raise the interest ceiling.

With the prospects of a constitutional convention at hand, Copeland began to work out the idea for an amendment to limit the amount the state could spend. The idea was not new, but it had never been approved anywhere. Hence, there were no guidelines to follow in preparing such a solution.

Copeland's first step was to enlist the aid of a few friends who saw things his way. Together, they began to draft an amendment that would do the job, win voter approval and, above all, be "responsible" and "workable."

At first, they considered constitutionally limiting the amount of taxes the state could collect, but eliminated this idea mainly because of the reaction to it by the Wall Street bond houses that arrange the state's borrowings. The bond houses thought that such an amendment would make it impossible for the state to sell long-term bonds because it would be constitutionally limited in the amount it could raise taxes in order to retire those bonds.

Then Copeland and his friends considered an amendment to simply put a lid on state spending. But this was also rejected as impractical. After all, what number do you pick for that spending limit?

Finally, they realized that what they were trying to do was *to limit the rate at which the state budget could grow* so that taxes would not continue to climb. Thus, the amendment they worked out was one which limited the growth of the state budget.

Even then they had a problem. Putting an arbitrary limit on budget growth did not mean that taxes could not grow. In fact, if growth leveled off, taxes might have to go up by 6 or 8 percent a year. And that was precisely what they were trying to avoid!

Finally, they hit upon the means that was to prove successful. They would propose an amendment to limit the growth of the state budget to a percentage of the growth of personal income in the state.

As originally conceived by Copeland, the heart of the amendment stated: "Spending by any unit of government of revenues it collects from its citizens shall rise no faster than the increase in Tennessee Personal Income, except to meet required increases due to administrative, legislative or judicial mandate of a superior unit of government, natural disasters, capital expenditures and debt service."

Now that Copeland and his little group had an amendment, they had to convince their fellow citizens that it belonged in the state constitution. This was to become a daily task for almost four years.

The initial problem was to get the electorate to make budget control part of the call for a state constitutional convention. Under Tennessee law, such a convention could be called by the voters in a referendum, but that convention must be limited to the specific issues included in the call. So Copeland formed an organization, the Taxpayers Coalition, and it settled down to its initial task.

Signatures were gathered and a spending item was placed on the August 1976 referendum on the convention call. The coalition then began a four-month campaign to convince the voters to include this in the formal call.

But spending limitation was not one of the burning issues of the day in 1976. Most people were just looking at the convention as a way of raising the interest ceiling so that the state could borrow, and to reorganize the state judiciary, which was badly outdated.

However, the coalition—which in those days really meant Copeland, a secretary, some supporters and mailing equipment—got some unexpected help: the state legislature voted to increase the sales tax in order to fund major budget increases. This angered enough voters in the state, and spending limitation was included in the convention call.

That began the second phase of the coalition's work: trying to influence the selection of the ninety-nine delegates to the convention. As Copeland remembers this phase, "We really were not that successful. The spending lid was still not that burning an issue and, while we were able to steer the election of a few delegates sympathetic to the idea in general, we were limited to making the problem known clearly to those who were elected."

The real work began in August 1977, when the convention opened. Over the four-and-a-half-month life of the convention, Copeland lobbied unceasingly for the amendment. Still, the idea had not really caught fire. Gradually, there emerged from the convention the feeling that perhaps some amendment on state spending should be offered to the voters but that it should be limited to simply a balanced annual budget and the legislature's providing the funds for all proposals it enacted.

But now the coalition had begun to get substantial help from outside organizations. The foremost of these was the National Tax Limitation Committee, which sent people into the state to help lobby the convention, donated money to help fund the financially strapped coalition, and helped arrange the single strategic move that is generally credited with getting the convention to put the spending limitation amendment before the voters.

The convention had broken down into committees and a twenty-member group was considering the Copeland proposal. The NTLC arranged for Dr. Milton Friedman, the Nobel prize-winning economist, to spend over an hour talking with members of the committee on a two-way telephone hook-up.

Friedman's eloquence and passionate defense of the idea proved to be the turning point. He was asked every question the opposition could conceive, parried every opposing thrust, and carried the day for the coalition. The committee was so impressed with Friedman's logical presentation that it voted overwhelmingly in favor on the measure.

For the first time, it became clear that the convention was going to give the voters a chance to approve a significant spending-limitation amendment. As things began to go their way, the coalition decided the time was ripe to try to eliminate other problems it saw with the way the state appropriated and spent its money. Chief among these was the problem of the state legislature's passing laws that required the cities or counties to fund projects. A requirement was added to the amendment that said the state could not impose an expenditure on a city or county unless it paid its share of the cost.

The next problem was the legislature's habit (one shared by Congress) of passing measures and then leaving it up to future legislatures to figure out where the money was going to come from. So another addition was made to the amendment, this one requiring the demise of any program that was passed by the legislature without any provision for first-year funding.

Last, they wanted to prevent the legislature from circumventing the spending limit by using long-term borrowing and capital expenditure to fund current state services, pretty much the same technique that New York City used for years to avoid its obligation for a balanced budget. A specific prohibition against this was also included.

The result was the following amendment:

"No public money shall be expended except pursuant to appropriations made by law. Expenditures for any fiscal year shall not exceed the state's revenues and reserves, including the proceeds of any debt obligation. No debt obligation, except as shall be repaid within the fiscal year of issuance, shall be authorized for the current operation of any state service or operation, nor shall the proceeds of any debt obligation be expended for a purpose other than that for which it was authorized.

"In no year shall the rate of growth of appropriations from state tax revenues exceed the estimated rate of growth of the state's economy as determined by law. No appropriation in excess of this limitation shall be made unless the General Assembly shall by law containing no other subject matter set forth the dollar amount and the rate by which the limit will be exceeded.

"Any law requiring the expenditure of state funds shall be null and void unless, during the session in which the act receives final passage, an appropriation is made for the estimated first year's funding.

"No law of general application shall impose increased expenditure requirements on cities or counties unless the General Assembly shall provide the state share of the cost.

"An accurate financial statement of the state's fiscal condition shall be published annually."

Thus began the last phase of the four-year campaign, the one to convince the voters to approve the amendment.

"Previously, we had no allies within the state," Copeland recalls. "Our only help came from tax-limitation groups from outside such as the NTLC and the Tax Limitation Task Force of the ACU (American Conservative Union). But now, really for the first time, we started to get much-needed help within the state."

Such groups as the Tennessee Farm Bureau, the Retail Merchants Association, the Manufacturers Association, and a number of retired-persons organizations suddenly came forward to help.

At the same time, the opposition began to form. Now that it appeared likely that this amendment, which for so long had been considered just the dream of one man, might actually become part of the state constitution, the forces that would be hit the hardest began to battle back. The opposition was formidable and included the state education association, organized labor, the League of Women Voters, and many of the political leaders of the state, especially Democrats.

In order to prevail, the coalition launched a major political campaign to win voter approval. A quarter of a million proamendment brochures were mailed out four weeks before the election. Meanwhile, local grass-roots organizations, which were established in every county to get out the vote, went full steam ahead. Phone banks were established and manned in every county and, in the two weeks before the March 7 vote, the staffers attempted to call as many households in each county as possible.

Five days before election day, radio commercials began airing statewide; as many as 20,000 individual spots were aired on the state's many radio stations. The weekend before the vote, full-page newspaper advertisements were run in all the papers in Tennessee.

On election day, proamendment supporters were in front of every polling place in the state, handing out literature and explaining the amendment to voters who did not understand it (they stayed just far enough away from the entrance to the polling places themselves to not violate election-day law).

The results were overwhelming: 65 percent of the voters approved the amendment and it became part of the state constitution.

How has the amendment worked in the short time that it has been a part of the Tennessee constitution? Many of the foes of spending ceilings say it is mainly cosmetic and of little practical use. Needless to say, Copeland does not agree. According to him, the amendment has already come into play four times in the first legislative session after it became effective:

1. A proposal was put forward in the legislature to use state money in place of local money as matching funds for the federal Title XX program. The proposal, which was considered a sure thing, was defeated because it would have violated the amendment.

2. A proposal was put forward that, in effect, would have required local school boards to raise teacher salaries by $150. Faced with the amendment provision that would have required the state to fund the increase (since it was requiring it), the measure was defeated.

3. A group of state workers was fighting to get its pensions automatically

increased. The amendment came into play and a $2.9 million increase was held to $2 million.

4. A property-tax-rebate proposal was passed by both houses of the legislature. It called for a $6 million rebate. But faced with the requirement that it must be funded in the same session as it was passed, the funding was held to $900,000, thus limiting the total amount to that figure.

Copeland says that the amendment probably saved the taxpayers over $20 million in its first four months alone.

A state economist argues that the amendment is really not all that important. He has calculated that, had it been in force the last seven years, it would have resulted in lessening expenditures only twice in that period. But Copeland has a counterargument.

"One of those two years," he says, "was 1976—and it would have resulted in a taxpayer saving that year of $101 million!"

But all that aside, the point is that the Copeland amendment is now the law of the land in Tennessee. Not because the people saw the need and came banging on Copeland's door, begging him to push for such an amendment; but because he and a few friends worked hard and took great care in producing a solution that was workable, responsible and appealing to the voters.

CHAPTER 7.

THE ELGIN EXPERIENCE: A SCHOOL-DISTRICT BATTLE

A TAX revolt need not be national, statewide or even citywide in scope. It could, for example, be directed at your local school board or school district.

One such battle was waged in the U-46 school district, the third largest in Illinois. It covers a three-county area northwest of Chicago and is centered in Elgin. The district contains 25,000 students and its tax levies are subject to approval by some 45,000 registered voters.

The U-46 district operates on an annual budget of $44 million, of which a third comes directly from the taxpayers of the district. The balance comes from state funds and from the federal government. But although only a third of its operating budget comes from the taxpayers of the district, to some of those taxpayers—particularly those who are retired or on fixed incomes—as much as 70 percent of their personal tax bills annually goes to the financing of the district.

Currently the school district levies an annual tax of $2.35 per $100 of assessed value of property within the district. In addition, another 40¢ per $100 of assessed value goes for the building and maintenance fund of the district, from which capital improvements and capital construction needs are met.

In early 1978, the school district said this assessment was not enough. Citing an Illinois state law which allows a school district to levy up to $4 per $100 of assessed value, the district asked for an increase of 55¢ for the regular operating budget and an additional increase of 4½¢ for the capital fund.

To some citizens of the three counties, this proposed increase was excessive. In their opinion, the school district had already grown fat and was spending a substantial sum annually on exotic programs which added nothing to the basic educational mission of its schools.

Opposition to the proposed school budget increase centered on Elgin attorney Eugene Devitt, head of the Elgin Taxpayer Watchdog Committee, whose membership is basically comprised of a small group of pensioners retired from the Elgin National Watch Company. This group determined that the proposed increase was simply not needed, and they geared up to fight it.

In the U-46 district, only a very small percentage of the registered voters traditionally turn out to approve school levies. Typically, only 8 to 10 percent of the district's registered voters go to the polls in such an election, and a substantial percentage of these are either teachers, friends of teachers, their families or people who are employed by businesses with a vested interest in a continually growing school budget.

The committee decided early on that they could defeat the levy simply by making it known to the general public that the election was taking place and what was at issue. The committee received help from James Tobin, head of the National Taxpayers Union of Illinois. Tobin and other NTU accountants examined the books of the school district and, using that data, charged that the district had a $20 million surplus which has been built up over the years, and had at least an additional $500,000 in long-term investments which could be cashed in at any time in order to meet operating expenses.

Using the NTU-supplied data, the committee also charged that substantial amounts of money were being wasted each year by the district, and therefore the increased levy was not necessary.

Traditionally, the school board refers to the financially oriented election as the "school-levy referendum." That sounds sufficiently boring to the electorate that not many voters become interested. So the first thing that Devitt's Watchdog Committee began to do is to call the referendum a "school-tax-increase election."

Looking around for possible allies to help it in its efforts, the committee began to contact the parents of schoolchildren attending the one Lutheran and two Catholic schools in the area, because their children in no way benefited from the increased levy. The committee found ready allies in many of these parents. Likewise, it found a receptive audience among senior citizens of the three-county area, the people on whom the biggest burden of the increase would fall.

As soon as it became apparent to the school board that there was organized opposition to the increase, some strange changes began to occur. Normally, budget referendums in the U-46 district take place on Saturdays, with the polling places open from 7:00 A.M. until 7:00 P.M. This year, however, the school board for the first time decided to hold the election on a Tuesday and to have the polling places open only from 11:00 A.M. until 6:00 P.M. In addition, the locations of some polling places were changed, in many cases requiring the climbing of steps or long walks from the nearest parking areas. The Watchdog Committee charged that this was being done in an attempt to dissuade older people from participating in the voting, and to keep working people away from the polls.

Then, over $10,000 worth of billboards suddenly appeared throughout the three-county area, urging people to vote in favor of the school levy. The school district denied any knowledge of the billboards. The Watchdog Committee was never able to discover exactly where the money came from for the billboards, but it is generally assumed in Elgin that businesses involved with the school district put up the money and that the billboards were purchased with the full knowledge and approval of the school board.

Additional pressure to approve the levy was applied by the superintendent of the U-46 district, who has a regular ninety-minute weekly radio talk show. Prior to the vote, he turned his talk show into a sounding board for those in favor of the increased budget and levy.

Allied against this well-heeled power structure were the twenty-five members of the Watchdog Committee, with a total operating budget for the campaign of $300. A substantial percentage of that amount went for the printing of 15,000 brochures, which were distributed throughout the three-county area.

The key to success was simply getting enough people to vote. Using very common grass-roots political organizing tactics, the Watchdog Committee was able to get 600 new voters registered in time for the referendum. They estimate that all 600 were in opposition to the proposed increase. In addition, on election day, phone banks were staffed by the committee, which called previously identified sympathetic voters throughout the area and urged them to go to the polls.

The result of this get-out-the-vote effort was staggering. Almost 30 percent of the registered voters of the three counties cast their ballots that day. This was a turnout at least three times as great as any previous referendum.

The results themselves were just as overwhelming: 70 percent of those going to the polls voting against the increased levy. The power, in the end, belonged to the people, not the power brokers!

CHAPTER 8.

THE MIAMI EXPERIENCE: HOW A SMALL ERROR CAN LEAD TO DISASTER

E ARLIER WE stressed the need for careful planning and meticulous attention to detail. Nothing could better point this up than the fiasco suffered
last year by the Dade Tax Revolt Group.

Taxpayers in the Miami, Florida, area seemed primed to join the tax revolt.
So a Coral Gables retiree, Harry L. Wilson, formed DTRG and drew up a tax
cut proposition which sought to reduce property taxes much in the style of
Proposition 13.

Wilson's group quickly gathered volunteers, and within a short period they
had gathered the necessary 15,000 signatures to put the initiative on the ballot
in a special election in September. But, to their horror, they discovered that
they had made a slight mistake in the wording of their petition. The present
tax rate in Dade County is 8 mills. Wilson wanted to cut it in half, to 4 mills.
But in drafting the petition the desired tax rate was expressed as "4 mills per
$1,000." If the petition had said simply "4 mills," the proposed rate would
have been $4 for each $1,000 of assessed valuation. But "4 mills per $1,000"
means $.004 for each $1,000. So instead of asking for a tax cut of 50 percent,
the Wilson petitions asked for a tax cut of 99.95 percent!

DTRG went to court to try to get a ruling to retroactively change the
petition or to allow the group to circulate new petitions with the correct
wording. But the court ruled that the requisite number of registered voters had
signed the petitions with the 4 mills per $1,000 wording, and that was what
the voters of Dade County would have to pass on.

Gleefully County officials laid out for the voters what a 99.95 percent tax
cut would mean. Among the things they said would be necessary would be
turning off all street lights, closing the county jail, firing approximately 9,000
of the county's total work force of 14,000 (including 60 percent of the fire
department and 50 percent of the police department) and closing Miami
International Airport. About the only thing that would have continued would
have been the school system, which is separately funded.

Faced with the court decision, Wilson tried to make the best out of the situation. He argued that another petition could be passed next year bringing the rate to 4 mills and that the county could easily survive a one-year 99 percent tax cut.

Armed with a budget estimated at $200,000, two groups, one made up of municipal unions the other a business and professional group, heaped ridicule on the proposed amendment. Wilson's DTRG, with a budget of little more than $5,000, was simply no match.

Better than seven out of every ten voters who went to the polls rejected the proposed cut—this in an area where public opinion polls showed voters ready to pass a Prop 13–type tax initiative. So the addition of three small words, "for each $1,000," turned what should have been an easy victory into a resounding defeat. Eleven months of hard work by an all-volunteer taxpayer organization went for naught.

SECTION III.

THE FEDERAL REVOLT

CHAPTER 9.

THE FEDERAL BUDGET

E ARLIER, WE pointed out that any tax revolt will only result in a partial savings to you because what you do not pay to a state or local government unit, you will have to include as income and pay taxes on at the federal level. This is why there are several movements afoot to launch a federal tax revolt. We will be discussing the major ones in this section. Before we do, however, we must take a look at the reason behind the federal taxes we pay—namely, the federal budget.

When Jimmy Carter ended that long walk down Pennsylvania Avenue and entered the White House to begin his presidency, he had a goal: he was going to get federal spending under control. His promise, he thought, was a realistic one. While it was clear to him that deficits would have to continue for awhile, he was certain that he could bring fiscal responsibility to Washington. So he bravely promised a balanced federal budget by fiscal 1980, his fourth year in the White House (and the year he could be expected to try and renew his lease with the landlords—us).

Well, Jimmy Carter has been in the White House for these four years, and the realities of the federal budget have finally sunk in. Gone are the days of a promised balanced budget. In its place were proud announcements by the White House that in fiscal 1980, through tight-fisted management, we would have a "prudent" and "fiscally responsible" budget that would result in only a $29 billion deficit. However, by January 1980, only three months into the new fiscal year, "in process adjustments" had raised the FY 1980 deficit estimate to $42 billion. And for FY 1981, an "austere" budget was offered, containing spending of $616 billion and a planned deficit of $16 billion (which many experts believe will be closer to $50 billion).

According to traditional economic theory, we should now be in a period of budget surpluses. We are in the second year of a high inflation and common sense would dictate that, as a result, tax income should be at record highs with surpluses as the end product. In fiscal 1980, for example, early estimates put federal tax revenue at $498 billion. Then when President Carter made up the budget, the revenue estimate had increased to $502.6 billion. Actual revenue is now estimated at $524 billion. For fiscal year 1981 revenue is pegged at $600 billion. Even-higher revenue should mean surpluses. In fact, state governments are running at about $31 billion annual surplus while the federal government continues to run its annual deficit. Why? The answer is really very simple. Federal spending has gone crazy.

It all started in the golden Great Society days of Lyndon Johnson. Since 1965, the federal government has been on a spending spree that is almost impossible to stop or even slow down. Most of this spending binge has been for various social programs. In terms of real dollars, we are spending a smaller share of the gross national product on defense today than we were in the Eisenhower years.

Some facts are both startling and illuminating. In the fiscal 1980 budget, fully 75 percent of all dollars are already mandated to continue existing programs, and most of these dollars do not represent real growth in these programs. The fact is that, since fiscal 1975, 68 percent of all the growth in the federal budget has resulted from inflation and not real growth. In other words, anyone wanting to cut the budget really does not have very much to cut from.

A trend was started in the Johnson years, built on optimistic economic forecasting and the feeling that continued growth was inevitable. The trend was toward open-ended programs indexed to various economic factors which guaranteed that they would grow year after year as surely as winter follows fall.

Most of the new social welfare programs, such as Medicare and Medicaid, were drawn up this way. And already existing programs, such as Social Security, were completely restructured with benefit levels pushed to ever-increasing highs because they were tied to the consumer price index, a move which guaranteed their ever-higher payments to recipients.

Just look at the numbers for the growth in federal spending for welfare programs in the last decade. In 1965, 20 million Americans were receiving an average of $84 a month under Social Security. Ten years later, 34 million were getting an average of $260 per month. In the same ten-year period, the number of people getting welfare rose from 4 million who were getting an average $621 to 11 million who averaged $948. In that period, the average Medicaid benefit has doubled and the average food-stamp recipient will get almost four times the amount when new increases are phased in this year. And perhaps the biggest culprits of all are the federal retirement programs, which paid out some $5 billion in 1965, paid out over $20 billion in fiscal 1979.

In 1970, the federal debt stood at about $400 billion. It had taken from 1789 on to accumulate this much debt, but we have somehow managed to double it—that's right, double it—to $800 billion in the last ten years. As a result, annual payments on the debt have risen to $52.3 billion a year and have become a very significant factor in the federal budget.

Jimmy Carter sounds like a fiscal conservative, but his fiscal 1979 budget was $27 billion greater than the estimate Gerald Ford made for fiscal 1979 in his last budget before surrendering the White House (despite a $5.5 billion cut in defense spending). While the present tenants at 1600 Pennsylvania Avenue might argue that Ford's estimates were outrageously low since he knew he would never have to live with them, the fact is that much of the increase is the result of today's political realities.

The Carter 1979 increases included over $12 billion for jobs and social services, $7 billion for income security, $3 billion for farm price supports, $3 billion for health payments and $1 billion for community development programs. Even the "austere" 1981 budget proposes at least $13.5 billion in new spending on social programs.

To many observers, the federal budget did not get out of hand by the mere passage of a couple of expensive laws. Rather, it is the cumulative effect of a lot of seemingly little measures, most of which, however, are openended. Some examples would be illustrative:

In 1976, Congress wanted to help some drought-stricken farmers in parts of the Southwest. So with all the good intentions in the world, it overwhelmingly passed a disaster-aid bill to be administered by the Small Business Administration and designed to give grants or very low-interest, long-term loans to the stricken farmers. The price tag on the bill, the day it was passed, was put at $20 million.

But no spending ceiling was put to the legislation. Nor, for that matter, was there any time limit attached to it. So far, under this $20 million program, almost $1.5 billion has been dispersed, and eventual loans under the program are liable to reach $3 billion.

As is typical of such hastily conceived programs, no overall eligibility rules were developed. As a result, low-interest loans have been given in two cases to farmers, one of whom has over $1 million worth of loan-free land and another who has more than $100,000 cash in the bank.

Things have gotten so bad, and so many farmers are applying for loans, that the SBA had to ask Congress to take the program away from it and give it to the Department of Agriculture. The SBA said that it simply did not have enough people to process claims nor enough people who know how to assess agricultural loss.

It would be nice to think that the tax revolt will result in something dramatic happening and that the course of federal spending will be reversed. But do not bet on it. Congress spends tax money in an atmosphere of intense political pressure. Everyone talks about tax reduction, and many of the current members of Congress were elected on a platform of cutting taxes, but the plain fact is that there is nothing, absolutely nothing, that gets a taxpayer and voter madder than to see some pet federal program being cut, especially if it is a program in which he or she has a direct interest or from which he or she will derive a direct benefit. And this means simply that for every proposed cutback, there are voters who, while being foursquare for tax reduction and spending cuts, are madder than hell because it was their program that was cut.

Given the political realities, it seems clear that, although Congress talks a good game of spending reduction, it is more likely that we will get more of the same in the coming years.

The only way we are ever going to get a break is if we get a hold of federal spending, either through a constitutional amendment or a legislative mandate to hold the line.

Several solutions are currently gathering support. Some are legislative, while others represent the constitutional amendment route. Taken as a whole, they represent the tax revolt come to Washington.

CHAPTER 10.

THE LAFFER CURVE: WHEN LESS MEANS MORE

A MONG THE present tax revolt economist-gurus, one must certainly include Arthur Laffer, a professor of business economics at the University of Southern California. Professor Laffer has made a career of studying taxation and tax revenues and his famous Laffer curve is providing the academic underpinnings for much of the present tax revolt.

As Laffer explains his theory: "What I've tried to emphasize and point out is that there are two effects of a tax-rate change. For example, if you cut tax rates, the first effect—which everyone knows about—is what we call the arithmetic effect: if you cut tax rates, you collect less revenue per dollar of tax-rate base. But then there's the second effect, the economic effect—which almost everyone overlooks: if you cut the tax rates, *you expand the tax base.* And total revenues depend upon both the arithmetic effect and the economic effect.

"As often as not, when you cut tax rates, it leads to an expansion of revenues, and not a reduction."

In other words, the more money you let people keep, the more money they will want to earn. The more money they earn, the more taxes they pay, even at the lower rate. And the more taxes they pay, the more money government gets to keep functioning.

For example, if taxes equaled 100 percent, everything people work for would be taken by the government. Obviously, the people would have no reason to work—at least, not for money—and you can bet that they will not work unless someone puts a gun to their heads. But if the tax rate were zero, then everything a person earned he or she could keep, thus providing the greatest incentive to work.

Laffer's theory, therefore, is that as the tax rate goes down, the incentive to work rises. This causes an increase in productivity and, although the productivity is being taxed at a lower rate, the increase in productivity more than makes up for the decline in rate. The result is greater revenue generated by the tax system.

One night, the good professor was sitting in a Washington restaurant, expounding on his theory to several congressmen. Using either a tablecloth or a napkin, he attempted to graphically show them just how his theory works. Thus was born the Laffer curve.

TAX REVENUES

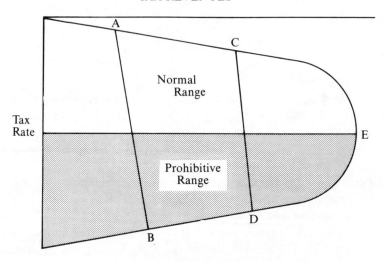

THE LAFFER CURVE

Here is what the curve means:

The vertical leg is the tax rate; the horizontal leg represents tax revenue. If you set the tax rate at zero, there would be no money to run government and the result would be no government—in other words, anarchy, a situation that might please some people but would horrify everyone else. If, on the other hand, you set the tax rate at 100 percent, the tax would be totally confiscatory, there would be no incentive to work within the money economy (meaning salaries) since people would lose everything they earned, and so they would revert to a barter economy (trading work for goods and services). Once again, the government would get no money from tax revenues because no one would be earning any money in the first place. Which brings us back to anarchy.

As the tax rate increases from point B to point D on Laffer's curve, the government obviously would be getting more money, but the people would not be losing enough money to throw in the towel or become less productive.

Coincidentally, as the tax rate declines from point A to point C, the government would also find its revenues increasing because, even though the rate is declining, more people would return to the money economy, and productivity would increase faster than the tax rate would drop.

Under Laffer's theory, the ideal point on the curve is Point E. Although it appears to be at the midpoint, it is not 50 percent. Rather, it is the maximum amount that people can be taxed and still maintain maximum productivity. It is at this point that government receives its maximum revenue. (Representative Jack Kemp, whose Kemp-Roth tax reduction bill is built around Laffer's theories, believes that mythical point beyond which we begin feeling the pinch is a peacetime tax rate of about 25 percent.)

Laffer says that we are now somewhere between point C and point E, with tax rates inching closer to point C. But if this trend could be reversed and tax rates begin to fall toward point E, tax revenues will actually increase.

There really is nothing new in Laffer's theory, as he himself is quick to point out. It was the mainstay of the economic theories of eighteenth-century writers and economists (such as Adam Smith, who, in his *Wealth of Nations,* discussed the limiting effects of high taxation). The theory was refined in the nineteenth century by two French economists, Jean Baptiste Say and Leon Walras.

In our own country, the theory was first put into practice by Andrew Mellon, who many people say was our greatest Secretary of the Treasury because he pushed through tax cuts in the early 1920s which fueled the economic growth of that decade.

Said Mellon at the time, "The history of taxation shows that taxes which are inherently excessive are not paid. The high rates inevitably put pressure upon the taxpayer to withdraw his capital from productive business and invest it in tax-exempt securities or find other lawful measures to avoid taxes. The result is that sources of taxation are drying out."

His prescription was a tax cut and it worked, Laffer points out. The same policy of tax reduction was put into effect in post-World War II West Germany. And, says Laffer, it is the tax reduction policies of West German finance minister Ludwig Erhard that are credited with the financial rebuilding of that war-ravaged nation.

In our own recent history, the 1963–64 tax cut pushed by President John F. Kennedy (against the advice of almost everyone in government) absolutely proves Laffer's point. In spite of the predictions of economic ruin, Kennedy cut back personal income tax rates by 20 percent and corporate rates by 4 percent. The government was getting less money in percentage from everyone, *but there was an actual growth in tax revenue.*

That is why Laffer says he is not worried about the effect of Proposition 13 on California. As he explains it:

"California has very high income taxes, very high property taxes, a very high sales tax, and the highest corporate profits tax of any state. We know that when you get very high rates and you cut these, the probability of tax revenue increasing is greatly enhanced. If you look at California, corporations will get the advantages [of lower property taxes] and, as a result, it will create more business there. You will get more income, output, employment and, as a result, you'll get more income taxes, more sales taxes, more profits taxes, and more construction.

". . . [Within] a very short period of time, total government revenues will increase.

"I don't think that the passage of this proposition will lead to a cut in services; in fact, I supported it because I believe that it will actually lead to an expansion of government services.

"Generally speaking, in cities that need an expansion of services, I don't see how, by raising the tax rate, you will generate the revenue for that additional increase."

One of the people who have expressed doubts about Laffer's theories is Herbert Stein, chairman of the Council of Economic Advisers under Presidents Nixon and Ford, and a bona-fide conservative.

Stein argues that there is no evidence to support the idea that a large tax cut of the kind called for by the Kemp-Roth bill would increase federal revenue. He points out that total government revenue has risen in all but three of the past thirty-two years, and the fact that revenues rose after the Kennedy cut "does not even faintly imply that they rose because of the tax cut or that they rose more than they would have risen without the tax cut."

He warns against "deluding ourselves into thinking that a large tax cut will be free." Stein puts his stress on cutting government spending as the only way to make a tax cut work.

CHAPTER 11.

THE KEMP-ROTH TAX
REDUCTION ACT

I N 1978, Representative Thomas P. "Tip" O'Neill, the Irish wit from Boston who is usually referred to as Speaker of the House, got off one of the more memorable lines of recent political days when he said of a much younger congressman of the opposing party, "He's got a pretty face but a lousy bill."

The man he was talking about was Jack Kemp, four-term Republican representative from Buffalo, New York, whose football team he once quarter-backed in the National Football League.

The bill is known as the Kemp-Roth Tax Reduction Act and is cosponsored by Senator William Roth, Republican of Delaware. It is a measure that would bring to the federal government the same revolution that Proposition 13 has brought to California.

Basically, as originally introduced in 1976 and again in July 1977, the measure in one fell swoop would have mandated *the largest single tax cut in the history of the Republic.* It was a simple bill, one that is easy to understand. As such, it was called things like "outlandish," "demagogic" and "totally irresponsible."

Its provisions were simple: personal income taxes would be cut by a third, from the present range of 14 to 70 percent to a range of 8 to 50 percent; the corporate tax rate would be lowered from 48 percent to 45 percent, and the floor for the maximum corporate rate would be raised from its present $50,000 to $100,000. These reductions would be phased in over a three-year period.

It sounded simple, and it was. The federal income tax for a family of four making $8,000 a year would be cut by 90 percent; the family of four making $15,000 would find its taxes cut by 40 percent; while the family of four making $20,000 a year would find its tax bill lowered by a third, from its present average of about $2,400 to $1,600.

What is less than simple is exactly what effect passage of Kemp-Roth would have on the federal treasury. Using the theories of Professor Laffer, the Kemp-Roth supporters argue that the results of this tax reduction will be an actual increase in federal revenues.

Washington economist Norman True created an economic model for the effects of Kemp-Roth after its implementation. His prediction was that, thanks to the tax reduction, the gross national product would jump initially by $43 billion in the first year, $95 billion in the second, and $157 billion in the third. Eventually, by 1985 (True assumed the law would be passed in 1978), GNP would grow by a total of $240 billion.

True estimated that the growth of the economy brought about by the tax cut would result in 1.2 million new jobs in the first year of the reduction, 2.5 million in the second, 4 million in the third and more than 5.5 million new full-time jobs eventually created by the shot in the arm to the economy. More important, to the prediction that tax revenues would increase, True added that capital investment would leap by $113 billion. Had the bill passed in 1977, the net result of all this would have been an increase in Washington's income of almost $1 billion in fiscal 1979, despite the substantially lower rates; at least, according to Kemp-Roth supporters.

Other economists called this nonsense. Even some who think that Laffer might be right over the long run, pointed out that True's estimates had to be substantially inflated. They claimed that the $113 billion predicted for the first year of Kemp-Roth in the growth of capital investment would represent a 30 percent increase in that category (when adjusted into real dollars to take out the impact of inflation). This is about the same as the entire growth in capital investment in the period 1965-72, a period of substantial growth. A jump of capital investment of this magnitude, they claimed, is simply not possible; you couldn't increase capital investment this much even if you had the money available. Yet for the forecast of increasing tax income under Kemp-Roth, such a growth in capital investment is probably necessary.

Further, the critics argued that even pro-Kemp-Roth economist True predicts that in later years, as the jump in GNP is slowed, the reverse will happen and revenues will fall off, perhaps by as much as $40 billion a year.

Opponents of Kemp-Roth said that if the bill were to become law, it would cost the treasury $80 billion a year and there is simply no way that the federal budget could sustain such a shock. Further, they argued, by putting that much more money in the public's pockets, an unprecedented spending boom would take place and would result in the largest leap in inflation ever seen in this country, not to mention the almost certain credit crunch that would follow.

Many proponents of the measure said, however, that, like the politicians in California after Proposition 13, maybe it is time that the Washington bureaucrats simply were forced to learn to live with $80 billion less and that the resultant inflationary pressures could be controlled if the White House had the bill to do so.

Kemp points out that his bill was simply modeled after the Kennedy tax-cut measure of 1964-65, when personal taxes were cut by a little over 20 percent and corporate rates were lowered from 52 percent to 48 percent. The effect of the Kennedy cut was to actually increase federal revenue, and led to a period of budget surpluses.

Senator Roth adds that, "Since 1946, every time we have had a tax cut, there were predictions of a decrease in revenue. But every time, the opposite has happened and revenue has actually increased."

Kemp is a conservative but he has some decidedly unconservative economic views. He says that he does not necessarily want to see a decline in federal spending and does not think that a balanced budget is all that important. He stresses that he wants to see a tax cut for the purpose of spurring the economy.

As he puts it, "I don't worship at the altar of the balanced budget. I would much rather have a growing economy and a budget that is unbalanced than one that is balanced in an era of contracting growth.

"In America, we now tax work, growth, investment, employment, savings and productivity, while we subsidize nonwork, consumption, welfare and debt. It's time we start to reverse this trend."

Kemp sees his present bill as only a beginning. Eventually, he would like to see the tax rate lowered to a minimum of 5 percent and a maximum of 25 percent, with the corporate rate set at 25 percent and a substantial reduction of both capital gains and estate taxes.

The Kemp-Roth Tax Reduction Act is not new. It was originally introduced into Congress in 1976. But with the influence of "Prop 13," it managed to gather 148 House cosponsors, as well as Senator Roth and nineteen other senators.

It was far from enough, however; Congress was not ready for such a wholesale cut. In 1978, therefore, a new bill emerged. It still is officially known as the Kemp-Roth Tax Reduction Act, but on Capitol Hill it is being called "Son of Kemp-Roth," or simply "Kemp-Roth II."

K-R II has three main features: (1) the K-R I 10 percent-a-year, three-year tax reduction, which would reduce taxes by almost a third over the period, is revived; (2) at the end of the three years, tax rates would be indexed to the rate of inflation to prevent a taxpayer from being pushed into a higher bracket without any real change in his or her income; and (3) a lid is placed on federal spending as a percentage of GNP.

Despite the fact that K-R II found substantial support in the 95th Congress, it did not stand a chance. It since has been reintroduced in the 96th Congress, and its proponents hope either to have it considered on its own merits or as part of the Revenue Act.

K-R II's chances this time around are unknown, but one thing is certain: the idea, considered radical when first proposed in 1976, has taken hold on the Hill. The basic changes contained in K-R I and K-R II have been embodied in other bills now pending in both houses. In fact, some of the bill's provisions are almost tame in comparison to a new bill introduced by Representative Robert Dornan (R-Calif.), which, considering its provisions, quite obviously is the brainchild of Howard Jarvis (see the following chapter).

For information on K-R II, contact Rep. Jack Kemp, 2235 Rayburn House Office Building, Washington, DC 20515.

CHAPTER 12

THE AMERICAN TAX REDUCTION ACT OF 1979

T HIS IS Howard Jarvis' national tax revolt bill and it is in keeping with his stated philosophy of slash, slash, slash. Introduced by Representative Dornan, the bill naturally is receiving the full support of Jarvis' American Tax Reduction Movement.

The bill is designed, as was Prop 13, to make major cuts in taxes. Specifically, the measure would: (1) provide for a federal surplus by no later than fiscal 1983 and thus, after that, for a reduction of the national debt; (2) place a permanent limit on federal spending at 18 percent of the total gross national product; (3) reduce federal individual income taxes over a four-year period by a total of $50 billion; (4) mandate a cutting back of the federal budget by $100 billion in the same period; (5) reduce by half the federal taxation of capital gains; and (6) index virtually all taxes—including income, corporate, capital gains, and estate and gift—to prevent all taxpayers from paying more simply because of inflation.

Jarvis claims the bill has the backing of 80 House members. He says that, by the time it is ready for committee passage (sometime in 1980), he will have lined up 140 cosponsors, 100 Democrats and 40 Republicans. This, he says, will show the measure has enough support to get it to the House floor, and once there, it will be passed because of public pressure. Or so he says.

"We are going to make this bill *the* test of whether a politician is really for tax cuts and reduced spending," Jarvis declares, "and no congressman will dare go back to face the voters in November of 1980 having voted against this bill."

CHAPTER 13.

CONSTITUTIONAL AMENDMENTS

O N JUNE 12, 1978, Representative Philip Crane (R-Ill.) introduced a constitutional amendment which, if passed and then approved by the requisite number of states, would mandate the total amount the federal government can spend in any one year.

What the Crane Amendment seeks to do is limit federal spending in any fiscal year to a sum equal to one-third of the average of gross national income in the three preceding years. When the amendment was introduced, it was considered quite radical and did not even merit much of a hearing from the House Judiciary Committee. However, this was before 30 states had issued a convention call for a constitutional amendment to balance the federal budget. So, when the 96th Congress convened in January 1979, hardly a day went by when some senator or representative did not offer up an amendment for consideration. Crane reintroduced his, and by early fall, it had been joined by 38 others in the House. Meanwhile, in the Senate, 20 separate amendments were introduced. These have been boiled down to a single compromise amendment, currently before the Judiciary Committee.

The amendments range from the very simple—e.g., "The Federal Government shall not spend any more than it takes in in any fiscal year"—to highly complex pieces of legislation covering many pages and including virtually incomprehensible language and mathematical formulas. The amendments do every from simply calling for a balanced budget to setting spending limitations based on indexing to seeking to eliminate the present national debt.

Several other measures have received substantial support from certain interest groups. Crane's, of course, is being supported by the American Conservative Union, which he headed prior to announcing his candidacy for the presidency. The National Tax Limitation Committee is throwing its weight behind a proposal introduced into the Senate by Senators John Heinz (R-Pa.) and Richard Stone (D-Fl.). The Heinz-Stone amendment seeks to limit total federal spending to growth in GNP, would reduce public debt through any tax surplus in any fiscal year and seeks to limit growth in federal grants to state and local governments.

In the House, it has been left up to two subcommittees to sort through all the proposed constitutional amendments to see if any consensus can be reached on language for a single amendment. On the Senate side, the Judiciary subcommittee on the Constitution, chaired by Senator Birch Bayh (D-Ind.), reached a compromise in early December 1979 and on December 20 reported it out to the full Judiciary Committee for consideration. In essence, the amendment would prohibit an unbalanced budget unless three-fifths of the members of both houses of Congress approved it. It would also prohibit the passage of any appropriations bill which would throw the budget out of balance.

The proposed amendment also states that "the receipts in any year shall not exceed, as a proportion of the national income, that collected in accordance with this section in the prior year, unless the bill directed solely at approving a specific increase in such proportion has been passed by each house of Congress by roll-call vote and such bill has become law."

On March 18, 1980, the Judiciary Committee, chaired by Senator Edward M. Kennedy, rejected the Bayh subcommittee amendment by a vote of nine to eight. The deciding vote was cast by Senator Charles C. Mathias of Maryland, the only Republican on the committee to vote against the measure.

On the House side, the House Judiciary Committee's Subcommittee on Monopolies and Commercial Law would seem to have an even greater problem in reconciling the 39 amendments before it. Its chairman, Representative Peter Rodino (D-N.J.), has chosen the approach of holding general hearings on the topic and then, it is hoped, being able to draft a subcommittee version of an amendment acceptable to all.

The chances of both Senate and House coming up with a single amendment that can be agreed upon and passed by both bodies do not appear great. It is not considered likely, therefore, that the present Congress will pass and forward to the states a balance-the-budget (or spending-lid or indexing) constitutional amendment. Unless, of course, public pressure demands it in an election year.

CHAPTER 14.

THE CONSTITUTIONAL CONVENTION TO BALANCE THE BUDGET

N EVER IN the history of our Republic has there been a convention called for the purpose of amending the Constitution. While the Constitution has been amended twenty-six times, in each case it has been Congress which first approved the amendment and then sent it off to the states for ratification. At one time or another, every state has called for an amending convention, but never has the requisite two-thirds issued the call at the same time or for the same reason.

Currently, two constitutional convention calls are underway. The one which has gotten the lion's share of publicity has been the one by the so-called right-to-life forces for an amendment against abortion. Nine states have approved the proclamation to call such a convention and right-to-life forces has trumpeted this as the most advanced convention-call effort ever.

Not so. Another convention call is underway, getting less publicity, but it is far more advanced in its effort to get thirty-four states to issue the call. This effort has been going on for five years and would lead to a convention called for the purpose of adopting an amendment that would require a balanced federal budget. The effort for the balanced budget amendment is being led by the National Taxpayers Union.

The proponents of the amendment see it as a starting place to get a hold of federal spending and to eventually force a cutback in federal taxes. They dispute the conventional economic thinking that says that governmental deficits fuel economic growth. They point out that in this country, as deficits have grown over the past decades, average annual growth of gross national product has declined.

In the decade 1961–70, the average annual deficit was $6 billion. In that decade, average unemployment was 4.6 percent and the average growth of GNP was 3.6 percent. In the first half of this decade, the annual deficit has grown to $22.2 billion annually. Yet unemployment has actually gone up, to an annual average of 6.4 percent, while economic growth, measured in GNP, has dropped to 1.5 percent.

The economic measure that has risen as fast as the deficit has been inflation, which is growing at the rate of 7.1 percent annually, up from an annual growth of 3.1 percent in the previous decade.

Further, the proponents of this amendment point out that in comparing the growth of various Western countries in the decade 1965–74, the countries showing the greatest growth have been those with central government budget surpluses or balanced budgets, while those showing the least growth had the largest budget deficits.

The NTU campaign points out that our national debt is now in excess of $700 billion, which is more than the total cost of running the country from its founding until 1950, including the full cost of both world wars. Also, if the national debt were charged to each man, woman and child in the United States, it would amount to more than $11,000 each.

The proponents think that they have an overwhelming percentage of the population behind them. They point to a 1976 Gallup Poll in which 90 percent of the respondents thought that it was "very important" to have a balanced federal budget and 76 percent were willing to amend the Constitution in order to accomplish it.

Thus, five years ago, the NTU began to organize a national campaign for the purpose of calling a constitutional convention. They are hopeful that thirty-four states will issue the call in approximately these words:

"Resolved: That, alternatively, this body makes application and requests that the Congress of the United States call a constitutional convention for the specific and exclusive purpose of proposing an amendment to the federal Constitution requiring in the absence of a national emergency that the total of federal appropriations made by the Congress for any fiscal year may not exceed the total of estimated federal revenues for the fiscal year."

So far, thirty states have issued the call. The proponents hope to line up the additional four states by the end of 1980.

This is easier said than done, however. Of the 20 remaining states (Hawaii, West Virginia, Washington, Vermont, Rhode Island, Minnesota, Wisconsin, Connecticut, Michigan, California, Alaska, Illinois, Ohio, Missouri, New Jersey, New York, Maine, Massachusetts, Kentucky and Montana), a number have already turned down the resolution. Another group has already adjourned biennial legislative sessions that will not meet again until 1981. Still another group has said it will not even hold hearings on the matter until the 1980 legislative session in each of these states. So, finding four states that might grant approval in the nearterm becomes a difficult task.

According to the organizers, the states now regarded as best bets for being the magic four are Montana (where one house of the legislature already has approved), Maine, Alaska and Kentucky; New Jersey and Minnesota are considered possibilities.

A problem that convention-call proponents have run into is that resistance to the idea now has become organized; earlier, before the publicity, the plan had sailed through many state legislatures because of the lack of opposition. Labor is against the plan, as are some elements of big business and, most important, the power structure of the Democratic Party. This opposition, led by Vice President Walter Mondale, has become a considerable force to reckon with.

Thus, the convention call is in a "so near yet so far" posture, much like the Equal Rights Amendment, and it now appears that the earliest the thirty-four state will issue a convention call is late in 1980, if ever.

Since no constitutional convention has ever been called before, the only background consists of various opinions by constitutional scholars. There is almost universal agreement that such a call is constitutional and legal, and once thirty-four states issue that call the convention must be held. But this general agreement breaks down somewhat as the experts debate the crucial details.

There is substantial agreement that the convention may be called only to debate a specific amendment and must be limited to that one subject. Where this agreement begins to falter is over the question of whether such a convention may also consider related matters. (For example, a number of states which have responded to the right-to-life campaign for a convention have issued the convention call for consideration of an amendment to abolish abortion and to consider other matters related to the family. Some experts see this convention call as invalid because it is a call for multiple purposes.)

A second problem that constitutional experts have raised is that the convention calls by the states cannot contain the specific language of the amendment sought because this would leave nothing for the convention to debate.

One problem thus far with most of the "calls" issued by the 30 states is that 26 of them give Congress an out. What these 26 states have done is to word their convention calls in such a way that would enable whichever Congress is meeting when the thirty-fourth state issues the call to pass its own balance-the-budget amendment and forward it to the states for the seven-year ratification process.

This means that if the thirty-fourth state does not issue its call until after Congress adjourns in October 1980, the clock will not start running until the new, 97th, Congress convenes in January 1981. This would give that Congress two years to act; if it did not, a convention would be called, but only until sometime in 1983 or even 1984.

However, some believe Congress may make the convention call moot by approving a constitutional amendment sometime in 1980 or 1981. As we saw earlier, Congress currently does not lack for ideas.

For further information on the Balance the Budget Convention Call, contact the National Taxpayers Union, 325 Pennsylvania Ave., S.E., Washington, D.C. 20003.

CHAPTER 15.

SUNSET LEGISLATION

A CCORDING TO most experts, one of the main problems with various tax-cutting or fiscal-control proposals, either constitutional or legislative, is that much of the federal budget is simply uncontrollable.

Some figures cited earlier are worth repeating. In the fiscal 1980 budget, fully 75 percent of all spending is mandated either for continuing programs or for things already contracted. Further, since fiscal 1975, fully 68 percent of the growth of the federal budget has been caused solely by inflation. Between the mandated programs and the continued rise in inflation, the budget by fiscal 1983 will reach about $700 billion.

If tax rates are kept at current levels, so that total federal tax revenue is kept at about its current level relative to gross national product about 21 percent —total revenue in fiscal 1983 will be $727 billion. This will mean that, given mandated programs and inflation, only $27 million will be available in fiscal 1983 either to use for new programs not yet on the books or, heaven forbid, for lowering the tax rate.

Given this situation, which is not speculative but is actually happening, the only way that money will be available for either new programs or reducing taxes will be to take it from existing programs. But as history shows, once Congress starts a program, short of absolutely gross mismanagement bordering on the criminal, or the complete disappearance of whatever problem the program is designed to combat, the program does not end. For to end it would be mean that Congress would have to admit to making a mistake in starting it in the first place, and Congress is not big on admitting mistakes.

Therefore, Senator Edmund Muskie, Democrat of Maine, chairman of the Senate Budget Committee, proposed a bill in the last three Congresses which now is formally known as the "Program Evaluation Act of 1979," but commonly known as the "Sunset Bill."

Under this law, all federal programs would be subject to a regular review and would have to be able to prove their continued worth if they are to be reauthorized and refunded. Under the law, a detailed ten-year, five-Congress cycle is set up to mandate which programs must be reviewed in each of the five two-year congressional terms. The schedule would include virtually every federal agency, program, commission and board. Any program not specifically reauthorized by the time Congress adjourns in the session in which it is up for review would automatically go out of business.

A review of the existing list of federal programs, over 1,100 administered by some 60 agencies, points out another problem that the Sunset Law is designed to overcome. The program listing, for example, shows thirty-six different programs under the general title of veterans aid, an additional twenty programs listed as veterans medical assistance, and yet another twenty-four separate programs, again all different, under the category of veterans job training. It is obvious that many of these programs overlap and that millions of tax dollars are being spend on duplicative services.

Under the Sunset Law, Congress would be mandated to reauthorize all programs of a single type at the same time. So the Congress which takes up the topic of veterans affairs would be required to review and reauthorize all veterans programs. Theoretically, overlapping and duplicate programs could thus be ferreted out and eliminated.

Still another feature of the legislation would be that since any agency or program not specifically reauthorized by the end of a session would go out of existence, Congress would be forced to act. It would be required to adhere to a strict work schedule and could not afford to become bogged down.

The final benefit of the legislation would be the establishment of a blue-ribbon, nongovernment (i.e., citizens) panel, with staff, to continually monitor the bureaucracy and recommend to Congress which agencies and programs deserve to be continued and which deserve to be terminated. This would give citizens their first direct monitoring authority over the government bureaucracy that they are paying for.

Some programs and agencies would be specifically exempted from the legislation. This would include the federal judiciary, the so-called contributory programs such as Social Security and Medicare, as well as interest on the national debt. Variously, federally funded retirement programs would be subject to the stringent ten-year review requirement but would not automatically go out of existence if not specifically reauthorized by the end of the congressional term.

In addition, the various federal regulatory agencies would be subject to the review but not the rules that they administer. Therefore, theoretically, if a regulatory agency were allowed to expire by not being reauthorized, the oversight of the rules that agency administers would automatically pass to the continuing regulatory agency whose function most closely resembles it.

As a safeguard against termination of any agency or program without a congressional vote either through a filibuster or other delaying tactic, the bill sets up a "privileged vote" status which mandates a vote within fifty hours after a reauthorization reaches the floor of either body.

As Muskie explains, "What it would do, what Sunset would do, would be to force the reauthorization of existing programs on a fixed schedule so that programs can be phased out if they can't be justified on their record of performance and on the record of their contribution to the national interest at that time."

But it appears that the Muskie concept of sunset, a strict construction that would actually cause programs to end if Congress does not act, does not sit well with many of our legislators. True, late in 1978 the Senate, by a vote of 87 to 1, did approve the Muskie bill, but it was with the knowledge that it was too late in the session for the House to act. Thus the vote was more a public relations gesture than an attempt to actually enact the Muskie bill into law.

At the start of the present legislative session, January 1979, Muskie reintroduced his bill, calling it the Program Evulation Act of 1979. But the substantial support, or at least lip service, it had in the previous session had largely evaporated. Faced with the prospect of actually passing the measure, the congressional leadership suddenly became very worried about what the review of all programs would do to its workload. So both the House and the Senate came up with new proposals that, while still called "sunset bills," are much watered down versions of the original Muskie concept.

The current Senate bill actually is an amended version of the original Muskie proposal. Proposed by Senators Charles Percy (R-Ill.), Jacob Javits (R-N.Y.) and Abraham Ribicoff (D.-Conn.), the measure would allow the congressional committee with oversight authority over a program to choose whether it wants to review the specific program.

Javits defends this version saying its purpose is to strengthen the sunset process. "I do not want to see us become bogged down in a nightmare of hearings, studies, reports and procedural problems on the floor," Javits said. "If this happens the sunset concept could fail under its own weight."

The House version of the new sunset bill (H.R. 5858) was introduced by Representative Gillis Long (D-La.), chairman of the Rules subcommittee on the legislative process. Like the Senate amendment, thc Long bill would require committees, every two years, to choose what programs they want to review. Further, no program could come to an end unless Congress votes affirmatively to kill it.

With many committee chairmen and senior members of both the Senate and the House opposed to the broad approach to sunset legislation that Muskie first proposed, it appears likely that if any bill emerges it will be along the lines of the Long bill. It will be labeled "sunset," but it will bear little resemblence to the original Muskie concept.

CHAPTER 16.

THE TAX EQUALIZATION
ACT OF 1979

I NFLATION, AS we all know, is manifested as the steady upward pressure of prices, which means that, despite the fact that we are earning more today than we did yesterday, we cannot buy any more than we used to (and probably less). No one, it seems, wins in an inflationary period except the federal government—which does so because of "taxflation," a steady increase in the revenues government takes in through taxes because of inflation.

Our income tax system is graduated. As a taxpayer's income increases, so does the percentage of that income he or she has to pay in taxes. In an inflationary period, such as we have been in for the last half decade, as wages rise to keep pace with inflation the taxpayer pays a higher and higher percentage of his or her wages in taxes even though buying power has not improved and, in fact, may be even worse. For instance, according to the fiscal year 1981 budget, personal tax income received by the federal government will increase by $35.7 billion. Of this amount, $14 billion will be solely due to this so-called bracket creep.

A bill has been introduced in Congress to try to elevate this problem. Known officially as the Tax Equalization Act of 1979, the proposed new law is also known as the "Dole-Gradison Indexing Act," after its cosponsors, Senator Robert Dole (R-Kan) and Representative Willis Gradison (R-Ohio).

What the bill is intended to do is make income taxes inflation-proof by automatically widening tax brackets according to the inflation rate. It would accomplish this by indexing tax brackets and personal exemption amounts to the consumer price index. Thus, if the CPI increases in a year by a certain percentage, tax brackets then would be upped by that percentage and personal exemption amounts would be similarly increased. This, say the bill's sponsors, would prevent a taxpayer from being pushed into a higher tax bracket and paying more tax simply because his or her income rose merely to keep pace with inflation. The only time a taxpayer would pay more is if his or her wages rose more than inflation and, thus, he or she enjoyed a real wage increase.

The bill is similar to one introduced by Senator Dole in 1978. That bill failed to clear the Senate Finance Committee by only two votes.

Several states—including California, Colorado and Iowa—already have indexed state taxes to the CPI in order to hold down the effects of inflation.

CHAPTER 17.

GROSS TAX PROPOSALS

T HERE ARE a number of experts in the federal tax system who argue that the present one has gotten so complicated and so cumbersome that the only real way to reform it is simply to throw the whole thing out and start over again from scratch.

One such proponent of this most basic of all means of tax reform is former secretary of the treasury William Simon, who made his proposal for a new basic tax system in a report issued during his last days in office in January 1977. The report was the result of a year-long study into basic tax reform, which he had ordered the Treasury Department and the Internal Revenue Service to conduct.

The report contains a new model tax system calling for the integration of corporate and personal income taxes, taxation of capital gains at full rates after allowing an adjustment for inflation and taxing many items that are not now taxed. It is a relatively simple system. It eliminates many exemptions and deductions, and it calls for replacing the present complex tax structures—the rates of which range from 14 to 70 percent—with only three tax brackets, ranging from a low of 8 percent to a high of 38 percent.

The key change in the Simon plan is the merging and integration of corporate and individual income taxes. Noting that corporations do not "consume," in the normal sense of the word, Simon proposes to eliminate the corporate income tax. Instead, there would be limits placed on the amount of profit a corporation could retain for future growth and the remainder would have to be paid out to its stockholders in the form of dividends. These dividends would then be taxed as part of the shareholders' income. In this way, a corporate income is fully taxed at rates appropriate to each of the shareholders.

Under this novel approach, capital gains also would be treated differently. Capital gains would become an increase in real wealth and not simply an artificial gain or loss through sale or exchange of an asset. Under the Simon plan, the capital gains would be fully taxable after adding in an inflation factor. Therefore, the capital gains that would be taxed would be the actual real gain of the value of an asset and not just the gain attributable to the natural rise of inflation.

In the Simon plan, deductions would be severely limited and would probably only consist of deductions for state and local taxes paid, interest paid, child-care expenses and payments to retirement systems. The normal standard deduction would also be eliminated; in its place would be more generous personal exemptions.

Simon and the experts he brought together to study the problem concluded that such a simplified system can work because it is "possible under the comprehensive income tax to raise the same revenue with roughly the same distribution of the tax burden by income class as under the present income tax system."

To do this, Simon proposes using only three income tax-rate brackets: 8 percent in the lowest bracket, 25 percent at the middle-income level, and 38 percent for upper-income taxpayers. Coupled with a generous personal exemption, it would be possible, Simon contends, to raise the same revenue while making the tax burden more equitable and, most importantly, by making the system easier to understand for the average taxpayer.

An individual's method of calculating his or her tax liability under this new system would be similar to the present method. However, the system would be much simpler and almost every taxpayer could easily figure his or her own taxes without the help of an outside preparer.

In addition, Simon says, since the burden of paying corporate taxes would in effect be shifted to the stockholder, corporations might withhold taxes from dividend payments much in the way employers currently withhold income taxes from paychecks. This would prevent taxpayers from being faced with large tax bills that they are unable to meet because they have already spent the money. It would also speed up the flow of the funds to the Treasury, as is now the case with the monthly payment by employers of taxes withheld from salaries.

Some tax reformers, however, have suggested an even more basic tax system, one that simply treats all income, from whatever source, as money earned and then taxed at a fixed rate, allowing few or even no deductions, exemptions or adjustments.

One such proponent of this basic revenue-collecting system is tax reformer Philip M. Stern. In his best-selling book on tax reform, *The Rape of the Taxpayer* (Random House, 1972), Stern suggests a system whereby the tax-payer would figure his or her taxes in a simple three-step operation:

1. Add up all your income for the year. Stern suggests a very broad definition of income: everything you receive that would give you the ability to buy something. This would include wages, all government benefits, any

money received by gift or inheritance and any money received through dividends or interest, including dividends on now tax-exempt government bonds.

2. Deduct from that total income a certain amount for yourself and each dependent at a rate to be fixed by Congress, as well as any costs you incurred in getting that income.

3. After making your deductions, figure your taxes based on a set of rates established by Congress.

There is substantial debate as to exactly what this range of tax rates would be. Stern estimates that they would be about two-fifths lower than the rates in existence in 1972, starting at approximately 8 percent to a top rate of no more than 40 percent. Brookings Institute economists Joseph Pechman and Benjamin Okner have done a computerized analysis of this type of tax system and suggest a rate schedule ranging from 7 to 44 percent in order to lighten the tax load on the lower-income taxpayer.

A Texas-based citizen's organization calling itself the Government Research and Development Corporation, headquartered in Blanco, Texas, is pushing for this type of basic tax system. Its managing director, Jim Jones, has on occasion appeared before congressional panels to testify in favor of it. His main efforts are to inform the press and public of the potential benefits of such a system.

Jones's system differs from Stern's in that corporate as well as personal taxes would be figured on this basis. Under Jones's system, as with Stern's, all income from whatever source would be added up, but with Jones's system no deductions of any kind would be allowed and a flat percentage of the total amount of income would be owed the federal government for income taxes.

Jones estimates that *as little as 1 to 3 percent* of this tax on gross income *would provide as much tax revenue as the federal government now receives* (although he admits that he has no hard data to support this contention).

Jones has made up a sample tax form, which in twenty-seven lines computes gross income, taxable income and income tax.

One obvious boon of any simplified tax plan, whether Simon's, Stern's or Jones's, is that the average taxpayer could figure out his or her tax bill in thirty seconds with no outside help, and the federal government could be saved millions of dollars annually because it could eliminate a vast percentage of the bureaucracy which now exists to collect taxes and to administer the progressively more complex tax structure.

SECTION IV.

THINGS YOU MUST KNOW

CHAPTER 18.

ON TAXES AND TAX REVOLTS

N ow you know everything you need to know about how to conduct a tax revolt, and you have seen how a few of those revolts worked. But there is a lot more information that you will need to know before you can even get started.

The very first thing you are going to have to know, as we pointed out in Step 1, is what kind of taxes you pay, to whom you pay it and why. In general terms, we will answer the first two parts of that question in this chapter. The last part, why you paid it, is something only your own research can answer.

What follows, then, are listings of the most common forms of taxation that you are probably required to pay, and a brief explanation. In some cases, you may not even realize that you are paying these taxes (Jarvis's 116 taxes on a loaf of bread, for example, or the taxes you pay on a gallon of gasoline). Not included in this list, however, are those "taxes" that come to you in the form of monthly bills for government services, such as water, garbage collection and the like.

Compare your lifestyle and your state or local community tax system to the following lists and you can begin to add up your total tax bill.

FEDERAL

Individual income: This is the most familiar type of tax, the one due IRS every April 15. The system is based on a theory of earned income, which is why, before you even begin to figure out what you owe Uncle Sam, you are allowed to deduct from your gross income (meaning every cent you earn) what it costs you to earn that income in the first place. The maximum rate on earned income is currently 50 percent.

Capital gains: Actually, the capital gains tax is not a separate tax but is part of your individual income tax. Simply put, when a taxpayer sells an asset (stocks, house, etc.) for more than he or she paid for it, a profit has been realized on that sale. This profit is treated as income to the taxpayer in the year in which the asset was sold, and that income must be treated as part of earned income in that year's federal return.

Corporate income: The amount that corporations must pay to the IRS is based on the concept of gross profits, that is, whatever is left after the various costs of doing business have been subtracted. Also subtracted are various tax credits that Congress has deemed necessary to promote a number of social needs (mainly toward the creation of new jobs). The maximum corporate rate is currently 48 percent. (It should be noted that, after corporations pay their taxes on gross profits, they distribute a substantial percentage of what is left to their stockholders in the form of dividends. In turn, these dividends are taxable to the individual stockholders as part of their earned income, in effect resulting in the double taxation of corporate profits.)

Estate and gift: If you come into money through inheritance, you must pay a portion of that money, after certain deductions, to the federal government in the form of an estate tax. The money is usually paid directly by the estate before the amount is distributed to the heirs. At the same time, if you make a gift of money or property, either personal or real, to an individual in an amount greater than $6,000 in a single year, you must pay a federal gift tax on that amount. Both these taxes are highly complicated, have any number of loopholes and the rates vary greatly, depending on the amounts involved. That should discourage you from wanting to lavish a lot of money on someone.

Excise: Excise sounds innocuous enough. But when you look at the myriad of little taxes that make up this category, you may be more than a little surprised. First, of course, are the biggies, the ones that are well known. These include the gasoline, liquor, tobacco, cigarettes (that's the finished product and amounts to about 8¢ a pack) and import (not to be confused with import duties, which is an amount that the federal government tacks on to an imported product to bring its eventual retail price more in line with a competing, more expensive, U.S.-made product).

But that is only the tip of the excise-tax iceberg. Federal excise taxes are also tacked on to thirty specific manufactured goods at the point of manufacture (everything from matches to tires to firearms to televisions), telephone calls, air transportation (and this is in addition to various fees, such as security fees, that are tacked on to ticket prices), produce transportation, amusement admissions, and a special retailers' tax on luxury items (including jewelry, furs, leather goods, perfume and luggage) and cabaret bills.

STATE

You still have money left? Fantastic, because the state has its hand out, too. (We have grouped the following taxes together although in some cases they may actually be levied by other local taxing bodies, or at the county or township level.)

Individual income: The state counterpart of the federal tax. In almost every state that levies a personal income tax, it is geared to the federal tax system and is based on a percentage of the federal tax less a credit for the amount of federal tax you have paid.

Corporate income: Again, like the federal corporate income tax, it is a tax on the profits of corporations either incorporated under the laws of the state or of "foreign" corporations (meaning chartered in other states) and doing business in the state.

Personal property: A once-a-year levy on the value of personal property owned by residents.

Real property: A once-a-year levy on the value of real property owned in the state. Since the most valuable asset most people own is their house, this is one of the highest taxes they pay. Also, it is a tax most likely due in a lump sum and one that is not withheld, making it particularly burdensome. On the other hand, it is one of the biggest sources of income for many state and local governments, and in many cases for school boards as well. Some school boards around the country get as much as 70 percent of their operating budgets from local property taxes.

Sales: An amount tacked on to retail sales at the point of final sale. Some states exempt certain necessities (food and drugs) from this tax. And if you don't think that the pennies add up, the fifty states in 1976 collected a total of $27 billion through this tax.

Excise: Just as in the federal system, this is in reality a series of state taxes applied to a whole list of items usually at the point of purchase. Also as in the federal system, the biggest revenue-producing excise taxes are on gasoline, cigarettes and tobacco and alcoholic beverages.

Inheritance and estate and gift: Thirty-four states and the District of Columbia levy an inheritance tax (sometimes known simply as a death tax), which can be as high as 30 percent. All the states, however, exempt amounts below a certain sum, depending on the state. An additional sixteen states levy state estate and gift taxes modeled after the federal taxes and in most cases are applicable only to amounts in excess of $10,000.

Pari-mutuel: In those twenty-seven states that allow racetrack gambling, both horse and dog, a percentage of every dollar bet at the track goes directly into the state's coffers. This is deducted automatically before the track figures out what a winning ticket will be paid (at the same time, the track takes its share). Again, this is no nickle-and-dime tax. In 1976, those twenty-seven states took in $719 million this way.

Unemployment compensation: Often not thought of as a tax, this is the amount withheld from each worker's paycheck and matched by a "contribution" from the employer. Although mandated by Congress, the money goes into state funds.

LOCAL

You really still have some money left? Thank goodness for small miracles. Because those guys at the local level are ready for their cut. (Remember, often what seems to be a state tax is actually locally controlled and what seems to be a local tax may really be mandated by the state.)

Individual income: A simple matter. After you figure out what you owe the federal government and the state, take a percentage and pay it to the local community. This tax does not exist in many communities but is especially high in some big cities, such as New York City. A variation of this is the so-called commuter tax, which is really an income tax levied against workers who work in one community but live in another.

Sales: Again, this is an amount levied against goods at their place of final sale.

If you still have anything left after all of this, and all that you have just shelled out does not bother you, close the book and go fishing, as we suggested earlier. But if the load is a bit too much, then read on. For now we get into the different kinds of tax revolt available.

KINDS OF TAX REVOLT

The current tax revolt campaigns that are sweeping the nation basically can be divided into two categories: those which seek to directly limit future increases in taxes or seek to do so indirectly by holding down spending, and those seeking to roll back specific taxes.

Tax Limitation: According to Lewis Uhler, president of the National Tax Limitation Committee, the only really basic tax reform that is going to work is a general across-the-board limitation of future tax growth. The only effective way this can happen is through the constitutional amendment process.

Actually, this can be accomplished in a number of different ways. One way would be to merely limit the amount of taxes a government unit can collect. Another way, and the most popular, is currently effective in Tennessee and is a tax revolt issue in Michigan and a dozen other jurisdictions. This way does not limit taxation; rather, it limits government spending and then ties the amount of tax that can be raised in any one year to the amount to be spent *in that year.*

The idea is to hold down future growth by putting a lid on future years' spending. Various methods to do this are being tried. The most basic is simply using the current fiscal year as a base and not allowing future spending to go above the current level. This is an absolute approach and does not allow for any government expansion, either as populations grow and more services are required, or as inflation drives up costs. Thus, to remain absolutely constant really means to go backwards in the future. For this reason, such an approach has been considered too radical and has not found much support.

A much better method is to allow some growth, either a predetermined amount each year or as much as is needed given a certain set of circumstances. In allowing predetermined growth, various factors are considered and a figure is arrived at as being an amount of growth that is within the affordable limits of the population. An amendment is then passed simply limiting each future year's budget to a maximum percentage. But this too is rather inflexible.

Therefore, it is advisable to devise a way for the budget to grow in accordance with the taxpayers' ability to pay. This can be accomplished by figuring out what percentage of the total real income of the state's taxpayers makes up the present budget. Assuming that what you are trying to do is hold down taxes to no more than what is being taken now, you index future budgets to that rate of personal income that exists in the current year, or perhaps has been in the average of the last three years.

This allows the budget to increase as income goes up because, as income goes up, so will the state's tax collections. Inflation, which drives up state government costs, also drives up salaries at about the same rate; this builds in an inflation factor. Further, as the state's population grows and more services are demanded, the budget will go up because more people are paying in more money, even though the rate remains constant.

This method was approved by the New Jersey state legislature, is before the voters in Michigan and is being proposed in one form or another in many jurisdictions. In Tennessee, the constitutional convention approved a play whereby, instead of using a predetermined rate, the budget is allowed to grow as fast as the state's economy, as defined by a computer-run economic model kept by the University of Tennessee.

Included in all these plans, of course, is the caveat that government cannot spend more than it takes in—in other words, a balanced budget—and the ability of the legislature to vote (usually by a two-thirds majority) a one-year spending increase in an emergency situation.

One interesting twist to this is being proposed in Utah. The initiative there calls for limiting future years' expenditures to an amount equal to the average of the state's personal income for the last three years (about 7 percent). The twist is that the proposed amendment allows the target percentage to be raised or lowered a specific amount in a vote of all the taxpayers. Such a vote could be called either by 5 percent of the voters or 25 percent of the legislature.

The thinking behind this is simple. Each election year, the party not in power will want to go to the voters and say, "We're the tax cutters." Because it will almost certainly represent at least 25 percent of the legislature, it will be able to call elections to lower taxes. Thus, the future pressure will be to lower and not to raise the rate and thus to lower taxes, not just to limit future growth.

Tax cuts: The other approach to the tax revolt is the one taken by the Jarvis-Gann initiative in California. It is a shotgun approach aimed at a major rollback in a single tax, be it the property tax (as in Proposition 13), sales taxes on food or other items, income tax or whatever. Jarvis-Gann accomplished its property-tax rollback by setting the maximum annual tax on any piece of property in the state at 1 percent of its actual cash value.

Organizations seeking to emulate Jarvis in other states have introduced similar measures. Some seek to limit the future growth of the property tax to a certain amount each year; others try to set a maximum rate, usually some-where between 1 and 1.6 percent of the fair market value of the property.

A WORD ABOUT TRADEOFFS

We must issue a warning to you at this point about tax tradeoffs. Be very careful about the taxes you cut. Know exactly what that money is being used for and be certain that it is something you can live without.

An example will suffice. In the Elgin, Illinois, school district case discussed earlier, an adult of the books showed that the district actually had a surplus of capital and had no need for any extra money. But if that audit had disclosed a serious deficiency in operating capital, it would have been irresponsible to seek to prevent the district from getting any new funds.

Do not just take the politicians' word for it. They are always going to cry poverty and most of the time it is just so much smoke to cloud your campaign. But do make every effort to propose a solution that is a responsible one and one that does not make it impossible for governmental authorities to continue functioning efficiently.

One of the reasons for taxes rising to such high levels, of course, is that government is not running efficiently today but is covered in many layers of bureaucratic fat. Cut just enough to trim that fat, but do not start getting into the bone structure.

CHAPTER 19.

HOW TO DETERMINE GOVERNMENT EFFICIENCY

H AVING THUS told you that the fat must be trimmed, we really owe it to you to give you some guidelines on how to find out where that at is.

First, you are going to have to learn how to read the financial statements put out by state and local government units. Then, you are going to have to be able to gauge the effectiveness of how those dollars are being spent.

You may be familiar with financial statements put out by corporations. If you are a stockholder, you undoubtedly receive annual reports from those companies in which you own stock. You may have glanced at the financial information contained in those reports. Well, forget all of that right now. There is a big difference between financial reporting by corporations and that done by governmental units. The purpose of a corporation is to make a profit for its stockholders. Therefore, its financial reporting is geared to disclosing how it is doing this. Quite obviously, it is not the business of government to make a profit; its financial reporting is geared to disclosing other things.

In business, there is clearly a bottom line—the one figure on which performance is based, net profit. Know this figure and know how it was arrived at and you know how well the business operated.

But there is no one figure that will tell you how well your government is operating. The purpose of government is to collect tax revenues and to spend them on providing a host of services.

Sometimes, you can look at a government financial report and see a surplus or a deficit. But this is not the same as a corporation's profit or loss. A government often bases what it will spend on projections of what it will take in. Therefore, a surplus or deficit may not really reflect good or bad management of programs but simply poor income forecasting, which resulted in either too much or too little income to the governmental unit. Actually, this is really what the governmental unit's financial report is designed to do—to tell you how closely it came to taking in the amount it forecast while, at the same time, telling you how it spent that money.

As outlined in the authoritative guide of the National Council of Governmental Accounting and the guidelines of the American Institute of Certified

Public Accounting, there are two elements that are basic to government accounting:

1. Government units base their annual expenditures on estimates of annual income. Therefore, their financial reports contain this data.

2. Most governmental units have set up the way they spend money into clearly separated funds. These funds are usually described in a separate report.

Therefore, the two basic documents that you will be dealing with in examining the finances of government will be the Combined Balance Sheet, which looks most like the corporate balance sheet that you may be used to, and the Statement of Fund Balances, which is mainly a revenue-expenditures statement.

THE COMBINED BALANCE SHEET

The main thing to be learned from this document, besides the financial position of your government unit, is what financial changes have occurred over the preceding year and, most important, what financial obligations exist for future years.

The Combined Balance Sheet most likely will be divided into the various funds (we discuss each of these in detail below). Perhaps the most crucial item to your examination at this point is the long-term debt account. This item should tell you the potential financial health of your government unit in the years to come, as well as possible future tax increases; that long-term debt will have to be repaid in the future and, since money does not grow on trees, it is going to have to come from taxes.

Just because your governmental unit has debts does not mean it is doing things all wrong. The question is whether this debt is piling up at an unacceptable rate, whether the administration of your governmental unit is simply pushing problems into the future.

Look at each of the individual funds and try to determine the following:

a. How has each done over the last year?
b. Does each have a positive cash position?
c. Does each show a larger balance at the end of the year than in the beginning?
d. How has each fund done this year as compared to last year or to the last several years? (If your financial statement does not contain comparative balance sheets for the last several years, you will have to obtain them in order to make this determination.)

Remember that, while the fact that the funds have gained over the year is not necessarily a sign of financial health, a drain of a fund is often a sign of potential trouble. Obviously, if there is a deficit, that deficit is going to have to be made up in a future year.

e. Does the individual fund have the ability to make up a deficit while the same level of services is being maintained, or is it obvious that either services are going to have to be cut back or additional funds (taxes) raised, or else the deficit will continue to grow?

This is the sign of true financial ill health.

If you see a fund in trouble, you will most likely want to study that fund in more detail. This brings us to the second document that will form the basis of your examination of the financial health of your government unit.

THE REVENUE-EXPENDITURE STATEMENT

This is the most common of all government financial reports. Simply put, it is a measure on a fund-by-fund basis of how much money was spent, how much was collected in comparison to what was expected, and how much of what was collected is not actually spent but is planned on being spent.

First, let us discuss the types of funds that will most likely be listed on such a statement. These funds are divided up into two general categories: "expendable," meaning those funds which are expected to be fully spent within a specific length of time, and "nonexpendable," meaning those not to be expended in a specific time, in many cases reserves for future contingencies.

Most likely, your statement will contain five general kinds of expendable funds:

1. General fund, which will include all current financial operations of the governmental unit and would be funded by taxes not specifically designated for a purpose.

2. Special revenue fund, an accounting of funds obtained for specific purposes but not including the following funds.

3. Capital projects funds, an accounting of funds for the purpose of the acquisition of major fixed assets (buildings, etc.).

4. Debt service, which includes funds earmarked to retire bonded indebtedness in future years.

5. Special assessment, which covers the collection and expenditure of funds collected for restricted purposes (property taxes which go to cover school costs, etc.).

At the same time, your statement will likely contain the following nonexpendable funds:

1. Enterprise funds, which are self-contained funds that pay for themselves (recreational facilities that are paid for by users fees, etc.).

2. Intergovernmental service, the amounts paid or collected by one governmental unit from another for service received.

In addition, the statement will likely contain two nonfund accounts: fixed assets (buildings, land, etc.) and long-term debt. Normally, depreciation of fixed assets is not considered in governmental accounting (because you are not trying to arrive at a profit figure). Therefore, fixed assets are listed at cost, no matter how old, and the age and need of replacement must be taken into consideration when looking at the fixed asset fund listing.

At the very least, all governmental units should have these two accounts, fixed asset and long-term debt, as well as, of course, a general fund.

The revenue-expenditure statement will undoubtedly contain certain terms that you should be familiar with. Some of these terms are the same as used in corporate accounting but have significantly different meanings in governmental accounting. These include the following:

Appropriation, the amount authorized to be spent for a specific purpose in a specified length of time.

Encumbrance, that part of an appropriation which has been committed but not already disbursed. May be covered by a contract, by a purchase order or by some other obligation device.

Surplus or *Deficit,* simply the excess of revenues over expenditures or the reverse, the excess of expenditures over income.

Inventory, normally expenditures that will be made when and if certain revenues are actually collected. This is a much different definition of inventory than found in corporate accounting.

Receivables, revenues that may be collected; again, a different definition from corporate accounting.

Now that you know what the forms are and what some of the terms mean, the key question is what to look for. First, you want to see how well the actual collection of taxes has measured up against the estimates. If there has been a significant shortfall, was it the fault of poor forecasting or of economic factors which could not be predicted but which continue to exist and will result in lower tax collections in the future?

A most important question: how closely do actual expenditures measure up against what was budgeted? If expenditures in certain areas were higher than budgeted, was this the result of some nonrecurring situation or was it the result of bad budgeting? If the latter, it may mean that this year's budget is also suspect.

Then, and almost obviously, how did actual expenditures in each area match up against actual revenues? Was each fund underbudget or overbudget? If it was overbudget, start asking some probing questions.

If there are overexpenditures or revenue shortfalls, are they unusual or is there a pattern? What about the spending trend, both overall and in individual accounts? Again, is there a pattern? Is there steady growth, and why? Is it all simply inflation or is there real growth?

Once you have reviewed the financial statements of your government unit, you will have a better idea of where your and your fellow taxpayers' dollars are going.

You may be able to see trouble spots that, if not attended to, will become a drain on the taxpayer in the future. You may have been able to see trends that speak to future trouble if not corrected. And, at the least, you will now be able to speak more intelligently about your tax dollars.

But the fact that you know where your tax dollars are going does not mean that you know if they are necessarily being well spent, or if there is any fat. And we promised to show you how to find the fat.

Actually, that is a tall order—too tall, in fact, for this book. But what we can do is provide some guidelines and suggest a place you can look for in-depth information: a new publication of the Washington-based Urban Institute on *The Procedure for Monitoring the Effectiveness of Municipal Services.* We highly recommend that you obtain a copy if you want to do a detailed evaluation of your own community's services. Just write to the Urban Institute, 2100 M. St., N.W., Washington, DC 20037; Publication No. URI 19500, $10.

The study breaks the basic community services into solid waste (garbage) collection, solid waste disposal, recreation, libraries, crime protection, fire protection, general transportation system, public transportation, water supply and handling citizen complaints. The study goes into great detail on how to evaluate each area of service; here are some general guidelines on each area:

Solid waste collection: How clean are your streets and alleys? Are they cleaner now than they were last year, or the year before? Do conditions vary in different parts of your area? Is your garbage collection service being done by the government itself, or by a private firm? What is the cost on a per capita basis? If it is being done by the government, are there other communities of your size where private firms are doing the collection and cleaning chores? Are they doing it as well? Cheaper?

Solid waste disposal: The simple aim of a municipal solid waste disposal program is "to provide for solid waste disposal in a safe, environmentally sound and esthetically acceptable manner." This is the yardstick you should be using in judging the system in use in your community. Just how does the system in use measure up to this standard? While many of the individual elements that go into the standard are highly technical in nature, enough are of the common sense variety and you should be able to come to some judgment.

Recreation services: Ask the simple question: how many citizens take advantage of the facilities and the programs, and what percentage of the population does this represent? What good is a program if no one takes advantage of it? If the programs are being under-utilized, why?

Libraries: As with recreational services, define the value of the library system in terms of its users. What percentage of the population takes advantage of the library system? Is the system too big or too expensive for the number of users? Is the use so low that the system has become an extravagance rather than a necessity?

Crime control and police protection: The very last service that anyone wants to see cut is police protection. Given this, you might believe that the bigger and more expensive the police department—actually, the whole justice system —the better. But as we have seen all too often, bigger is not necessarily better. And that is just as true here as anywhere else.

The Urban Institute says the objective of crime control is "to promote the safety of the community and a feeling of security among the citizens, primarily through the deterrence-prevention of crime and the apprehension of offenders, providing service in a fair, honest, prompt and courteous manner to the satisfaction of the citizens." But add to that definition the concept of "cost efficient."

National figures show that as much as 90 percent of a police force's annual budget is taken up with personnel costs. And the simple fact is that it costs the average police force about 50 percent more for a sworn uniformed officer than for a civilian employee.

Ask yourself how many jobs on your own local force are being performed by uniformed officers that could just as easily be done by civilian employees. These would include such jobs as dispatcher, clerical jobs and functions such as public or community relations. Even jobs such as traffic control are being handled in some cities by civilians who perform the jobs quite well, and at a significantly lower cost than using highly trained uniformed officers. And this has the addition of freeing more officers for crime-control duties.

Fire protection: Next in line after police protection, the service that most taxpayers least want to see cut back is fire protection. Again, as with our brief discussion of police protection, it is generally assumed that bigger is better, or in this case, safer. To hear most fire departments tell it, if a single dollar is cut from their budgets, the cities they protect will surely burn down. To cut the fire budget is to invite a holocaust.

But is this true? There is one amazing story that should be told here. The city of Scottsdale, Arizona, has done something that is almost unique in the United States. Instead of running its own fire department, as every other community does, it has contracted out to a private, profit-making company to provide the same typical fire services as every municipal fire department does.

And do you know what? It's much cheaper. Scottsdale has a per capita cost for fire protection that is only about a third as great as other Arizona cities of about the same size.

To hear the fire fighters' unions of these other cities tell it, if you live in Scottsdale then without a doubt you are going to roast in your bed some night soon. But the people who write fire insurance apparently believe this is absurd and are willing to back that belief with their money. Their cooperative rating system, the Insurance Services Office, recently reinspected Arizona communities and rates Scottsdale in the same risk categories with most other cities of its size and water-supply situation, including some where the per capita cost for fire protection is four times higher.

General transportation system: Basically put, the general transportation system refers to whether citizens *who have their own transportation* generally have rapid, easy, convenient and safe access to their desired destinations. This takes into consideration such questions as design, traffic control, street and highway condition, parking availability, etc.

Mass transportation: This question is the same as in the general transportation area except that it is asked about those citizens who do not have their own form of transportation. Here, perhaps more than in the general transportation area, cost enters into the equation. And again we stress, bigger and more expensive is not always better.

Water supply: The central question here is simple: is the supply of fresh water sufficient, dependable and healthy, and is it being provided at the lowest possible cost both to the consumers and to the community as a whole?

Handling citizen complaints and requests: At one time or another, almost every household in the community will come in contact with the government by making a complaint, by seeking services, by seeking information or by making a suggestion. How are each of these being met? This is at the heart of the day-to-day communication between government and its citizens, and plays one of the most important roles in how an individual views his or her government.

Let us dwell on this point for a moment. Often, it may not be how well a government is functioning on some objective scale that is important, but how well the citizen thinks it is functioning.

The only real way to find out is by taking a survey, which is one of the tasks outlined for the research committee in Step 4. One of the best such surveys was done by the city of Nashville, and contains seventy-nine questions geared to obtaining a cross-section of the attitudes of the city's population to the services provided by the city. The survey is reprinted in the appendix of the Urban Institute book referred to earlier and can serve as a model for your own survey.

You are not trying to be scientific about this. All you want to know is how do people think government is doing its job, which part of government is doing that job best or worst, etc.

You have already examined the financial status of your community and evaluated the effectiveness of its services. Now, with the citizen input from the survey, you will have all of the information that you need to target your tax revolt and get the people behind you. You will have the facts and figures needed to make a sensible decision, and you will know what parts of government you can attack and have the majority of the people shake their heads and say, "We knew it all the time."

CHAPTER 20.

WHAT'S HAPPENING: A STATE-BY-STATE ROUND-UP

A s WE said back in Step 3, one of the first things you must do is determine what other tax revolts are brewing in your geographical area. While we cannot list all the various local-level campaigns, we can give you some idea of what is happening around the nation. What follows is a complete state-by-state round-up as of mid-December 1979 (if your state is not listed, there was no tax revolt brewing as of then):

ALABAMA

A statewide taxpayer movement is growing where one did not exist two years ago. The state legislature on several occasions has made promises of significant tax relief. None has been forthcoming, although a special session did put a cap on the annual growth of the property tax. The big issue is the lack of a voter initiative process. The Alabama Taxpayers Union is leading a major effort to get voter initiative so taxpayers will have some way around the balky legislature. Gov. Fob James has promised to push for the adoption of the initiative process, and the ATU hopes this will happen in 1980.

ALASKA

A major effort is underway to put a tax-slashing amendment on the 1980 ballot. The proposed amendment would cut state income taxes by 80 percent. Proponents say such a large cut, about $120 million, is possible because state revenue from North Slope oil is so high. They have gathered enough signatures to put the measure on the November 1980 ballot.

ARIZONA

There will be two initiatives on the November ballot. The first will be a Prop 13–type property-tax-cutting measure sponsored by "Citizens for Tax Relief," a statewide organization. The measure seeks to cut property taxes to 1 percent of assessed value. The second initiative seeks to remove food from state taxation at all levels, from the farm to the consumer. A similar measure failed in 1978.

ARKANSAS

A move to exempt food and drugs from the sales tax failed in 1978. But the effort woke up state legislators, who, during the 1979 session, introduced and passed into law several significant tax breaks. Those favoring the food and drug exemption say they will make another attempt to get voter approval in 1980 in hopes of reversing the narrow 1978 defeat.

CALIFORNIA

Once again California is at the head of the tax revolt movement. On top of Proposition 13, Proposition 4 is now on the books. But tax revolt groups in the state are not done. Three new tax-slashing initiatives will likely be voted on this year, one in the June primary and two others on the November 1980 ballot.

The most sweeping is one proposed by Howard Jarvis himself. His new group is called "Cut Income Tax Committee," and it seeks to do just that. The proposal the group is pushing would cut all state income tax rates by 50 percent. It would also abolish the state tax on business inventories. Additionally, the measure would seek to keep taxpayers' income tax liabilities from growing each year from inflation by indexing tax rates to the inflation rate. If the initiative passes, California taxpayers will save an estimated $2.6 billion annually. The measure will be voted on in June.

The second initiative expected to be on the November ballot is designed to give taxpayers control over growing school budgets. The measure would allow a California taxpayer who pays any money, either to private or public schools, to deduct up to $1,200 per child of that money from his state taxes.

The third initiative would phase out the state's sales tax over a five year period. It would allow local jurisdictions to impose a sales tax for up to five years by a favorable vote of two-thirds of a jurisdiction's voters. After six years, the sales tax would have to be voted on again, effectively a "sunset" of this sales tax. This initiative also would require a two-thirds vote to impose any new tax or fee by any jurisdiction. If this initiative passes, the average California family would save an estimated $1,200 a year.

COLORADO

Taxpayer organizations are still trying to regroup following the defeat in 1978 of an initiative aimed at putting a cap on state-spending growth. The groups are trying to organize a new petition campaign to put the measure on the ballot again in 1980.

CONNECTICUT

In the past, taxpayer groups have worked mainly on a local level—usually seeking county-by-county spending limits. Now, however, an umbrella organization has been formed and it is trying to get a statewide spending limitation measure on the November 1980 ballot.

FLORIDA

In 1979, the Florida State Legislature increased state spending by 31 percent. As a result, taxpayer groups are working to place two initiatives on the November 1980 ballot.

The first, which is being described as a "model" proposal (it may be copied by other tax revolt organizations), would gradually reduce total state revenue to 6 perecent of gross personal income (it is about 9 percent today). Any revenues collected in excess of this 6 percent "cap" would be rebated to taxpayers in the form of reduced sales taxes the following year.

The second measure would cap local revenues. All local taxes would be cut by 10 percent and increases would be limited to one percent a year. Any new local taxes would need the approval of two-thirds of the voters in the jurisdiction.

Finally, the Dade County proponents of last year's defeated property tax cut proposal are back at work again with a redrafted initiative, this time correctly stating what the new tax rate should be. (See chapter 8 for what happened in their last attempt.)

GEORGIA

This is another state where most tax revolt activity is on the local level. Local organizations have been mainly fighting against proposed bond issues and new taxes. Last year (1979) voters in Fulton County (Atlanta) defeated a proposed increase in the sales tax from 4 to 5 percent. City and county officials had indicated that the additional funds would be used to hire additional police and fight crime, but voters rejected the measure by almost a two-to-one margin. Some statewide organization is underway but specific goals have yet to be chosen.

HAWAII

A petition drive is underway to put an initiative on the 1980 ballot to exempt food, drugs and all health care items from the state sales tax.

IDAHO

In the wake of a successful 1978 campaign to pass a Prop 13–type property-tax cut, Idaho tax reform groups are turning their attention to the educational tax credit issue. A group calling itself Educational Tax Credit for Idaho has begun a campaign to place an initiative on the 1980 ballot that would allow taxpayers to deduct educational expenses for their children from their state tax returns. The effort to get the measure on the ballot is expected to succeed.

ILLINOIS

There are citizens' organizations throughout the state working hard for various forms of tax reform. Because of the political structure in Illinois, most of this activity is centering on getting the state legislature to act.

A leader in this effort is State Representative Don Totten, whose "Taxpayers Rights Amendment" passed the Illinois House but failed in the Senate after the governor threatened to veto the measure.

Totten's amendment would limit the state's ability to raise revenue to a ratio of revenue to the personal income of the state as defined by the U.S. Department of Commerce. In Illinois for the last four years, that ratio has been 6.8 percent, so the Totten bill pegged it at 7 percent (Note: in Totten's bill, that 7 percent would include taxes from income, sales, gasoline and cigarettes.)

Under the Totten measure, the voters could increase the limit by referendum. It also contains an emergency provision for the legislature to raise revenue in an extraordinary situation. Further, the amendment prohibits the state from reducing the proportion of state money going to all local units of government, including school districts, below the 1975 level, and it requires that all new local programs mandated by the state be paid for by the state.

Totten believes that various citizens' organizations within the state can put sufficient pressure on the governor to get him to reverse his stand, and expects the measure to pass in 1979 and to be placed before the state's voters in 1980.

At the same time, a number of taxpayer organizations—particularly the National Taxpayers United of Illinois—are preaching actual tax revolt in its purest sense. As a result, a substantial property tax "strike" is underway in several counties, including Chicago's Cook County.

Many residents of Cook County simply refused to pay property taxes until the legislature was willing to provide some relief. The result was a so-called circuit-breaker bill, which put a lid on property-tax increases and had the net result of a $60 million tax cut.

The tax strike is beginning to spread to other counties in the state as property owners demand not simply a lid on the future growth of property tax but an actual tax rollback.

A move is now underway by NTU-I to use a little-noticed law which does allow for initiative procedures on a very local level. Thus, the organization is trying to get on the ballot, on a local taxing district (school district, county, etc.) basis, measures that would cut property taxes in those districts by 25 percent. This effort, however, is likely to face a court challenge before local balloting can proceed.

IOWA

Efforts here are aimed at getting the state legislature to pass taxpayer initiatives. A statewide organization called Iowans for Tax Relief was successful in getting the legislature to partially index the state's personal income tax. The group intends several measures for tax relief to go before the state legislature in 1980.

KENTUCKY

Statewide efforts by a group called The Taxpayers Action Group are limited to convincing the state legislature to approve the balance-the-budget federal convention call during the 1980 legislative session.

MASSACHUSETTS

In no state in the nation have taxes risen as fast as they have in the Commonwealth of Massachusetts. In fact, taxes in the Bay State are so high that it ranks 48th in per capita after-tax disposable income, ahead of only Vermont and Mississippi.

With tax rates so high, it was inevitable that the tax revolt would find its way back to Massachusetts, where, you might say, it all started over 200 years ago with that famous tea party.

For the last several years, Citizens for Limited Taxation, one of the best-organized taxpayers' organizations in the nation, has been fighting to keep Massachusetts's taxes down. In 1976, it successfully lead a fight to reject a proposed graduated income tax. With this victory in hand, it turned its attention to trying to win a constitutional amendment to put a lid on future state spending.

In Massachusetts, it is difficult to get a constitutional amendment before the voters. You must first gain sufficient signatures on petitions to get the matter before the state legislature. Then, at least 25 percent of both houses meeting in special session must approve it in two consecutively elected sessions of the legislature. After the second approval is granted, the measure is placed on the next available general election ballot and, if a majority of the voters approve it, the constitution is amended.

CLT took the first step in 1977 when it collected 87,000 signatures on petitions. Then, as both houses of the state legislature met in special session, the requisite number gave their consent and the amendment, called the Tax Limitation Amendment, was halfway home. The second approval came in 1979. Now the measure will be on the ballot in 1980.

The CLT amendment proposes that a lid be placed on state spending and the amount of money that can be raised by the state. The ceiling is figured by dividing average state revenues for the past three years by average state personal income, yielding the percentage of taxpayer income diverted to the state, currently about 9 percent. Under the ceiling, the state could not raise or spend more than that average.

The proposed amendment would impose annual limitations both on the revenue raised and expenditures made by the commonwealth. The proposal forbids appropriating more money than the "state revenue limit" described below, and would require that all tax money raised in excess of the limit be returned to the taxpayers. The state could no longer mandate local programs without making corresponding state appropriations.

A newly created Economics Estimate Committee would have the responsibility for calculating and publishing the annual "state revenue limit." The limit would be determined each year in accordance with the mathematical formula contained in the proposed amendment. First, the "limitation ratio" would be computed by dividing the average gross state budget for the three fiscal years immediately preceding the proposed amendment's effective date by the average total personal income of Massachusetts for the three calendar years immediately preceding that date. Then, the average total personal income of Massachusetts for the previous three calendar years would be multiplied by the limitation ratio and the resulting figure would be the state revenue limit.

The limit could then be increased or decreased only by statewide popular vote. The commonwealth could not raise more money than that limit except for the specific purposes of providing local property-tax relief or for state pension obligations incurred before the effective date of the proposal.

The proposal requires creation of a special reserve fund which is not subject to the state revenue limit and which could be utilized to meet emergency financial situations, and also for imposition of short-term, specific new taxes or tax increases to meet those emergencies. The use of bonds is restricted to financing capital improvements.

The CLT amendment is very similar to the one enacted in Tennessee and the one being pushed in Michigan. The Massachusetts organization received substantial help in its campaign from the National Tax Limitation Committee and its experts.

According to CLT director Don Fedder, the organization has spent about $50,000 thus far on its campaign. If the amendment continues its steady course toward adoption, it will not go before the voters until 1980 and therefore its effect will not be felt on the Massachusetts budget until 1982.

But CLT believes that the states taxpayers want relief now. So the organization is backing another proposal, this time for a referendum, on a statute that they are calling "Proposition Two-and-a-Half." Basically, this statute calls for limiting property tax increases to 2½ percent, forbids the legislature from mandating local programs to be paid for by local units of government and requires the Boston Transit Authority to operate on a balanced budget. CLT tried this before, in 1977, but failed. Now it is aiming the referendum for a special election sometime in 1980.

However, the tax revolt has already had effect in Massachusetts. The Massachusetts Taxpayers Foundation, a forty-year-old organization funded by business and banking interests in Boston, sponsored a bill which freezes Massachusetts' property taxes at 1977 levels plus a maximum of 5 percent increase for inflation. It was easily passed by a special legislative session. This was a critical bill; Massachusetts' property taxes are about the highest in the nation because the commonwealth requires residential property to be taxed at 100 percent of actual value.

With property taxes so high, it is clear that Massachusetts is also ripe for a Proposition 13-type proposal. In fact, one modeled after the Jarvis-Gann initiative was placed before the special session of the legislature but it was rejected out of hand. A number of taxpayers' organizations in the Bay State are considering a Proposition 13-type revolt by constitutional amendment; but as can be seen in the CLT experience, it is a long and complicated process.

NEVADA

Voters passed a Prop 13–type property-tax-cutting measure in 1978. The way the state constitution is structured, amendments, to take effect, must be passed in two successive elections. A new petition effort has placed the measure on the 1980 ballot. Judging by the margin of victory the first time around, it should easily qualify and again pass. A second initiative also is being circulated. Nevada currently has no state income tax. This new measure would make a state income tax unconstitutional. The new measure also would require a two-thirds vote of the legislature to raise any existing state tax or fee.

NEW JERSEY

This is a state where no direct voter initiative is possible. Therefore a taxpayer group calling itself United Taxpayers of New Jersey has started a drive to force the legislature to establish a voter initiative and also to pass the balance-the-budget federal convention call.

NEW YORK

This is another state where no direct voter initiative exists. A group calling itself United Taxpayers of New York State, like its sister organization in New Jersey, is concentrating on getting the state legislature to approve a direct voter initiative and the balance-the-budget constitutional convention call. Several other taxpayer groups are working with the National Tax Limitation Committee to lobby the legislature to pass an act that would limit the growth of state spending.

NORTH CAROLINA

A statewide taxpayer organization calling itself United Taxpayers of North Carolina has been formed and is starting to add local affiliates. As of now the organization has no specific goals except to lobby the state legislature to hold down spending and not to legislate any new taxes.

OHIO

An attempt is being made by Ohioians to Limit State Taxes to gather 300,000 signatures to put a spending limitation amendment on the November ballot.

OKLAHOMA

An initiative will be on the 1980 ballot to allow using federal tax deductions when preparing state returns. This would result in a 20 percent tax cut for most taxpayers. The measure is facing stiff opposition, especially from state legislators who are threatening to raise taxes 20 percent if the measure passes.

OREGON

The Oregon Taxpayers Union is trying to rebound from a 1978 defeat at the polls when voters rejected a tax-cutting initiative. A petition is circulating to place a similar measure, one which limits growth in property tax to one percent a year, on the November 1980 ballot.

SOUTH DAKOTA

Citizens for a Dakota Proposition, a statewide taxpayer group, is circulating a petition to try to qualify a Prop 13–type property tax cut for the November 1980 ballot. As of this writing it is not clear if they will succeed.

UTAH

A coalition of taxpayer organizations is circulating petitions to place on the 1980 ballot a measure that would eliminate all taxes on the production and distribution of food. Called the "Food Chain Initiative," the measure is aimed mainly at the retail sales tax and is given a good chance of passage.

WASHINGTON

Washington state voters approved the so-called Initiative 62 on the November 1979 ballot. The measure called for the restricting of state spending growth to the growth in state personal income. It would also restrict the ability of state and local governments to pass new spending programs.

Now, the Washington Taxpayers Union is pushing a proposal to get the legislature to adopt a sunset review of all tax measures every ten years. This would mean that any tax would cease at the end of ten years unless it was renewed by the legislature. The new proposal also calls for indexing of state income tax rates.

In the past, Washington taxpayer organizations have had difficulty getting initiatives qualified for the ballot. In 1977 an initiative called "Initiative 358" tried but failed despite a rather novel court ruling. A state court ruled that proponents of that measure did not have to circulate petitions in the normal manner. Rather, the court said proponents could take out newspaper ads with coupons that voters could clip and mail in. Despite this ease of circulation, Initiative 358 failed to make the ballot.

In addition to the above states, taxpayer organizations are in the formative stages in several others. These include Minnesota, Montana and Vermont.

CHAPTER 21.

INITIATIVES, REFERENDUMS, LOBBYING: FINDING OUT WHAT YOUR STATE ALLOWS

O KAY, throughout the first section of this book and much of this section, we have been throwing some fancy words around: initiatives, referendums, lobbying campaigns. And, while it is not too difficult to understand in general terms what these mean, you are not really certain. More important, you probably have not the slightest idea under which system your tax revolt must operate in your state.

INITIATIVES

An initiative is a process whereby voters can *directly change the state constitution* or *directly enact laws*. There are two basic kinds of initiative processes:

1. Direct initiative. This is the most common process. Under it, an amendment or proposed law is put on the ballot for consideration by the electorate after a certain number of eligible voters sign petitions supporting the change. The number of required signatures is mandated by law.

2. Indirect initiative. This process applies only to the enactment of new laws, not amendments to state constitutions. Under it, citizen sponsors of the new law must file petitions signed by a required number of eligible voters. If the petitions qualify, the state legislature has a certain amount of time to consider the requested change and act upon it. That period of time is mandated by law. If the state legislature fails to act within the prescribed time, or if it votes it down, then it goes to the voters.

Some states use the direct initiative system for both amendments and laws. Others use the direct process for constitutional amendments and the indirect process for laws. Still others allow direct or indirect initiatives only for amendments or only for new laws.

Following is a rundown of those states that allow voter initiatives. Petitions must be filed with the secretary of state unless otherwise designated; in all cases, a simple majority is needed to pass an initiative.

Alaska: No initiatives allowed for constitutional amendments. Direct initiatives for statutes (Alaska Const. Art. XI; Stats. 15.45.010). Petition requirement: 10 percent of those voting in the last general election for governor in each of two-thirds of the state's electoral districts. Petitions may be filed at any time with the lieutenant-governor designated to receive them.

Arizona: Direct for both laws and amendments (Arizona Const. Art. 4, Pt. 1). Petition requirement is 15 percent for constitutional amendments and 10 percent for laws, with the percentage based on the amount of votes cast in the last general election for governor. Petitions must be filed at least four months before the election.

Arkansas: Direct for both (Const. Amend. 7). Petition requirement is 10 percent for constitutional amendments and eight percent for laws, again based on those voting in the last general election for governor, including at least 5 percent in each of fifteen counties. Petitions must be filed four months before an election with notice of petitions being circulated at least thirty days before that.

California: Direct for both (Const. Art. 4). Petition requirement is 8 percent of those voting in the last general election for governor. A notice of intent must be filed with the state attorney general prior to the start of petitioning; the secretary of state is designated to receive the petitions, however.

Colorado: Direct for both (Const. Art. 5). Petition requirement is 8 percent of those voting in the last general election for secretary of state. They must be filed four months before election.

Florida: Direct for both. Petition requirement is 8 percent of those votes cast in each of one-half of the state's congressional districts in the last general election for presidential electors. (In other words, if you get 10,000 signatures in District A representing 7 percent, and 8,000 signatures in District B representing 9 percent, you have only qualified in District B.)

Idaho: Direct for statute only; not allowed for constitutional amendments (Idaho Const. Art. III, Sec. 1). Petition requirement is 10 percent of those voting in the last general election for governor. They must be filed four months before the election.

Maine: Indirect for statutes only; not allowed for constitutional amendments (Maine Const. Art. IV, Sec. 3). Petition requirement is 10 percent of those voting in the last general election for governor. It must be filed with the secretary of state within fifty days after the legislature convenes. Once the petitions are certified as qualifying, they are forwarded to the legislature. If it rejects it or does not act upon it during the session in which it is submitted, the initiative is placed on the ballot.

Massachusetts: Indirect for both (Const. Amend. Art. 48, Pt. 1). Petitions must be submitted to the legislature. Petition requirement for initial filing is 3 percent of those voting in the last general election for governor; not more than a quarter of the signatures can come from any one county. Constitutional amendments must receive an affirmative vote in two successive special joint sessions, following which it is presented to the voters. Laws must be passed by the first Wednesday in May; if they are not, then new petitions containing an additional .5 percent of the votes cast for governor will force release and placement on the ballot.

Michigan: Direct for amendments and indirect for laws (Const. Art. 2). The petition requirement is 10 percent for constitutional amendments and 8 percent for laws of those voting in the last general election for governor. Statutory initiatives (meaning, initiatives for new laws) must be submitted to the legislature ten days before the start of the legislative session and must be enacted or rejected within forty legislative days. If rejected, they are placed on the ballot. Initiatives on amendments must be filed 120 days before the election.

Missouri: Direct for both (Const. Art. 3, Sec. 49). Petition requirement is based on those voting in the last general election for governor, amounting to 8 percent for constitutional amendments and 5 percent for laws in each of two-thirds of the state's congressional districts. They must be filed four months before the election.

Montana: Direct for both (Const. Art. 3, Sec. 4 and Art. 14, Sec. 9). Petition requirement is 10 percent of the qualified voters in each of at least two-fifths of the state's legislative districts; the total must equal 5 percent of the state's total qualified voters. Filing is 120 days before election for constitutional amendments and ninety days for laws.

Nebraska: Direct for both (Const. Art. III, Sec. 2). Petition requirement is 10 percent for constitutional amendments and 7 percent for laws of those voting in the last general election for governor. Filing is four months before the election.

Nevada: Direct for constitutional amendments; indirect for laws (Const. Art. XIX, Sec. 2). Petition requirement is 10 percent of those voting in the last general election in 75 percent of the state's seventeen counties. Initiatives on statutes must be submitted to the legislature. If rejected or not passed within forty legislative days, they are then presented to the voters. Filing of amendments is ninety days before the election; laws must be filed thirty days before the start of the legislative session.

North Dakota: Direct for both (Const. Art. II, Sec. 25). Petition requirement is 10,000 qualified voters. Filing is ninety days before election.

Ohio: Direct for constitutional amendments; indirect for laws (Const. Art. II, Sec. 1). Petition requirement is 10 percent for amendments and 3 percent for laws of the state's qualified voters. Laws must be presented to the legislature ten days before the start of the legislative session; if rejected or not passed within four months after being presented, they can be forced on the ballot by the filing within ninety days of new petitions equal to three percent of the state's qualified voters. Petitions for amendments must be submitted ninety days before the election.

Oklahoma: Direct for both (Const. Art. V, Sec. 1). Petition requirement is 15 percent for constitutional amendments and 8 percent for laws of those voting in the last general election for the state official who received the largest number of votes. Petitions must be filed within ninety after the first date signatures are solicited.

Oregon: Direct for both (Const. Art. 4, Sec. 1). Petition requirement is 8 percent for amendments and 6 percent for laws of those voting in the last general election for governor. They must be filed four months before the election.

South Dakota: Direct for both (Const. Art. XXIII). Petition requirement is 10 percent for amendments and 5 percent for laws of those voting in the last general election for governor. Initiatives for laws are submitted to the state legislature (by the secretary of state, who is the only one entitled to receive them); they are submitted to the voters whether the legislators approve or reject the laws. Filing of amendments is one year before the election; no time limit is set for laws.

Utah: Indirect for statutes only; not allowed for constitutional amendments (Const. Art. VI, Sec. 1). Petition requirement is 10 percent of the voters from a majority of counties. They must be submitted to the legislature ten days prior to start of a regular session. If the legislature does not enact the new law, then it may be forced on the ballot by the filing of new petitions with all new signatures equal to 10 percent of the state's voters.

Washington: Both direct and indirect on statutes only; the choice is up to you. No constitutional amendments are allowed by initiative (Const. Art. 2, Sec. 1). Petition requirement is 8 percent of those voting in the last general election for governor. They must be filed at least ten days prior to the start of the legislative session. If going the direct route, petitions must be filed four months before the election; if going the indirect route, at least ten days prior to the start of the legislative session.

Wyoming: Direct for statutes only (Const. Art. 3, Sec. 52). Petition requirement is 15 percent of those voting in the last general election for governor in at least two-thirds of the counties. Petitions may be filed at any time but cannot be filed within five years of the failure of a similar initiative.

REFERENDUMS

A number of states allow the voters directly through the referendum procedure to repeal or change *existing laws.* You cannot create new law by using the referendum process; that is what initiatives are for. Unfortunately, a number of states prohibit the use of referendums on revenue measures, which means that this process cannot be used for a tax revolt in those states.

Basically, there are three categories of referendums available in the various states.

1. Direct referendum. The electorate by direct petition (normally done by obtaining a requisite number of signatures from eligible voters) can place a measure on the ballot for approval by the electorate as a whole.

2. Indirect referendum. The state legislature may on its own motion voluntarily put an issue directly to the voters (in effect, this is not much more than an advisory vote to give a show of voter sentiment on controversial issues before the legislature finally commits itself).

3. Mandated referendum. In some states, the state constitution mandates that certain issues be put directly to the people in the form of a referendum. (Note: This is different from other types of referendums, which allow the voters to change or repeal existing laws.)

Following is a state-by-state rundown of the referendum process. Unless otherwise specified, all petitions must be filed with the secretary of state; in all cases, a simple majority of the voters are needed to approve the referendum:

Alaska: Direct. Petition requirement is 10 percent of the votes cast in the last governor's race in at least two-thirds of the state's electoral districts. Filing must be made with the lieutenant-governor within ninety days following adjournment of the legislative session in which the law was passed or amended. It may not be used against revenue measures. Referendum is also available at local government levels.

Arizona: Direct, mandated. In direct referendums, petition requirement is 5 percent of all qualified voters. They must be filed within ninety days after passage of the targeted law. For mandated referendums, the legislature must place before the voters certain measures, including any constitutional amendments it initiates. Referendum is also available at local government levels.

Arkansas: Direct, indirect. Petition requirement for direct referendums is six percent of the votes cast in the last race for governor. The state legislature may initiate referendums. Referendum is also available at local government levels.

California: Direct, indirect. Petition requirement for direct referendums is 5 percent of the last vote for governor. A notice of intent must be filed with the state attorney general prior to the start of petitioning; the secretary of state is designated to receive the petitions, which must be filed within ninety days of enactment of the target law. Referendum is *not allowed* in order to repeal or change revenue or taxing measures used to meet *current* expenses. Certain measures must be put directly to the voters. Laws that have been amended by the referendum process can only be repealed or changed in a new referendum.

Colorado: Direct; indirect. Petition requirement is 5 percent of the last vote for secretary of state. They must be filed within ninety days following adjournment of the legislature that passed the target law. It may not be used against appropriations measures. Issues may be submitted by the legislature. Referendum is also available at local government levels.

Florida: Mandated. Constitutional requirement that certain issues go directly to voter. Referendum is also available at some local government levels.

Georgia: Mandated; indirect. Certain issues must be placed before the voters. The state legislature has submitted referendums to the voters in the past, although there is no specific provision for this in the state constitution. Referendum is also available at local government levels.

Idaho: Direct. Petition requirement is 10 percent of the vote cast for governor in the last election. Filing must be within sixty days following final adjournment of the legislative session in which the target law was passed. Referendum·is also available at local government levels.

Illinois: Indirect. Referendum is also available at local government levels.

Iowa: Mandated. Constitutional requirement on certain issues only. Referendum is also available at local government levels.

Kansas: Mandated. Constitutional requirement on certain issues only. Referendum is also available at local government levels.

Kentucky: Direct on issues involving the classification of property and differential taxation on that property; mandated. Petition requirement for direct referendums is 5 percent of the votes cast for governor in the last election. The state constitution requires that certain issues go directly to the voters. Referendum is also available at local government levels.

Maine: Direct, indirect; mandated. Petition requirement for direct referendums is 10 percent of the votes cast for governor in the last election. Filing is within ninety days of the end of the legislative session in which the target law was passed. The legislature may also submit referendums and the state constitution requires that certain issues go directly to the voters. Referendum is also available at local government levels.

Maryland. Direct; indirect. Petition requirement for direct referendums is 3 percent of the votes cast for governor in the last election. Filing must be made by June 1. The state legislature may also submit. Referendum is also available at local government levels.

Massachusetts: Direct. Petition requirement is 2 percent of the total votes with not more than a quarter of the signatures coming from any one county. A notice of intent must be filed within thirty days of the effective date of the target law. Filing of actual petitions must be made within ninety days of that effective date. Referendum is also available at local government levels.

Michigan: Direct; indirect; mandated. Petition requirement for direct referendums is five percent of the votes cast for governor in the last election. Filing must be within ninety days after adjournment of the legislature in which the target law was passed. Referendums may also be submitted by the legislature and there is a constitutional requirement to put certain issues before the voters. Referendum is also available at local government levels.

Missouri: Direct; indirect. Petition requirement for direct referendums is 5 percent of the legal voters in each of two-thirds of the congressional districts. Filing is within ninety days after enactment of the target law. The legislature may also submit referendums to the voters. Referendum is also available at local government levels.

Montana: Direct. Petition requirement is 5 percent of the state's qualified voters and at least 5 percent in each of one-third of the state's legislative districts. Filing must be made within six months after adjournment of the legislative session in which the target tax was passed. Referendum is also available at local government levels.

Nebraska: Direct. Petition requirement is 5 percent of the votes cast for governor in the last election. Filing must be made within ninety days after adjournment of the legislative session in which the target law was passed. Referendum is also available at local government levels.

Nevada: Direct. Petition requirement is 10 percent of the votes cast for governor in the last election. Filing must be made four months before the election. Referendum is also available at local government levels.

New Hampshire: Indirect. No referendum is available at local government levels.

New Jersey: Indirect; mandated for certain issues. Referendum is available at local government levels.

New Mexico: Direct. Petition requirement is 10 percent of the votes cast for governor in the last election and at least 10 percent of the qualified voters in each of three-quarters of the state's counties. Petitions must be filed four months before the election. Submission of petitions with 25 percent of the necessary signatures within ninety days after enactment of the target law will suspend that law until the referendum is held. No referendum is available at local government levels.

New York: Mandated on certain issues only. No referendum is available at local government levels.

North Carolina: Indirect; mandated on certain issues. No referendum is available at local government levels.

North Dakota: Direct. Petition requirement is 7,000 signatures. Petitions must be filed within ninety days of adjournment of the legislature in which the target law was passed. Referendum is available at local government levels.

Ohio: Direct. Petition requirement is 6 percent of the votes cast for governor in the last election. Petitions must be filed within ninety days of the target law's being signed by the governor. Referendums may not be used against *current* expenditures. Referendum is available at local government levels.

Oklahoma: Direct; mandated. Petition requirement for direct referendums is 5 percent of the votes cast for the state official who received the greatest number of votes in the last election. Petitions must be filed ninety days after adjournment of the legislature in which the target law was passed. The state constitution requires that certain issues go directly to voters. Referendum is available at local government levels.

Oregon: Direct; indirect. Petition requirement for direct referendums is four percent of the votes cast for governor in the last election. Filing is within 90 days after passage of the target law. The legislature may also submit certain issues directly to the voters. Referendum is available at local government levels.

Pennsylvania: Mandated on certain issues only. Referendum is also available at local government levels.

Rhode Island: Mandated on certain issues only. Referendum is also available at local government levels.

South Carolina: Indirect; mandated on certain issues. Referendum is also available at local government levels.

South Dakota: Direct. Petition requirement is five percent of the votes cast for governor in the last election. Filing must be made within 90 days of adjournment of the session in which the target law was passed. Referendum is also available at local government levels.

Utah: Direct. Petition requirement for direct referendums is 10 percent of the votes cast for governor in the last election. Filing is within 60 days after the legislative session in which the target law was passed. Referendum is also available at local government levels.

Vermont: Indirect. Referendum is available at local government levels.

Virginia: Indirect; mandated on certain issues. Referendum is available at local government levels.

Washington: Direct; mandated. Petition requirement for direct referendums is four percent of the votes cast for governor in the last election. Filing within 90 days after the legislative session in which the target law was passed. The state constitution requires that certain issues go directly to the voters. Referendum is also available at local government levels.

Wisconsin: Indirect; mandated on certain issues. Referendum is available at local government levels.

Wyoming: Direct; mandated. Petition requirement for direct referendums is 15 percent of the votes per county that were cast for governor in the last election, and from at least two-thirds of the counties. Petitions must be filed within ninety days of enactment of the target law. Referendums may not be used against revenue measures. The state constitution requires that certain issues go directly to voters. Referendum is also available at local government levels.

In addition, the following states have referendum processes available only to local units of government: Minnesota, South Carolina, Texas and West Virginia.

LOBBYING

In those states where it is up to the legislature to put a constitutional amendment or a new law on the ballot for voters to decide, or where no direct citizen input is allowed, the only way to get things done is through lobbying

—in other words, convincing a majority of the legislators to see things your way.

In most instances, such lobbying is regulated, and you will have to check local law to determine how you can go about this task.

One of the tools you can use in lobbying efforts is the gathering of signatures on petitions (a fuller discussion of this can be found under Step 8 in Section 1). In most cases, there is no specific law regarding the wording or filing of such petitions.

But there is in Illinois, where 680,000 signatures from qualified voters are required. Even then, the legislature is not obligated to do anything about your request, although it would be foolish for it simply to ignore 680,000 signatures, which could represent 680,000 voters on election day.

CHAPTER 22.

GROUPS THAT CAN HELP YOU

THE NTU

The National Taxpayers Union is the granddaddy of tax-revolt organizations. It is also the one with the hardest line on taxes. Its goal: across-the-board tax and spending cuts, period. Anything less is not good enough.

Says the NTU: "We are not simply for holding down future tax increases or holding down the rate of government spending; we want to see spending cuts and tax cuts and we want to see them now. We will support measures that hold down future government growth and future tax increases, but to us this is only a temporary starting point. We not only want to stop future growth, we want to cut back from where we are today."

The group was founded in 1969. James Davidson, NTU's current chairman and one of its founders, recalls the group's early days:

"We started as a group to oppose what we saw as the crazy spending practices of the federal Congress and to try to call attention to the growing national debt and what was the reckless disregard for the taxpayers money, a disregard that really hasn't changed much in the last eight years. Our goal was to change federal spending policies and today this continues to be our goal.

"In the early days, we primarily testified against those projects we considered wastefullsuch as the SST [the U.S. version of the British-French Concorde supersonic airliner], various aspects of foreign aid and especially the federal government's payroll and pension practices.

"At the same time, we tried to educate the press so they could begin to educate the public as to the real cost of government."

As an example of its successes, the NTU points to the elimination of the so-called 1 percent add-on, which automatically allowed federal retirement paychecks to actually keep ahead of inflation, something often denied to us poor mortals who are not fortunate enough to be federal civil servants. It was NTU research that discovered the add-on and brought it to the attention of friendly legislators and the public. A bitter fight ensued, but the add-on was eliminated from the pension system.

Today, the organization has grown and its goals have broadened. It lists as its present activities:

—*"Lobbying for the taxpayer.* NTU's citizen lobbyists present the taxpayer's point of view. In Congress and in state capitals, we work to counter the arguments, propaganda and armtwisting by those who want more and more of your money."

Among the current campaigns it is waging are lobbying efforts against national health insurance and other federal spending issues currently before Congress, including continued massive government support for the National Passenger Service Corporation, better known as Amtrak. Many of the rail line's routes are losing vast sums of taxpayer money and the federal subsidies are reaching the point of absurdity. As an example, it has been estimated that federal subsidies on the New York-to-Miami run amount to $134 for every ticket sold. That means that *it would actually be cheaper for the federal government to buy a first-class airplane ticket for anyone who wanted to take the train to Miami.*

At the same time, the NTU is waging a battle for things which it believes will save the taxpayers money in the long run. These include such things as the deregulation of the airline and trucking industries and the containment of soaring hospital costs.

—*Local organizing.* As Jim Davidson explains it, the most fertile ground for fighting the battle for tax reform in recent years has been at the state and local level. So NTU has begun forming "a national coalition of taxpayer groups . . . to beat back the special interests, repeal wasteful laws and defeat the politicans who waste your money."

The NTU currently has a field staff that is working with more than 200 local organizations. As an example, it aided the Proposition 13 fight in California with both money and organizational support.

—*Research and education.* NTU's research department regularly publishes information about the federal budget in an effort to educate both legislators and taxpayers to what it says are the real facts. For example, NTU researchers claim that the long-term debt of the American taxpayer is at least ten times greater than what is usually referred to as "the national debt" by public officials.

The organization also publishes a monthly newsletter, entitled "Dollars and Sense." Tax topics are discussed in every issue and there is a section on absurd government spending.

—Setting federal spending limits. For the last three years, the NTU has been leading the fight for a constitutional amendment to balance the federal budget. The idea has caught on and 30 states have backed a call for a constitutional convention for that purpose. If the call succeeds, it would be the first such convention since the Constitution was adopted nearly 200 years ago. (There is a further discussion of this in the section on federal tax revolts.)

—Local government center. The NTU's Local Government Center is head-quartered in Santa Barbara, California, and is headed by urban planner Robert Poole. It functions as a research center to plan more efficient and cost-effective local government services, and acts as consultants to municipalities or citizen groups trying to keep down the cost of local government.

The NTU began with just a couple of people working out of their homes. It now has a staff of twenty and its planned operating budget for 1980 is $800,000. It claims to have more than 60,000 direct dues-paying members and the approximately 200 groups that it is working with are said to have a combined membership of more than a million people.

For further information, write to the National Taxpayers Union, 325 Pennsylvania Ave, S.E., Washington, DC 20003.

THE NTLC

The National Tax Limitation Committee is the first national organization formed for the specific purpose of limiting the taxing and spending powers of government through the use of constitutional amendments.

The organization was founded by three men: California attorney Lewis Uhler, New York economic consultant William Rickenbacker, and Illinois publisher and businessman Jameson Campaigne Jr., who also is a vice-chairman of the American Conservative Union. Rickenbacker is no longer affiliated with NTLC.

NTLC is a totally nonpartisan organization actively engaged in assisting citizens, legislators and organizations who are trying to force the passage of constitutional amendments in their states limiting taxes and/or spending.

It provides advice on economic, political and legal matters to local organizations, active staff assistance, nationally known speakers and financial aid to those groups engaged in actual statewide campaigns.

One of the organization's biggest victories came about in Tennessee, which in March became the first state to limit spending by constitutional amendment (a full discussion of the Tennessee case is included elsewhere in this book). It has also been active in both Michigan and Massachusetts, and in 1980 is working in New York, Pennsylvania, Ohio, and Illinois, where spending-limitation amendments are currently being pushed by citizen groups.

According to NTLC President Uhler, "Our efforts so far have been to work with state organizations like the ones in Tennessee and Michigan, which are working toward limitation amendments. We think that, over the near term, our work will be primarily at the state level. However, our ultimate goal is an amendment to the federal constitution providing for a limitation on taxation and spending by the federal government."

To that end, Senators John Heinz (R-Pa.) and Richard Stone (D-Fla.) have introduced a joint resolution (S.J. Res. 56) proposing an amendment to the U.S. Constitution which would limit percentage increase in the total outlay of the U.S. government in any one year to no more than the percentage increase in the gross national product. In any year in which inflation is greater than 3 percent, government spending would have to be reduced by a quarter of a percent for each percent the inflation rate is higher than 3 percent.

The NTLC is backing the Heinz-Stone amendment and is trying to gather grass-roots support for it because, as Uhler recently told *Time* magazine, "We know that this is going to be a long, tough, no-nonsense battle."

Uhler recently told *Time* magazine, "We know that this is going to be a long, tough, no-nonsense battle."

NTLC recently formed the nonprofit Tax Limitation Research Foundation for the purpose of conducting research on the general subject of constitutional tax limitation. The foundation has, in turn, entered into a research contract with the Center for the Study of Law Structures at California's Claremont College.

One of the first research projects being undertaken is a computer analysis of what effect a constitutional spending amendment would have had on each of the fifty states had it been in effect for the last twenty years.

Besides Uhler, Campaigne, and Rickenbacker, the founders of NTLC included: C. Austin Baker, a vice-president of Hornblower, Weeks, Noyes and Trask, Inc.; Robert Carleson, former U.S. commissioner of welfare; George Champion, former chairman of Chase Manhattan Bank; Milton Friedman, the Nobel prize-winning economist; Arthur Godfrey; Allan Grant, president of the American Farm Bureau; James Hall, a California businessman; former ambassador Clare Boothe Luce; Vern McCarthy, a businessman; newspaper publisher John McGoff; William Niskanen, chief economist for Ford Motor Company; William Shaker, founder of Taxpayers United of Michigan; Frank Shakespeare, former director of the U.S. Information Agency; Professor William Stubblebine of Claremont College; and Gen. A. C. Wedemeyer, USA-Ret.

NTLC is now run by a five-man board: Uhler; Campaigne, Robert Carlson, former U.S. commissioner of welfare; Prof. William Stubblebine of Claremont College, who also runs the Tax Limitation Research Foundation; and William H. Shaker, founder of Taxpayers United of Michigan. Shaker is the executive vice-president of NTLC and works full time in the Washington office.

For further information, write to the National Tax Limitation Committee, P.O. Box 513, Loomis, California 95650; or 1707 H Street, N.W., Washington, DC 20006.

THE AMERICAN TAX REDUCTION MOVEMENT

The American Tax Reduction Movement is the new guy on the tax revolt block. It is the brainchild of California's Howard Jarvis, the other father of Prop 13.

The ATRM philosophy is the Howard Jarvis philosophy: slash, slash, slash! It is a hardline organization, and the unwillingness of other national tax revolt groups to take as hard a line or give Jarvis the freedom he wanted resulted in his going into competition with them.

In typical Jarvis style, the organization was launched with a half-hour national television program aimed at gathering members and money. This was quickly followed by a large-scale national direct mail fund-raising campaign.

ATRM is already active on three separate levels. At the national level, Jarvis has had his tax cut proposal introduced into the House of Representatives as the American Tax Reduction Act of 1979. It is a radical measure calling for a surplus in the federal budget by 1983, placing an 18 percent of GNP lid on federal spending, instituting a massive cut in individual taxes, and indexing all tax rates to inflation in order to prevent people from being moved into higher tax brackets merely because of inflation. The bill is before the House Ways and Means Committee, but so far, because it is considered so radical, it has generated little support.

At home in California, Jarvis and ATRM are gathering petition signatures in an effort to place a new tax-slashing measure on the 1980 ballot. Jarvis, who is not satisfied with Prop 13 results so far, wants the state's income tax cut by a flat 50 percent, coupled with a massive reduction in the state inventory tax businesses must pay once a year. Slightly over 500,000 signatures are needed to put the measure on the ballot. Jarvis says he will get 2 million.

On the grass roots level, ATRM is starting to work with organizations in various states to put Prop 13–type initiatives on those ballots. In addition, the organization has begun raising money and has formed a political action committee to distribute that money to candidates in the 1980 elections who agree to support tax-cutting measures both on the federal and state level.

The American Tax Reduction Movement can be reached at Suite 350, 6333 Wilshire Blvd., Los Angeles, CA 90048.

ACT NOW

Americans to Cut Taxes Now is a project of the American Conservative Union and grew out of the ACU's Tax Limitation Task Force. Chaired by former ACU Chairman Representative Philip Crane, Act Now has Nobel prize-winning economist Militon Fried.nan as its technical adviser. Additionally, its honorary chairman is former South Carolina Governor James Edwards, and its honorary vice-chairman is Senator James McClure (R-Ida.).

Obviously, as the name implies, the main thrust of the organization is to limit taxes. In announcing the formation of the task force last fall, Representative Crane said, "We will carry the fight to limit taxes to every individual state with a view to trying to get constitutional amendments in the states, and after a sufficient number of states have acted positively on this idea, then to go for a national constitutional amendment."

Act Now works closely with the National Tax Limitation Committee and shares that organization's philosophical commitment to the idea of tax limitation. As such, the ACU task force worked hard in Tennessee for the passage of that state's new constitutional amendment and on similar efforts that narrowly failed in Illinois and South Dakota.

Members of the task force include: Dr. William Allan, professor of economics, University of California; Robert Carleson, former U.S. Commissioner of Welfare; Dr. Kenneth Clarkson, professor of economics, University of Miami; State Representative David Copeland of Tennessee, State Senator Fred Eckert of New York; State Representative Edgar Fredricks of Michigan; Charles Hobbs, an author of California's Proposition 13; Norman Hughes, Metamora, Michigan; Richard Kazan, a member of California's Task Force on Tax Limitation which was set up in 1972 by Ronald Reagan, then governor of the state; Dr. J. Clayburn LaForce, University of California; former Treasury Secretary William Simon; Edwin Thomas, another member of the Reagan task force; James Tobin, president, Illinois Taxpayers United; Dr. Jay Tontz, dean of the School of Business, California State University; State Representative Donald Totten of Illinois; Frank Walton; and State Representative Hal Wick of South Dakota.

Members of the task force travel throughout the nation to help organize other taxpayer limitation efforts. In recent months, they have aided groups in Minnesota and Missouri.

Representative Crane has now put his idea of a federal constitutional spending limitation amendment into written form and has introduced it into the House of Representatives. The task force is backing the proposal. (There is a discussion of this in the section on federal tax revolts.)

The organization's most recently announced project: "A Modern-Day Tea Party." The idea, according to Crane, is for "all disenchanted taxpayers to mail a tea bag to any government official who they feel is squandering excessive amounts of taxpayer funds. By sending a tea bag to their state and federal officials, this message will be reinforced in the minds of the legislators that the overtaxed citizen has had enough."

The ACU also sees Act Now as an umbrella organization for various tax reform groups nationwide. It intends to hold national meetings to bring these various groups together and to coordinate their efforts nationally. The ACU has budgeted $100,000 for Act Now for the next year.

For further information, write to Mr. Gary Jarmin, Act Now, American Conservative Union, 316 Pennsylvania Ave., S.E., Washington, DC 20003.

THE TRRG

TRRG is part of a Ralph Nader umbrella organization called "Public Citizen." It was formed several years ago primarily to lobby for tax reform on the federal level. In mid-1978, however, it became actively involved in lobbying for state and local tax reform.

According to a spokesman, the organization works "for reform of federal, state and local taxation, as well as the fair and efficient administration of those laws by the Internal Revenue Service and local tax administrations."

Its main efforts go into trying to persuade Congress to "protect the interests of middle-income taxpayers and consumers during consideration of tax and energy legislation."

In addition, the TRRG continued its strong involvement in efforts to reform the operations of the Internal Revenue Service. Through the active participation of the organization's director as a public interest representative on the IRS Commissioner's Advisory Group, TRRG has continued to push for what it believes are necessary reforms within IRS, including:

—fuller disclosure of IRS operations, including its procedures for issuing rulings and regulations;
—more notice to taxpayers of their rights;
—stronger congressional oversight of IRS operations;
—simpler procedures for appeal of IRS rulings;
—low-cost legal representation for middle-income taxpayers;
—the right of citizens to sue IRS over improper rulings and regulations.

In 1978, TRRG began branching out, working with groups on state and local levels as an integral part of its tax reform efforts. TRRG has focused on tax issues of state and local concern to average taxpayers. In this area, the group has:

—lobbied against an international tax treaty between the United States and the United Kingdom;
—provided expertise and technical assistance on state tax issues to state-wide citizen action and union groups;
—encouraged property tax reform efforts throughout the country through clearinghouse activities, speaking engagements, workshops and news journal columns.

TRRG has also supplied information to tax reformers, citizen and church groups, unions and the Congress itself through studies and testimony.

It has a major book on the tax system available: *Tax Politics: How They Make You Pay and What You Can Do About It,* and the TRRG monthly newspaper, *People and Taxes,* now claims a monthly circulation of 85,000.

TRRG operates with a full-time staff of eight, including five tax professionals, and a budget in excess of $100,000 annually.

For further information, write to the Tax Reform Research Group, P.O. Box 14198, Ben Franklin Station, Washington, DC 20044.

THE ALEC

The American Legislative Exchange Council is a nonprofit, nonpartisan, tax-exempt public affairs and research organization for state legislators from across the nation. Its membership also includes private citizens interested in state legislative issues.

The primary purpose of ALEC is to help elected representatives throughout the nation share ideas and legislative proposals in all areas of public policy, with emphasis on strengthening "grass-roots" government as the alternative to centralized government in Washington.

ALEC also serves as a forum for the exchange of sound, imaginative ideas for reducing and controlling the bureaucracy, promoting fiscal responsibility, lowering the tax burden and safeguarding precious individual liberties.

To further these objectives, ALEC provides legislators and the general public with factual analyses, research information and model legislation on a wide range of issues concerning local, state and national government.

Annually, ALEC compiles and distributes its "Suggested State Legislation," containing model statutes that its member-legislators may want to introduce. One of its suggested statutes forms the basis for the Tennessee constitutional amendment which was adopted this year. On its 1980 listing of model statutes is a state constitutional tax limitation amendment, a tax indexing act, and a spending and debt limitation constitutional amendment.

ALEC also sponsors an annual series of national conferences on various legislative issues. Its most recent conference was on tax limitation, which it cosponsored with the National Tax Limitation Committee.

For further information, write to the American Legislative Exchange Council, 418 C Street, N.E., Washington, DC 20002.

THE TAX FOUNDATION

The Tax Foundation is a publicly supported, nonprofit organization, founded in 1937 to engage in nonpartisan research and public education on the fiscal and management aspects of government.

Its purpose, characterized by the motto "Toward Better Government Through Citizen Understanding," is to aid in the development of more efficient and economical government.

It serves as a national information agency for individuals and organizations concerned with problems of government expenditures, taxation and debt.

The foundation is known for its periodicals, among them the biennial and authoritative *Facts and Figures on Government Finance,* the monthly *Tax Review* and *Handbook of State and Local Government Finance.*

The foundation is currently embarked on a research program on the basic revisions necessary to improve the federal income tax system. Among the topics currently being researched are "taxation and capital formation," "the effects of reducing the rate of tax on capital income" and "financing social security."

In addition, the foundation sponsors a series of annual conferences, including a national and several regional meetings for state associations and state executives.

Of particular interest to people involved in state tax issues are three annual surveys published by the foundation: "State Tax Prospects," "State Tax Action in 1979" and "Allocation of the Federal Tax Burden by State."

For further information, write to the Tax Foundation, Inc., 1875 Connecticut Ave., N.W., Suite 903, Washington, DC 20009.

MODEL PRESS RELEASE

EFFECTIVE TAX REVOLT, INC.
77-44 Harmony Lane
City, State ZIP

For Further Information: For Immediate Release
Al Jones, Publicity Chairman   April 15, 1979
(800) 999-8888

Group Seeks Property Tax Rollback

City—The recent increase in the property tax, which takes effect next January, has had a side effect unforeseen by the legislators who voted for it—a tax revolt in this city.

According to Effective Tax Revolt, Inc., which was formed recently, the 32 percent increase in the property tax rate will make it a lot more difficult for an average family of four to keep its home going.

"When you consider the high cost of living, the ever-rising rate of inflation, the never-ending climb in prices, you have to wonder how people manage to make ends meet as it is," says ETR Chairwoman Margaret Smith. "The added 32 percent is only going to make things a whole lot worse. Government is supposed to help people, not make their lives miserable or force them to sell the homes they worked so hard forA"

Smith said her group intends to push for legislation rolling back the property tax rate to its current level. ETR has already lined up several legislators who have agreed to sponsor the legislation the group has prepared. The legislators are: James McAdams, D-County; Horace Banner, R-Municipality; Alice Baker, D-City; and Seth Taylor, I-Community.

Effective Tax Revolt, Inc., intends to obtain 100,000 signatures on petitions supporting the legislation and to launch a letter-writing campaign "to let the legislators know how the people feel about this hideous new burden," Smith said. In addition, the group intends to conduct a door-to-door campaign in favor of the rollback in the district of each legislator who supported the rate increase in the first place.

"We will call off the campaign in any given district where the legislator agrees to vote in favor of the rollback," Smith said, adding, "I hope they haven't forgotten that this is an election year."

Smith emphasized that her group is not affiliated with any political party.

"We have two Democrats, one Republican and one independent supporting us in the legislature," she said. "We won't be campaigning for anybody or against anybody. We will only be campaigning in the districts of those legislators who voted for the rate increase originally, and only for as long as they fail to agree to the rollback."

Other members of ETR's executive committee are Arnold Saltzman, a local druggist; Dave Klein, an attorney; Lisa Caroll, owner of an antiques shop; and Al Jones, an advertising executive.

Effective Tax Revolt, Inc., is located at 77-44 Harmony Lane.

MODEL PRESS CONFERENCE ANNOUNCEMENT

EFFECTIVE TAX REVOLT, INC.
77-44 Harmony Lane
City, State ZIP

For Further Information:
Al Jones, Publicity Chairman
(800) 999-8888

What: A press conference announcing a campaign to roll back the recently passed 32 percent hike in the property tax rate

Where: VFW Post 14 Auditorium
31-56 Main Street, City

When: 11 A.M., Tuesday, April 22, 1979

Who: The executive committee of Effective Tax Revolt, Inc., plus—

Leg. James McAdams, D-County
Leg. Horace Banner, R-Municipality
Leg. Alice Baker, D-City
Leg. Seth Taylor, I-Community

SAMPLE BIOGRAPHY FOR USE
IN A PRESS KIT

EFFECTIVE TAX REVOLT, INC.
77-44 Harmony Lane
City, State ZIP

For Further Information:
Al Jones, Publicity Chairman
(800) 999-8888

Margaret Smith
Biography
(with photo)

Margaret Smith was born in Eastchester, N.Y., and moved to City five years ago.

A graduate of Fashion Institute of Technology, she currently owns and operates The Boutique, which sells her own Margo line of women's clothing. Her office in the back of The Boutique also serves as the headquarters for Effective Tax Revolt, Inc., of which she is chairwoman.

She is married to Paul Smith, an accountant. The couple has two children, Molly (age 9) and J.J. (age 6).

"We are the perfect average family of four," she says.

STATE TAX-AND-SPENDING-LIMITATION AMENDMENTS

THE NOW-FAMOUS PROPOSITION 13: THE JARVIS-GANN INITIATIVE

Section 1. (a) The maximum amount of any ad valorem tax on real property shall not exceed one percent (1%) of the full cash value of such property. The one percent (1%) tax to be collected by the counties and apportioned according to law to the districts within the counties.

(b) The limitation provided for in subdivision (a) shall not apply to ad valorem taxes or special assessments to pay the interest and redemption charges on any indebtedness approved by the voters prior to the time this section becomes effective.

Section 2. (a) The full cash value means the County Assessors valuation of real property as shown on the 1975–76 tax bill under "full cash value", or thereafter, the appraised value of real property when purchased, newly constructed, or a change in ownership has occurred after the 1975 assessment. All real property not already assessed up to the 1975–76 tax levels may be reassessed to reflect that valuation.

(b) The Fair market value base may reflect from year to year the inflationary rate not to exceed two percent (2%) for any given year or reduction as shown in the consumer price index or comparable data for the area under taxing jurisdiction.

Section 3. From and after the effective date of this article, any changes in State taxes enacted for the purpose of increasing revenues collected pursuant thereto whether by increased rates or changes in methods of computation must be imposed by an Act passed by not less than two-thirds of all members elected to each of the two houses of the Legislature, except that no new ad valorem taxes on real property, or sales or transaction taxes on the sales of real property may be imposed.

Section 4. Cities, Counties, and special districts, by a two-thirds vote of the qualified electors of such district, may impose special taxes on such district, except ad valorem taxes on real property or a transaction tax or sales tax on the sale of real property within such city, county, or special district.

Section 5. This article shall take effect for the tax year beginning on July 1 following the passage of this Amendment, except Section 3 which shall become effective upon the passage of this article.

Section 6. If any section, part, clause, or phrase hereof is for any reason held to be invalid or unconstitutional, the remaining sections shall not be affected but will remain in full force and effect.

THE COLORADO SPENDING-LIMITATION AMENDMENT

Be It Enacted by the People of the State of Colorado:
That the constitution of the state of Colorado be amended by the addition of a new Article to read:

Article Limitation on Per-Capita Expenditures of Units of Government

Section 1. *Definitions.* As used in this article and in any statute or statutes enacted pursuant to its provisions, the following terms shall have these meanings:

(1) The term "unit of government" means and includes the state of Colorado itself and every county, city and county, city, town, school district, special district, and any other political subdivision of and within the state, whether now existing or hereafter created;

(2) The term "fiscal year" means any accounting period of twelve consecutive months;

(3) The term "aggregate expenditures" means the total amount of moneys, derived from all sources other than the federal government, appropriated for expenditure by a unit of government during any fiscal year for all purposes except for payment of interest and principal on lawfully incurred indebtedness;

(4) The term "population" means the aggregate number of persons officially estimated or otherwise determined to be residing within the boundaries of each unit of government on the first day of any fiscal year;

(5) The term "per-capita expenditure" means the quotient derived from dividing aggregate expenditures by a unit of government during any fiscal year by its population on the first day of that particular fiscal year, except that in the case of a school district per-capita expenditure shall be determined by dividing aggregate expenditures of such school district during any fiscal year by the average number of pupils actually enrolled, or estimated to be enrolled, in the public schools of such school district during that particular fiscal year;

(6) The term "increase in the cost of living" means any increase in the Consumer Price Index (all items) for the United States, or in any comparable index, published by the Bureau of Labor Statistics, United States Department of Labor or by any successor agency, occurring during the first twelve months of the eighteen-month period immediately preceding the beginning of the fiscal year of a unit of government;

(7) The term "emergency" means an event or happening which could not have been reasonably foreseen or prevented.

Section 2. *Limitation on the per-capita expenditure of the state government.* Beginning July 1, 1979, the per-capita expenditure of the state government during any fiscal year shall not be increased over its per-capita expenditure during the immediately preceding fiscal year by a percentage any greater than the percentage of increase occurring in the cost of living of its residents during the period of time specified in section 1 (6) of this article, unless a greater percentage of increase shall be authorized by a majority of the votes cast by the registered electors of the state voting on the question in a special election. Such special election shall be held prior to the beginning of the fiscal year on such date as shall be prescribed by law, and only one such special election may be held in any year. Any act appropriating any amount of money in excess of the permitted or voter-approved percentage of increase shall be void and of no effect.

Section 3. *Limitation on the per-capita expenditure of each local unit of government.* Beginning January 1, 1980, the per-capita expenditure of each local unit of government during any fiscal year shall not be increased over its per-capita expenditure during the immediately preceding fiscal year by a percentage any greater than the percentage of increase occurring in the cost of living of its residents during the period of time specified in section 1 (6) of this article, unless a greater percentage of increase shall be authorized by a majority of the votes cast by its lawfully qualified electors voting on the question in a special election. Such special election shall be held prior to the beginning of the fiscal year on such date as shall be prescribed by law, and only one such special election may be held in any year. Any measure appropriating any amount of money in excess of the permitted or voter-approved percentage of increase shall be void and of no effect.

Section 4. *State-imposed costs—indemnification of local units of government.* The state government shall not impose on any local unit of government any part of the costs of new state programs or the costs of increased levels of service under any existing state programs. All such costs shall be fully defrayed by the state government.

The aggregate amount of money payable by the state government to any local unit of government for all purposes during the calendar year 1980 shall not be reduced below the aggregate amount of money paid by the state government to such local unit of government for all purposes during the calendar year 1979.

Section 5. *Adequacy of annual appropriations to ensure payment of future benefit obligations.* If the state government or any local unit of government enacts any measure providing for future payment of benefits, or if any such measure is presently in effect, annual appropriations of money made pursuant to the provisions of any such measure shall be adequate to ensure timely payment of the amount of such future benefits when judged under commonly accepted accounting principles and actuarial practices.

Section 6. *Emergencies.* Whenever the governor and two-thirds of the members of each house of the general assembly agree upon the existence and nature of an emergency and public announcement is made of the manner in which the costs of meeting the emergency will be defrayed, the limitation on the per-capita expenditure of the state government than in effect may be exceeded, but only for a period not longer than twelve consecutive calendar months in duration. Any expenditures required to meet any such emergency shall not operate to modify the per-capita expenditure limitation then in effect, but such limitation shall continue to constitute the base for computing the per-capita expenditure during the next following fiscal year.

In the case of a local unit of government, whenever two-thirds of its governing body and its chief executive officer, if such there be, agree upon the existence and nature of an emergency and public announcement is made of the manner in which the costs of meeting the emergency will be defrayed, the limitation on the per-capita expenditure of such local unit of government then in effect may be exceeded, but only for a period not longer than twelve consecutive calendar months in duration. Any expenditures required to meet any such emergency shall not operate to modify the per-capita expenditure limitation then in effect, but such limitation shall continue to constitute the base for computing the per-capita expenditure during the next following fiscal year.

Section 7. *Transfer of responsibility for defraying costs.* Whenever by law or by court order the responsibility for defraying the costs of a program or programs is transferred from one unit of government to another unit, the per-capita expenditure of the unit of government to which such responsibility was transferred shall be commensurately increased and the per-capita expenditure of the unit of government from which such responsibility was transferred shall be commensurately decreased, to the end that no net increase in the cost of such program or programs shall occur as a result of such transfer.

Section 8. *Excess of revenue receipts over expenditures.* The governing body of every unit of government shall diligently seek to avoid consistent receipt of annual revenues in excess of annual expenditures as limited by the provisions of this article.

Any excess of state government receipts over state government expenditures occurring during any fiscal year shall, at the end of such fiscal year, be transferred to a surplus fund. The balance in said surplus fund at the beginning of any fiscal year shall be limited to an amount no greater than five percent of the aggregate amount appropriated for expenditure during said fiscal year, and any amount in excess of said limitation shall be used by the general assembly for reduction in tax rates, for tax credits, or for tax refunds.

Section 9. *Implementation of provisions.* In its first session following the adoption of this article, the general assembly shall by law prescribe a method for estimating or determining the population of the state and of each local unit of government therein as of the first day of each fiscal year required by the provisions of this article, and shall enact such other statutes as may be necessary to implement and enforce all other provisions hereof.

Section 10. *Local units of government hereafter created.* The general assembly shall by law prescribe the manner by which any local unit of government created after the adoption of this article shall determine its per-capita expenditure during the first three years of its existence.

Section 11. *Severability.* If any expenditure category of any unit of government is expected or exempted from the limitations imposed upon per-capita expenditures by the provisions of this article, the limitations upon per-capita expenditures imposed by the provisions of this article shall be adjusted accordingly, but such limitations shall remain in full force and effect with respect to all expenditure categories not excepted or exempted.

THE ILLINOIS TAX-LIMITATION AMENDMENT

Resolved, by the House of Representatives of the eightieth general assembly of the state of Illinois, the senate concurring herein, that there shall be submitted to the electors of this State, at the general election next occurring at least 6 months after the adoption of this resolution, a proposition to amend Article IX of the Constitution by adding Section 11 thereto, the added Section to read as follows:

Article IX

Section 11. LIMITATIONS ON TOTAL OF STATE TAXES AND SHARE COMMITTED TO LOCAL GOVERNMENT—PROHIBITION OF MANDATE OF LOCAL PROGRAMS WITHOUT STATE FUNDING

(a) There is hereby established a limit on the taxes imposed by the legislature for any fiscal year. Effective with the first fiscal year beginning after approval of this Section by the electors, and for each fiscal year thereafter, the legislature shall not impose taxes of any kind which, together with all other revenues of the State, shall exceed 7 percent of the personal income of Illinois for that fiscal year except as provided in subsection

(b) of this Section. "Personal income of Illinois" means the total income received by persons in Illinois from all sources, as defined and officially reported by the United States Department of Commerce or its successor agency. "Revenues of the State" means all public funds received by the State but does not include federal aid nor the contributions to and earnings of trust funds in the custody of the State Treasurer.

(b) An Emergency Fund equal to two-tenths of one percent of the personal income of Illinois in each fiscal year shall be established. Revenues shall be allocated to this emergency fund and shall be included in the total level of allowable taxation as limited by subsection (a) of this Section. Expenditures from this fund shall be allowed only upon the Governor's declaration of an emergency situation and the affirmative vote of three-fifths of the members of each house of the legislature.

If it is determined that the amount in the Emergency Fund is less than what is needed to meet an emergency situation taxes in excess of the limitation in subsection (a) may be imposed and collected only if all of the following conditions are met:

1. The Governor requests the legislature to declare an emergency.
2. The request shall be specific as to the nature of the emergency, the dollar amount of the emergency and the method by which the emergency will be funded.
3. Upon receiving this request the legislature declares an emergency in accordance with the specifications of the Governor's request by a 2/3 vote of the members elected to each house. The emergency must be declared in accordance with these provisions prior to incurring any of the expense which constitutes the specific emergency request. The tax limitation level may be exceeded only for the fiscal year in which the emergency is declared; in the next and subsequent fiscal years the tax limitation of subsection (a) of this Section shall again take effect.

Income earned from the funds maintained in the Emergency fund shall accrue to the fund. At the end of each fiscal year any balance in the Emergency Fund in excess of the amount estimated to be required by this subsection for the Emergency Fund for the succeeding fiscal year shall be distributed to the following:

1. The State Employees' Retirement System of Illinois
2. The Teachers' Retirement System of Illinois
3. The State Universities Retirement System
4. The Judges Retirement System of Illinois
5. The General Assembly Retirement System

The distribution of the excesses shall be determined by the Bureau of the Budget and shall be in the proportion that the actuarial reserve deficiency of each fund bears to the total of the actuarial reserve deficiency of all of those funds. If the actuarial reserve deficiencies of all of those funds are eliminated the excess shall be used to retire general obligation bonds sold by the State.

(c) For any fiscal year, in the event that revenues of the State exceed the limit established in subsection (a) of this Section, the excesses shall be distributed to the following:

1. The State Employees' Retirement System of Illinois
2. The Teachers' Retirement System of Illinois
3. The State Universities Retirement System
4. The Judges Retirement System of Illinois
5. The General Assembly Retirement System

The distribution of the excesses shall be determined by the Bureau of the Budget and shall be in the proportion that the actuarial reserve deficiency of each fund bears to the total of the actuarial reserve deficiency of all of those funds. If the actuarial reserve deficiencies of all of those funds are eliminated the excess shall be used to retire general obligation bonds sold by the State.

(d) For any fiscal year beginning after the approval of this Section by the electors, that proportion of State expenditures paid to all units of local government and school districts shall not be reduced below that proportion in effect in fiscal year 1975 and no new program, or increase in the level of service under an existing program shall be mandated by the legislature to units of local government or school districts unless an appropriation has been made by the legislature to pay the costs of the mandated program or service.

James R. Thompson Governor

The following is an analysis of the major provisions included in HJRCA 22 and the technical problems associated with them.

Provision: *Taxes and all other revenues of the State* (except federal aid and trust funds) *for any fiscal year* shall not exceed 7 percent of the personal income of Illinois (reported by U.S. Department of Commerce) for the *"latest known fiscal year".*

Problems: Revenues of the State" exclude federal aid and trust funds. For fiscal year 1976, revenues by this definition totaled $5.82 billion (Comptroller's Annual Report). *Revolving funds should also be excluded to avoid double counting.* In addition, bond financed funds should be excluded since bonding represents long term expenditure commitments rather than taxes.

"Revenues . . . for any fiscal year shall not exceed 7 percent of . . . Illinois personal income for the latest known fiscal year." The "latest known fiscal year" is a key restriction. At the time of the adoption of the fiscal year 1976 budget, fiscal year 1974 Illinois personal income was the latest known fiscal year. FY1974 Illinois personal income was $66.93 billion. *In FY1976, revenues exceeded 7 percent of the latest known fiscal year's (FY1974) personal income for illinois.* In fact, FY1976 revenues were 8.7 percent of FY1974 Illinois personal income.

Presently, the latest known fiscal year's Illinois personal income is $87.45 billion for fiscal year 1977. If this provision existed today, the fiscal year 1979 appropriation request from state revenues could not exceed 7 percent of $87.45 billion or $6.12 billion. The FY1979 budget request from state revenues is $7.11 billion. Thus, *the proposed budget from state revenues for FY1979 exceeds 7 percent of the latest known fiscal year's personal income.* The FY1979 budget request is 8.1 percent of FY1977 personal income. This means that the Governor's FY1979 budget would have to be reduced by $1.0 billion.

The Department of Commerce personal income data is subject to major revisions both quarterly and annually. Therefore, which figure will be the benchmark?

Provision: An Emergency Fund equal to 0.2 percent of Illinois personal income for the *latest known fiscal year* shall be established. Revenues shall be allocated to this fund (which is included within the 7 percent constraint) and *expenditures from the Emergency Fund shall be allowed only upon the Governor's declaration of an emergency situation and the affirmative vote of three-fifths of the members of each house of the legislature.*

Problems: Of the $6.12 billion of state revenue that would be available for FY1979 under HJRCA 22, *$175 million would not be available for appropriation* since it would have to be distributed to the emergency fund. This revenue could be appropriated upon the Governor's declaration of an emergency situation and an affirmative vote of the General Assembly. *Under HJRCA 22, it is likely that the state would always be in a declared emergency situation in order to spend revenues from the emergency fund.*

The method for distributing revenue into the emergency fund is not known. Would the fund receive a portion of the revenue from each fund or from one tax source?

Provision: In the event revenues exceed the 7 percent constraint, the excess shall be distributed to:

(a) The State Employees' Retirement System of Illinois,
(b) The Teachers' Retirement System of Illinois,
(c) The State Universities' Retirement System,
(d) The Judges' Retirement System of Illinois, and
(e) The General Assembly Retirement System.

Problem: There is no provision for excess revenue in the event that the pension funds become fully funded. In this case, benefits paid from retirement systems could become excessive. Alternatively, state employees may not be required to match the state's contribution.

Provision: Units of local government and school districts shall be held harmless *proportionately* to the proportions of expenditures in effect in fiscal year 1976. New programs or increases in existing services mandated by the legislature to units of local government and school districts shall be paid by the State.

Problems: Even though HJRCA 22 provides for local govenrments and school districts to be held harmless proportionately to fiscal year 1976, local governments would likely receive less state revenue under the provisions of HJRCA 22 than they would otherwise. This means that *the future state revenue that local governments are anticipating will have to be made up by local taxes, primarily property taxes.*

Advances in school financing, road improvements, health, energy and the environment which would have been funded by the state would be virtually impossible under HJRCA 22. Any court decision requiring the state to assume a larger role in funding a program would result in less funding for existing services.

Recommendation: HJRCA 22, as presently structured, would *not* result in the continuation of existing state services as argued by the proponents. *Limiting state revenues to 7 percent of Illinois personal income for the latest known fiscal year (FY1977) would result in a $1.0 billion cut for fiscal year 1979 in the programs financed by state revenues.* As a result of this limitation, along with the numerous other technical problems of the provision, the Bureau of the Budget *opposes* HJRCA 22.

SOUTH DAKOTA'S PROPERTY TAX–REDUCTION AMENDMENT AND PETITION

INITIATIVE PETITION FOR CONSTITUTIONAL AMENDMENT WE, THE UNDERSIGNED duly qualified electors of the State of South Dakota, do hereby petition that the following Amendment be added to the Bill of Rights, Article VI, Section 28, of the Constitution of the State of South Dakota, and which shall be submitted to the electorate of the State of South Dakota for their approval at the 1980 general election, or at any earlier statewide election held prior to that general election, or as otherwise provided by law. The following is a full and correct copy of the title and text of the proposed Amendment:

Title: INITIATIVE CONSTITUTIONAL AMENDMENT—REAL PROPERTY TAX LIMITATION

Text: BE IT ENACTED BY THE PEOPLE OF THE STATE OF SOUTH DAKOTA That Article VI, Section 28 be added to the South Dakota Constitution to read:

Section 1. (a) The maximum amount of the existing real property taxes in force and effect by the present statutes of this State on real property shall not exceed one per cent (1%) of the full and true valuation of such real property. The one per cent (1%) tax is to be collected by the counties and apportioned according to law to the districts within the counties.

(b) The limitation provided for in subdivision (a) shall not apply to assessments to pay the principal, interest and redemption charges on any indebtedness approved prior to the time this section becomes effective.

Section 2. (a) The full and true valuation shall be the County Assessor's valuation of real property as shown on the 1977 tax statements under "full and true valuation", or thereafter, the appraised value of newly constructed real property which shall be based upon the 1977 assessment valuation guidelines. All real property not already assessed to the 1977 full and true valuation levels may be reassessed to reflect that valuation.

(b) The full and true valuation may annually reflect an inflationary rate not to exceed two per cent (2%) for any year subsequent to the 1977 taxable year. A decline in the full and true valuation, as shown by the United States Department of Labor Consumer Price Index, shall be reflected in a commensurate tax decrease in the full and true valuation.

Section 3. From and after the effective date of this article, any changes in State or Local taxes enacted for the purpose of increasing revenues collected pursuant thereto, whether by increased rates or changes in methods of computation, must be imposed by an act passed by not less than two-thirds of all members elected to each of the two houses of the Legislature, provided that no new taxes on real property or sales taxes on the sales of real property may be imposed.

Section 4. Cities, counties and special taxing districts, by a two-thirds vote of the qualified electors of said districts, may impose special taxes on said districts, except that no new taxes on real property within said City, county or special taxing districts may be imposed.

Section 5. This article shall take effect for the taxable year beginning on January 1, following the passage of this Amendment, except Section 3 which shall become effective upon the passage of this article.

Section 6. If any section, part, clause or phrase hereof is for any reason held to be invalid or unconstitutional, the remaining sections shall not be affected but shall remain in full force and effect.

The names and addresses of the sponsors of this proposed Amendment are as follows: Danielle M. Samuelson, Box 649, Keystone, South Dakota 57751 G. Wester Samuelson, Box 649, Keystone, South Dakota 57751 Robert L. Christensen, R#2 Box 133, Rapid City, South Dakota 57701 Warren H. Hilt, 2433 Covington Dr., Rapid City, South Dakota 57701 Alfred C. McDonald, Cliff Drive, Canyon Lake Heights, Rapid

City, South Dakota 57701 Maxine M. Terry, 1668 Zinnia, Rapid City, South Dakota 57701 Lamny Callen, Rt. 8 Box 700, Rapid City, South Dakota 57701 Lee Terry, 1668 Zinnia, Rapid City, South Dakota 57701

INSTRUCTIONS TO SIGNERS:

1. Signers to this initiative petition must individually sign their name in the form they are registered to vote.

2. Each signer or circulator must add the mailing address of his residence and the date of signing. Place of residence shall be shown by name of city or town, with street and number, if any; if residence is outside of a city or town he should designate the township or precinct or route and box number. (DO NOT USE POST OFFICE BOX NUMBER.)

3. Abbreviations, including DITTO MARKS, can be used.

| NAME | RESIDENCE | DATE OF SIGNING |
| | (With Street and No. If Any) | |

1. _____

2. _____

3. _____

THE TWO ARIZONA PROPERTY TAX–RELIEF AMENDMENTS

Article XXVII. Residential Property Tax Limitation.

Section 1. The maximum tax on residential land and residential improvements in Arizona shall not exceed one (1%) percent of the fair market value of the residential land and residential improvements.

Section 2. The fair market value of residential land and residential improvements shall not be increased above two (2%) percent per year, except upon change of ownership. When ownership changes, the fair market value of the property may be increased above two (2%) percent.

Section 1. (a) The maximum of tax on property, land, and improvements shall not exceed (1%) one percent of the full cash value of such property, land, and improvements. The (1%) one percent tax to be collected by the counties and apportioned according to law.

(b) The limitation provided for in subdivision (a) shall not apply to property, land and improvements, to pay the interest and redemption charges on any indebtedness approved by the voters prior to the time this section becomes effective.

Section 2. (a) The full cash value means the county assessor's valuation of property, land, and improvements as shown in the 1970 tax under full cash value, or there after the appraised value of property, land, and improvements, including real property and improvements, when purchased, improvements after 1970 based on ($10.00) ten dollars per square foot, on new improvements, or a change in ownership has occurred after 1970 assessment, all property, land, and improvements not already assessed up to the 1970 tax levels may be reassessed to reflect that valuation.

(b) The full cash value base may reflect from year to year the inflationary rate not to exceed (2%) two percent for any given year or reduction as shown in the consumer price index or comparable data for the area under taxing jurisdiction.

Section 3. From and after the effective date of this article any changes in state, county or cities for the purpose of increasing revenues collected pursuant there to whether by increased rates or changes in methods of computation must be imposed by an Act passed by not less than (⅔) two thirds of all members elected to each of the two houses of the legislature except that no new property, land and improvements, or sales taxes, or transaction taxes, or income taxes, or other types of taxes for the recovery of revenue may be imposed.

Section 4. Cities, counties and special districts, by a (⅔) two thirds vote of the qualified electors of such district, may impose special taxes on such district, except property, land, and improvements taxes, or sales taxes, on the sale of property, land and improvements within such city, county or special district.

Section 5. This article shall take effect for the tax year beginning on January 1, following the passage of this Amendment, except Section 3 which shall become effective upon passage of this article.

Section 6. This article includes all commercial, industrial, and private lands and improvements.

Section 7. If any section, part clause, or phrase hereof is for any reason held to be invalid or unconstitutional, the remaining section shall not be affected but will remain in full force and effect.

TAXPAYERS UNITED'S MICHIGAN TAX–LIMITATION AMENDMENT

Sec. 25. Property taxes and other local taxes and state taxation and spending may not be increased above the limitations specified herein without direct voter approval. The state is prohibited from requiring any new or expanded activities by local governments without full state financing, from reducing the proportion of state spending in the form of aid to local governments, or from shifting the tax burden to local government. A provision for emergency conditions is established and the repayment of voter approved bonded indebtedness is guaranteed. Implementation of this section is specified in Sections 26 through 34, inclusive, of this Article.

Sec. 26. There is hereby established a limit on the total amount of taxes which may be imposed by the legislature in any fiscal year on the taxpayers of this state. This limit shall not be changed without approval of the majority of the qualified electors voting thereon, as provided for in Article 12 of the Constitution. Effective with fiscal year 1979–1980, and for each fiscal year thereafter, the legislature shall not impose taxes of any kind which, together with all other revenues of the state, federal aid excluded, exceed the revenue limit established in this section. The revenue limit shall be equal to the product of the ratio of Total State Revenues in fiscal year 1978–1979 divided by the Personal Income of Michigan in calendar year 1977 multiplied by the Personal Income of Michigan in either the prior calendar year or the average of Personal Income of Michigan in the previous three calendar years, whichever is greater.

For any fiscal year in the event that Total State Revenues exceed the revenue limit established in this section by 1% or more, the excess revenues shall be refunded pro rata based on the liability reported on the Michigan income tax and single business tax (or its successor tax or taxes) annual returns filed following the close of such fiscal year. If the excess is less than 1%, this excess may be transferred to the State Budget Stabilization Fund.

The revenue limitation established in this section shall not apply to taxes imposed for the payment of principal and interest on both, approved by the voters and authorized under Section 15 of this Article, and loans to school districts authorized under Section 16 of this Article.

If responsibility for funding a program or programs is transferred from one level of government to another, as a consequence of constitutional amendment, the state revenue and spending limits may be adjusted to accommodate such change, provided that the total revenue authorized for collection by both state and local governments does not exceed that amount which would have been authorized without such change.

Sec. 27. The revenue limit of Section 26 of this Article may be exceeded only if all of the following conditions are met: (1) The governor requests the legislature to declare an emergency; (2) the request is specific as to the nature of the emergency, the dollar amount of the emergency, and the method by which the emergency will be funded; and (3) the legislature thereafter declares an emergency in accordance with the specifics of the governor's request by a two-thirds vote of the members elected to and serving in each house. The emergency must be declared in accordance with this section prior to incurring any of the expenses which constitute the emergency request. The revenue limit may be exceeded only during the fiscal year for which the emergency is declared. In no event shall any part of the amount representing a refund under Section 26 of this Article be the subject of an emergency request.

Sec. 28. No expenses of state government shall be incurred in any fiscal year which exceed the sum of the revenue limit established in Sections 26 and 27 of this Article plus federal aid and any surplus from a previous fiscal year.

Sec. 29. The state is hereby prohibited from reducing the state financed proportion of the necessary costs of any existing activity or service required of units of Local Government by state law. A new activity or service or an increase in the level of any activity or service beyond that required by existing law shall not be required by the legislature or any state agency of units of Local Government, unless a state appropriation is made and disbursed to pay the unit of Local Government for any necessary increased costs. The provision of this section shall not apply to costs incurred pursuant to Article VI, Section 18.

Sec. 30. The proportion of total state spending paid to all units of Local Government, taken as a group, shall not be reduced below that proportion in effect in fiscal year 1978–79.

Sec. 31. Units of Local Government are hereby prohibited from levying any tax not authorized by law or charter when this section is ratified or from increasing the rate of an existing tax above that rate authorized by law or charter when this section is ratified, without the approval of a majority of the qualified electors of that unit of Local Government voting thereon. If the definition of the base of an existing tax is broadened, the maximum authorized rate of taxation on the new base in each unit of Local

Government shall be reduced to yield the same estimated gross revenue as on the prior base. If the assessed valuation of property as finally equalized, excluding the value of new construction and improvements, increases by a larger percentage than the increase in the General Price Level from the previous year, the maximum authorized rate applied thereto in each unit of Local Government shall be reduced to yield the same gross revenue from existing property, adjusted for changes in the General Price Level, as could have been collected at the existing authorized rate on the prior assessed value.

The limitations of this section shall not apply to taxes imposed for the payment of principal and interest on bonds or other evidence of indebtedness or for the payment of assessments on contract obligations in anticipation of which bonds are issued which were authorized prior to the effective date of this amendment.

Sec. 32. Any taxpayer of the state shall have standing to bring suit in the Michigan State Court of Appeals to enforce the provisions of Sections 25 through 31, inclusive, of this Article and, if the suit is sustained, shall receive from the applicable unit of government his costs incurred in maintaining such suit.

Sec. 33. Definitions. The definitions of this section shall apply to Section 25 through 32 of Article IX, inclusive.

"Total State Revenues" includes all general and special revenues, excluding federal aid, as defined in the budget message of the governor for fiscal year 1978–1979. Total State Revenues shall exclude the amount of any credits based on actual tax liabilities or the imputed tax components of rental payments, but shall include the amount of any credits not related to actual tax liabilities. "Personal Income of Michigan" is the total income received by persons in Michigan from all sources, as defined and officially reported by the United States Department of Commerce or its successor agency. "Local Government" means any political subdivision of the state, including, but not restricted to, school districts, cities, villages, townships, charter townships, counties, charter counties, authorities created by the state, and authorities created by other units of local government. "General Price Level" means the Consumer Price Index for the United States as defined and officially reported by the United States Department of Labor or its successor agency.

Sec. 34. The Legislature shall implement the provisions of Sections 25 through 33, inclusive, of this Article.

Sec. 6. (New language capitalized) Except as otherwise provided in this constitution, the total amount of general ad valorem taxes imposed upon real and tangible personal property for all purposes in any one year shall not exceed 15 mills on each dollar of the assessed valuation of property as finally equalized. Under procedures provided by law, which shall guarantee the right of initiative, separate tax limitations for any county and for the townships and for school districts therein, the aggregate of which shall not exceed 18 mills on each dollar of such valuation, may be adopted and thereafter altered by the vote of a majority of the qualified electors of such county voting thereon, in lieu of the limitation hereinbefore established. These limitations may be increased to an aggregate of not to exceed 50 mills on each dollar of valuation, for a period of not to exceed 20 years at any one time, if approved by a majority of the electors, qualified under Section 6 of Article II of this constitution, voting on the question.

The foregoing limitations shall not apply to taxes imposed for the payment of principal and interest on bonds APPROVED BY THE ELECTORS or other evidences of indebtedness APPROVED BY THE ELECTORS or for the payment of assessments or contract obligations in anticipation of which bonds are issued APPROVED BY THE ELECTORS, which taxes may be imposed without limitation as to rate or amount; OR, SUBJECT TO THE PROVISIONS OF SECTIONS 25 THROUGH 34 OF THIS ARTICLE, to taxes imposed for any other purpose by any city, village, charter county, charter township, charter authority or other authority, the tax limitations of which are provided by charter or by general law.

In any school district which extends into two or more counties, property taxes at the highest rate available in the county which contains the greatest part of the area of the district may be imposed and collected for school purposes throughout the district.

Provisions of Existing Constitution Altered or Abrogated
by this Amendment if Adopted Article IX, Section 6

Section 6. Except as otherwise provided in this constitution, the total amount of general ad valorem taxes imposed upon real and tangible personal property for all purposes in any one year shall not exceed 15 mills on each dollar of the assessed valuation of property as finally equalized. Under procedures provided by law, which shall guarantee the right of initiative, separate tax limitations for any county and for the townships and for school districts therein, the aggregate of which shall not exceed 18 mills on each dollar of such valuation, may be adopted and thereafter altered by the vote of a majority of the qualified electors of such county voting thereon, in lieu of the limitation hereinbefore established. These limitations may be increased to an aggregate of not to exceed 50 mills on each dollar of valuation, for a period of not to exceed 20 years at any one time, if approved by a majority of the electors, qualified under Section 6 of Article II of this constitution, voting on the question.

The foregoing limitations shall not apply to taxes imposed for the payment of principal and interest on bonds or other evidences of indebtedness or for the payment of assessments or contract obligations in anticipation of which bonds are issued, which taxes may be imposed without limitation as to rate or amount; or to taxes imposed for any other purpose by the city, village, charter county, charter township, charter authority or other authority, the tax limitations of which are provided by charter or by general law.

In any school district which extends into two or more counties, property taxes at the highest rate available in the county which contains the greatest part of the area of the district may be imposed and collected for school purposes throughout the district.

THE MASSACHUSETTS TAX–LIMITATION AMENDMENT

Section 1. Tax Revenue Limitation. (1) There is hereby established a state revenue limit for each fiscal year. Except as specified in sub-sections (2) and (3) below, for the first fiscal year commencing after the effective date hereof and for each fiscal year thereafter, the maximum state tax revenue shall be the amount determined by multiplying the limitation ratio by the average personal income of Massachusetts for the three previous calendar years.

(2) Additional revenue may be raised specifically for the purpose of local property tax relief.

(3) Additional revenue may be raised specifically for the purpose of providing for the state's pension obligations incurred prior to the effective date of this chapter.

Section 2. Revenue Limitation Adjustments. (1) If a program is transferred between the state and any other level of government, the state revenue limit shall be commensurately adjusted by the new limitation ratio thereby created.

(2) The State Tax Revenue Limit may be increased or decreased by a designated dollar amount by a majority vote of the people at a Statewide election approving a measure placed on the ballot by the Legislature by a roll-call vote entered into the journal, two-thirds of the membership of each house concurring, or placed on the ballot as an initiative petition pursuant to Article XLVIII of this Constitution. A measure so approved shall take effect the day after the election, unless the measure provides otherwise.

(3) If Federal Taxes are reduced on condition that the State increase expenditures by an amount equivalent to the Federal reduction, the Tax Revenue Limitation may be increased by such an amount.

Section 3. Appropriation Limitation. No appropriation shall cause an expenditure during any fiscal year of tax revenues in excess of the Tax Revenue Limitation for that fiscal year, other than for disposition of surplus revenues as provided in Section 4 or for Emergency situations as provided in Section 6.

Section 4. Disposition of Surplus Revenue. If the state revenue for any fiscal year exceeds the state revenue limit for that fiscal year, the excess shall be distributed pro rata on the income taxes annual returns next filed following the close of such fiscal year.

Section 5. Restriction on Mandating Programs. (1) No new program, or increase in level of service under an existing program, shall be mandated to units of local government, or authorities created by the state, or of political subdivisions of the state, unless a specific state appropriation is made sufficient to pay the local unit of government, authority, or political subdivision for the costs of that program. Such appropriation shall not be considered property tax relief under Section 1.

(2) The proportion of state revenue paid to or for all units of local government, authorities created by the state, and political subdivisions of that state, taken as a group, shall not be reduced below that proportion in effect in the fiscal year next preceding the effective date of this Amendment.

Section 6. Special Reserve Fund. (1) A special reserve fund not to exceed 0.2 percent of the state personal income shall be established and maintained by the legislature. Moneys appropriated to the Special Reserve Fund shall be from state tax revenues and shall be subject to the state revenue limit.

(2) Upon the governor's declaration of an emergency situation and the exhaustion of such funds as may be available from other sources such as internal borrowing or federal emergency funds, the legislature may, by a two-thirds vote of each house make appropriations from the special reserve fund to meet the emergency or, if that fund is exhausted, the legislature may, by a two-thirds vote of each house provide for a specific tax increase or a specific new tax designated solely to meet the emergent situation. Any tax so enacted shall remain in effect no longer than two years, unless its continuation is approved by a majority of the votes cast at a state, general or special election.

Section 7. Economic Estimates Committee. (1) There shall be an Economic Estimates Committee consisting of the State Treasurer, an appointee of the Governor as designated by him who is not a member of the legislature or an employee of the Commonwealth, an attorney in the private practice of law appointed by the Massachusetts Board of Bar Overseers, a designee appointed by the State Senate who is not a member of the

Legislature or an employee of the Commonwealth, and the dean of the School of Business from an accredited college or unviersity within the Commonwealth appointed by the Governor. Actions by the Committee shall require the concurrence of three of its members. The Committee Chairman shall utilize the resources of existing State agencies in carrying out its duties.

(2) The Committee shall determine and publish, prior to April 1, of each year, the State Revenue Limit for the following fiscal year by making and publishing all necessary estimates and calculations as provided in this Amendment. The Committee shall determine the State Revenue Limit for the fiscal year next following enactment as soon as it can act. If it does not act prior to the July 1, next following, the State Revenue Limit for such fiscal year shall be the amount the Tax Revenue Limit would have been for the present fiscal year had this Amendment been in existence. The Committee shall also determine and publish such estimates of the State Revenue Limit as are necessary for the orderly and proper development of State Budgets. If the Committee does not act to determine the State Revenue Limit before July 1, of a fiscal year, the State Revenue Limit for that fiscal year shall remain the same as for the previous fiscal year.

Section 8. Future Obligations and Use of Bonds. (1) If the state enacts a law which provides for future payments or benefits, or if such a law or laws currently exist, any appropriation made pursuant thereto shall be adequate when judged by sound or commonly accepted accounting and actuarial practices to assure such future payments or benefits.

(2) Bonds shall not be used to finance operating expenses but may be used only to finance capital improvements. Revenue anticipation notes may be used providing the redemption date on such notes is not subsequent to the end of the then current fiscal year.

Section 9. Severability. If any expenditure category or revenue source shall be exempt or excluded from the limitation herein stated, pursuant to final judgment of any court of competent jurisdiction and any appeal therefrom, this spending limit shall be adjusted accordingly; the spending limit will remain in full force and effect with regard to all other expenditure categories and revenue sources.

Section 10. Definitions. (1) "Personal Income of Massachusetts," the total income received by persons in Massachusetts from all sources, including transfer payments, as defined and officially reported by the U.S. Department of Commerce or its successor agency.

(2) "Limitation Ratio," the quotient formed by dividing the average gross state budget for the three fiscal years immediately preceding the effective date hereof by the average personal income of Massachusetts for the three calendar years immediately preceding the effective date hereof.

(3) "State Revenue Limit," that amount of dollars equivalent to the average total personal income of Massachusetts for the previous three calendar years multiplied by the limitation ratio.

(4) "State Tax Revenue," the revenue of the state from every tax, penalty, receipt and other monetary exaction and interest in connection therewith. Included revenue will be all taxes including but not limited to retail sales and use, motor vehicle fuels, business and occupation, excise, public utility, alcoholic beverage, food and restaurant, tobacco, inheritance, estate; excluded revenue shall mean federal grants and revenue sharing, proceeds from bond issues, earnings on investments, tuition, fees, service

charges and other departmental revenues, and employment trust fund income.

(5) "Internal Borrowing," the procedures whereby State funds borrow from other State funds on a temporary basis to meet a cash-flow deficiency.

(6) "Federal Emergency Funds," are funds available through Federal programs such as Public Law 91.606 The National Disaster Assistance Act.

(7) "Local Property Tax Relief," are funds raised by the State for this purpose to be distributed to the cities and towns according to an equitable schedule within 120 days of the end of the fiscal year in which raised to be utilized by the cities and towns to proportionately reduce property taxes.

THE TENNESSEE TAX–LIMITATION AMENDMENT

Section 24. Appropriation of public moneys.—No public money shall be expended except pursuant to appropriations made by law. Expenditures for any fiscal year shall not exceed the state's revenues and reserves, including the proceeds of any debt obligation, for that year. No debt obligation, except as shall be repaid within the fiscal year of issuance, shall be authorized for the current operation of any state service or program, nor shall the proceeds of any debt obligation be expended for a purpose other than that for which it was authorized.

In no year shall the rate of growth of appropriations from state tax revenues exceed the estimated rate of growth of the state's economy as determined by law. No appropriation in excess of this limitation shall be made unless the General Assembly shall, by law containing no other subject matter, set forth the dollar amount and the rate by which the limit will be exceeded.

Any law requiring the expenditure of state funds shall be null and void unless, during the session in which the act receives final passage, an appropriation is made for the estimated first year's funding.

No law of general application shall impose increased expenditure requirements on cities or counties unless the General Assembly shall provide that the state share in the cost.

An accurate financial statement of the state's fiscal condition shall be published annually.

NEBRASKA'S TAX–LIMITATION AMENDMENT

Initiative Petition

The object of this petition is to submit to the legal voters of the State of Nebraska, at the General Election to be held on November 7, 1978, a proposed amendment to the Constitution of the State of Nebraska relating to budgets of political subdivisions of the State of Nebraska authorized to levy a tax or cause a tax to be levied, providing in substance that the budgets of such political subdivisions shall not be increased in excess of 5% of the actual amount budgeted for the previous fiscal year, unless the question of the increase is first submitted to an election at which a majority of the qualified voters voting at such election approve the increase, unless the Legislature, by a four-fifths vote, allows a greater increase, or unless a population growth in excess of 5% is experienced.

The legal effect of the filing of this petition will be to invoke the power of initiative (whereby the Constitution of the State of Nebraska may be amended by the electors as provided in Article III, Section 2 of the Constitution of the State of Nebraska) to make this proposal a part of the Constitution of the State of Nebraska. To the Honorable Allen J. Beermann, Secretary of State for the State of Nebraska:

We, the undersigned legal voters of the State of Nebraska, and the county of   being severally qualified to sign this petition, respectfully demand that the following proposed amendment to the Constitution shall be submitted to the voters of the State of Nebraska for their approval or rejection at the general election to be held on the 7th day of November, 1978, and each for himself say: I have personally signed this petition on the date opposite my name; I am a legal voter of the State of Nebraska and of the county of   , and am qualified to sign this petition; my street and street number or voting precinct, and my city, village or post-office address, are correctly written after my name.

Proposed amendment to the Constitution of the State of Nebraska: BE IT ENACTED BY THE PEOPLE OF THE STATE OF NEBRASKA:

That Article VIII of the Constitution of the State of Nebraska be amended by adding six new sections, to be numbered 12, 13, 14, 15, 16 and 17, as follows:

Section 12. Every political subdivision of the state authorized to levy a tax or cause a tax to be levied shall limit its budget for the 1979–80 fiscal year to an amount not to exceed five percent more than its budget for the 1978–79 fiscal year, except as provided in Sections 13 through 16 of this Article; and for each fiscal year after the 1979–80 fiscal year, its budget shall not exceed the previous fiscal year's budget by more than five percent, except as provided in Sections 13 through 16 of this Article. Budget shall mean and include all funds except such funds as are used for employer's contributions under the Federal Insurance Contributions Act and as are used to pay interest on or for retiring, refinancing, or servicing bonded indebtedness during the upcoming fiscal year, and amounts referred to in Section 16 of this Article. No tax shall be levied or an amount budgeted in excess of the limitation contained in this section for the purpose of acquiring buildings, the erection of buildings, and additions to buildings without a majority vote of the qualified electors voting in any such election, which election shall be conducted as the Legislature shall provide by general law; provided, no such election shall be required as to any buildings acquired, erected or added to under the Provisions of Article XIII, Section 2 of this Constitution.

Section 13. Any political subdivision of the state authorized to levy a tax or cause a tax to be levied which experiences a growth in population in excess of five percent during the calendar year per annual official estimates made as the Legislature shall provide by general law, may increase its budget for the fiscal year which follows by the same percentage increase as the percentage increase in the population growth, up to a population growth of ten percent; and for each percent of population growth in excess of ten percent may increase its budget one-half of one percent for each percent of increase in population growth in excess of ten percent. Common school districts' populations shall be measured by student enrollments.

Section 14. Each year, the Legislature may by resolution suspend, by a four-fifths vote, the budget limitations provided for in Sections 12 and 13 of this Article. In the resolution to suspend the Legislature shall set forth (1) the reasons for the suspension, (2) the political subdivisions affected by the suspension, and (3) the allowed increase in excess of the limitations for the upcoming fiscal year provided for in Sections 12 and 13 of this Article; Provided, any political subdivisions affected under such suspension may include the allowed increase in their budget for the fiscal year following such year of suspension. No resolution suspending budget limitations shall be effective for more than one fiscal year.

Section 15. If the governing body of any political subdivision of the state authorized to levy a tax or cause a tax to be levied determines that a budget higher than that permitted in Section 12, Section 13 or Section 14 of this Article is needed, it shall by resolution call for a special election of such political subdivision for that purpose. The budget increase above the limit permitted in Section 12, Section 13 or Section 14 of this Article may be adopted if approved by a majority of the qualified electors voting in such election. The resolution calling for the election, the election notice, and the proposition appearing in the election ballot shall refer to Section 12, Section 13 or Section 14 of this Article, and shall state that the limitation contained therein is proposed to be exceeded and show the proposed increase in the budget amount in terms of dollars and percentages over the limitation as computed in Section 12, Section 13 or Section 14 of this Article, and in terms of dollars and the percent of increase over the current budget. All such elections shall be held on the third Tuesday in July of the year in which taxes will be levied to fund the budget. The form of submission upon the ballot shall be as follows:

FOR exceeding the constitutional budget limit.

AGAINST exceeding the constitutional budget limit.

Section 16. To the extent any budget category or revenue source is increased as the result of a decision based upon the provisions of the Constitution of the United States, by a court of competent jurisdiction, the amount of the increase in the budget limit or revenue source for that category shall not be considered a part of the budget for purposes of Section 12, Section 13 or Section 14 of this Article.

Section 17. The provisions of Sections 12 through 16 of this Article shall be self-executing, but the Legislature may enact legislation to facilitate their operation.

FLORIDA'S GREENE AMENDMENT

The Greene Amendment

The Greene Amendment would put a provision in Florida's Constitution which would limit further increases in state spending, allowing additions to our budget each year only insofar as they reflect actual population growth and the actual effect of inflation.

The actual technical language of the Greene Amendment would be: "There is added to Article VII, Section 1, a new subsection (e), to read:

The Governor shall not propose, nor shall the Legislature enact, an appropriation act for any year, in which the total amount appropriated from general revenue, trust fund and working capital sources under such act, per capita and in constant dollars, exceeds the per capita amount of such funds under the previous year's appropriations act. The maximum dollar amount of any such appropriation shall, therefore, be calculated by multiplying the total dollar amount for the prior year by the quotient which results from dividing the population of the state at the beginning of the current year, as estimated by the United States Bureau of the Census, by such population at the beginning of the prior year, and by further multiplying that product by the quotient which results from dividing the United States Department of Labor Cost-of-Living Index amount for the beginning of the current year by such amount for the beginning of the prior year. However, upon determination by the Legislature that a specific emergency exists requiring the expenditure of additional state funds, an appropriation in excess of such maximum dollar amount may be made, but only with the approval of three-fourths of the members of the House and three-fourths of the members of the Senate.

This petition form issued by the Committee for the Greene Amendment (with the assistance of *VOICE*—Voters Organizations for Intelligent Control of Expenditures), Wilbur Canning, Treasurer, 490 First Ave. So., St. Petersburg, Florida 33701, a committee of Florida citizens duly registered with the Office of the Secretary of State, Tallahassee, Florida.

THE ARIZONA TAX–LIMITATION AMENDMENT

A Concurrent Resolution

Proposing an amendment to the constitution of Arizona relating to public debt, revenue and taxation; limiting state appropriations to a percentage of state personal income; providing for the establishment of an economic estimates commission; prescribing powers and duties; providing for adjustments, and amending Article IX, Constitution of Arizona, by adding Section 17.
Be it resolved by the Senate of the State of Arizona, the House of Representatives concurring:

1. The following amendment to the Constitution of Arizona, by adding article IX, section 17, is proposed, to become valid when approved by a majority of the qualified electors voting thereon and upon proclamation of the governor:

17. *Economic estimates commission; appropriation limitation; powers and duties of commission*

Section 17. The Economic Estimates Commission shall be established by law, with a membership of not to exceed three members, and shall determine and publish prior to February 1 of each year the estimated total personal income for the following fiscal year. By April 1 of each year the commission shall determine and publish a final estimate of the total personal income for the following fiscal year, which estimate shall be used in computing the appropriations limit for the legislature. For the purposes of this section, "total personal income" means the dollar amount that will be reported as total income by persons for the State of Arizona by the U.S. Department of Commerce or its successor agency. For purposes of this section, "state tax revenues" shall be defined by law.

The legislature shall not, by appropriation for any fiscal year, cause the expenditure of state tax revenues for that fiscal year to exceed seven per cent of the total personal income of the state for such fiscal year as determined by the economic estimates commission, except upon affirmative vote on each such appropriation of two-thirds of the membership of each house of the legislature.

In order to permit the transference of governmental functions between the federal and state governments and between the state govenrment and its political subdivisions without abridging the purpose of this section to limit state spending to a percentage of total personal income, the legislature shall provide for adjustments by the Economic

Estimates Commission of the appropriation percentage limitation of total personal income consistent with the following principles:

1. If, by order of any court or by legislative enactment, the costs of a program are transferred from a political subdivision of this state to the state, the appropriation percentage limitation may be commensurately increased provided the tax revenues of the affected political subdivisions are commensurately decreased.

2. If, by order of any court or by legislative enactment, the costs of a program are transferred from the state to a political subdivision of this state, the appropriation percentage limitation shall be commensurately decreased, and the tax rates of the political subdivision may be commensurately increased.

3. If federal taxes are reduced on condition that the state increase expenditures by an amount equivalent to the federal reduction, the appropriation percentage limitation may be increased by such amount.

4. If the costs of a program are transferred from the state to the federal government, the appropriation percentage limitation shall be commensurately decreased.

5. The adjustment provided for in this section shall be made in the first fiscal year of transfer or operation. Such adjustment shall remain in effect for each subsequent fiscal year.

2. The proposed amendment (approved by a majority of the members elected to each house of the legislature, and entered upon the respective journals thereof, together with the ayes and nays thereon) shall be by the secretary of state submitted to the qualified electors at the next regular general election (or at a special election called for that purpose), as provided by article XXI, Constitution of Arizona.

ARIZONA'S SALES TAX–REMOVAL AMENDMENT

Article 1. We, the undersigned, citizens and qualified electors of the state of Arizona, respectfully demand that the following proposed amendments to Title 42, chapter 8, Arizona Revised Statutes, shall be submitted to the qualified electors of the state of Arizona for their approval or rejection at the next regular general election and each for himself says:

I have personally signed this petition with my first and last names. I have not signed any other petition for the same measure. I am a qualified elector of the state of Arizona, county of

A full and correct copy of the title and text of the amendments to Title 42, chapter 8, article 1, Arizona Revised Statutes, so proposed to be initiated, is as follows:

An initiative measure relating to taxationG proscribing levy of transaction privilege tax on food or food products: defining food or food products, and amending Title 42, chapter 8, article 1, Arizona Revised Statutes, by adding section 42-1312.02.

Be it enacted by the people of the state of Arizona:

Section 1. Title 42, chapter 8, article 1, Arizona Revised Statutes, is amended by adding section 42-1312.02, to read: 42-1312.02. *Transaction privilege tax on food; prohibition; definition*

A. Notwithstanding any provision of law to the contrary, transaction privilege taxes shall not be levied on food or food products for human consumption by this state nor by any political subdivision, except as provided in section 42-1313.

B. Food and food products include cereal and cereal products, milk and milk products, meat and meat products, fish and fish products, vegetables and vegetable products, fruit and fruit products, margarine, cooking oils and fats, spices, salt and salt substitutes, sugar and sugar products, including candy and confectionery and sugar substitutes, coffee and coffee substitutes, tea, cocoa and cocoa products, soft drinks, sodas and beverages. Food and food products do not include any spiritous liquor or wine, as defined in section 4-101.

MODEL TAX-LIMITATION AMENDMENT OF THE AMERICAN LEGISLATIVE EXCHANGE COUNCIL

To prevent taxes from increasing year after year, a state constitutional amendment has been suggested that would limit the total amount of taxes that can be imposed by the state. The tax revenue limit would be an appropriate percentage of total annual personal income in the state, and has ranged between 6 per cent and 14 per cent in those states where the amendment has been proposed.

The advantages of the suggested constitutional limitation on state taxation are (1) the state would have to encourage economic growth that increases personal income in the private sector in order to increase its own revenue for government programs; (2) state agencies would be forced to compete for state funding and demonstrate that they need the funds they receive; and (3) the legislature would be forced to review all existing government programs each year before approving new programs.

The suggested constitutional limitation on state taxation would prohibit the state from forcing municipalities to pay for certain state-mandated programs. It would further assure that any state revenue surplus is returned to taxpayers through tax refunds.

Suggested Legislation (Title, etc.)

Section 1. [*Text of proposed amendment.*] Be it resolved by the Legislature of the State of [name of state], two-thirds of the members of each house concurring, that there shall be submitted to the electors of the State of [name of state], for their approval or rejection in the manner provided by law, a proposal to amend Article [cite appropriate number] of the Constitution of the State of [name of state] by adding thereto a new section to read as follows:

§ [cite appropriate number] *Limitations on state taxation; prohibition against mandating local programs without state funding*

A. The levy of a new tax, an increase in an existing tax, or a repeal of an existing tax exemption shall require the enactment of a law by two-thirds of the elected members of each house of the legislature. No amendment to any such measure by one house shall be concurred in by the other, and no conference committee report shall be concurred in by either house except by the same vote required for final passage of the bill. The vote thereon shall be by record vote.

B. A state tax revenue limit shall serve as a check on uncontrolled increases in state tax revenues. The state tax revenue limit for any fiscal year shall be [cite appropriate percentage] of state personal income. State personal income is the dollar amount that is reported by the United States Department of Commerce or its successor agency as total income by persons in the State of [name of state] for the calendar year in which the fiscal year commences. State tax revenues include sales, severance, income, gift, inheritance, excise, property, license, corporation, and all other taxes collected by the state during the fiscal year. State revenues collected in excess of the state tax revenue limit and all interest thereon shall be placed in a tax surplus fund in the state treasury which shall be used only for annual income tax [or other appropriate tax] refunds as provided by law.

C. No law requiring increased expenditures for wages, hours, working conditions, pension and retirement benefits, vacation, or sick leave benefits of political subdivision employees shall become effective until approved by ordinance enacted by the governing authority of the affected political subdivision or until the legislature appropriates funds for the purpose to the affected political subdivision and only to the extent and amount that such funds are provided.

Section 2. [*Date of election.*] This proposed amendment shall be submitted to the electors of the State of [name of state] at the next general election on [a certain date].

Section 3. [*Text of official ballot.*] On the official ballot to be used at said election, there shall be printed the following description of the proposed amendment:

FOR the proposed amendment to Article [cite appropriate number] of the Constitution of the State of [name of state] to add a new Section [cite appropriate number] to limit the state's taxing authority by requiring a two-thirds vote of the legislature to raise taxes, to establish a state tax revenue limit, and to prevent the imposition of costs on local government.

AGAINST the proposed amendment to Article [cite appropriate number] of the Constitution of the State of [name of state] to add a new Section [cite appropriate number] to limit the state's taxing authority by requiring a two-thirds vote of the legislature to raise taxes, to establish a state tax revenue limit, and to prevent the imposition of costs on local government.

Section 4. [*Procedure for voting.*] Each elector voting on this proposition for amending the Constitution shall indicate his vote relative thereto in the manner provided by the election laws of the State of [name of state].

MODEL STATUTES CIRCULATED
BY ALEC

1. CONTROLLING THE SIZE OF THE BUREAUCRACY

Section 1. [*Short title.*] This act may be cited as the Zero Government Growth Act.

Section 2. [*Statement of purpose.*] The purpose of this act is to enact procedures which will control the level of state employment and, when appropriate, lead to an orderly reduction, through attrition, in the number of state employees without a reduction of state services and without endangering the public safety and welfare.

Section 3. [*Definitions.*] For the purpose of this act, the term—

(1) "Executive branch" means all departments, boards, commissions, agencies and other entities declared by the constitution or by law to constitute a part of the executive branch and all such entities, other than local political subdivisions and district offices, declared by the constitution or by law not to be within the legislative or judicial branches of government.

(2) "Legislative branch" means the Senate and House of Representatives, their officers and committees, and all legislative agencies headed by an officer or employee selected by the legislature or a legislative committee including, without limitation, the Legislative Council, the legislative auditor, and the legislative fiscal officer.

(3) "Judicial branch" means the courts created or recognized by the constitution, or created by the legislature pursuant thereto, the Judiciary Commission, and all agencies, boards and commissions or other entities created by the courts.

(4) "Reporting agencies" means the Civil Service Commission, the commissioner of administration and the Legislative Fiscal Office.

(5) "Position of new employment" means any position of employment which has been authorized, for which a budget has been approved and for which an appropriation has been made or a transfer of funds effected pursuant to law, but which position has never been filled or occupied by the employment of any person.

(6) "Vacancy" means any position of employment which has been authorized, for which a budget has been approved and for which an appropriation has been made or a transfer of funds effected pursuant to law, and which position has previously been occupied but, due to termination of employment, is unoccupied.

Section 4. [*Prohibition against filling of vacancies or positions of new employment.*] No vacancy in any position of permanent employment shall be filled, nor shall a new position of permanent employment be created or filled, within the executive or legislative branches of state government except in the manner authorized by this act or pursuant to the exceptions contained herein.

Section 5. [*Executive branch; filling of vacancies or positions of new employment.*]

A. No vacancy in any position of permanent employment shall be filled, nor shall a new position of permanent employment be created or filled, within the executive branch without the express written approval of the governor or his designated representative. Each secretary or other head of any department, board, commission, agency, office or other entity shall file a written request with the governor for permission to fill a vacancy, to create a new position of employment or to fill the same and such request shall include a justification for the filling or creation of such position. The governor may, by executive order, provide additional procedures for the filing of written requests, including the promulgation of standard forms.

B. The following exceptions shall apply to this section:

(1) Vacant or new positions of employment among faculty members at all state colleges and universities.

(2) Vacant positions which must be filled in order to prevent an emergency directly affecting the public safety or welfare or necessary to be filled to prevent a serious disruption of public services. Notice of such appointment shall be made within ten calendar days to the governor. No appointment under this provision shall extend for longer than thirty calendar days, nor shall a further appointment be made thereto, without the express approval of the governor given in accordance with the procedures established by Subsection A hereof.

(3) Vacancies or new positions specifically mandated by or effected to accommodate any court order. However, notification of appointment made under this provision shall be given to the governor within ten calendar days of such employment, and the governor may rescind such employment by written order.

(4) Transfers, promotions and reallocations within a department or agency and between departments or agencies, which will not increase the aggregate number of employees within the department or agency after the action has occurred. Notice of such transfers, promotions and reallocations shall be given to the governor within ten calendar days of such action, and the governor may rescind such employment by written order.

C. Each secretary or other head of any department, board, commission, agency or other entity shall, not later than the tenth calendar day of each calendar quarter, file with the governor a statement for the previous quarter which shall specify employment figures by job classification at the beginning and the end of the quarter, and shall indicate the number of vacancies filled or positions created within the quarter and indicate the authority under which such positions were filled. The report shall specify with particularity the number and nature of all positions remaining unfilled at the end of the quarter, whether new positions or vacancies, and shall otherwise reflect a full accounting of all personnel changes within the department or other agency, including transfers, promotions and reallocations, within the quarter. The first quarter shall commence July 1, 1978 and end September 31, 1978.

D. No secretary or other agency head shall obtain from the Department of Civil Service applicant lists with which to fill vacant or new positions until approval for the filling thereof shall have been given in accordance with the provisions of Subsection A hereof.

E. All requests to fill vacancies; requests to create and fill new positions; notices of emergency appointments; notices of appointment and creation of new positions pursuant to court order; notices of transfers, promotions and reallocations; approvals, rejections or orders rescinding appointment by the governor and quarterly reports shall be sent to the reporting agencies simultaneously with the original transmittal and shall be public records.

Section 6. [*Legislative branch; filling of vacancies or positions of new employment.*] A. No vacancy in any position of permanent employment shall be filled, nor shall a new position of permanent employment be created or filled within the legislative branch without the express written approval of the Budgetary Control Council [or other appropriate agency]. Each head of any legislative office or agency shall file a written request with the Budgetary Control Council for permission to fill a vacancy, to create a new position of employment or to fill the same. Such request shall include justification for the filling or creation of such position. The Budgetary Control Council may, by rule, provide additional procedures for the filing of written requests, including the promulgation of standard forms.

B. The following exceptions shall apply to this section:

(1) Employment of personnel who are employed for the duration of legislative sessions only.

(2) Transfers, promotions and reallocations within an office or agency which will not increase the aggregate number of employees within the office or agency after the action has occurred. Notice of such transfers, promotions and reallocations shall be given to the Budgetary Control Council and the reporting agencies within ten calendar days of such action.

(3) The employment of legislative staff by individual members of the legislature.

C. Each head of any legislative office or agency, not later than the tench calendar day of each calendar quarter, shall file with the Budgetary Control Council a statement for the previous quarter which shall specify employment figures by job classification at the beginning and the end of the quarter, and shall indicate the number of vacancies filled or positions created within the quarter and indicate the authority under which such positions were filled. The report shall specify with particularity the number and nature of all positions remaining unfilled at the end of the quarter, whether new positions or vacancies, and shall otherwise reflect a full accounting of all personnel changes within the office or agency, including transfers, promotions and reallocations, within the quarter. The first quarter shall commence July 1, 1978 and end September 31, 1978.

D. All requests to fill vacancies; requests to create and fill new positions; notices of transfers, promotions and reallocations; approvals and rejections by the Budgetary Control Council; and quarterly reports shall be sent to the reporting agencies simultaneously with the original transmittal and they shall be public records.

Section 7. [*Severability clause.*]

Section 8. [*Repealer clause.*]

Section 9. [*Effective date.*]

2. CONTROLLING THE SIZE OF STATE DEBT

Public Debt Limitation—State Constitutional Amendment

The growing cost of state government has caused legislators in many states to propose both constitutional and statutory changes to control state spending and to prohibit or limit state debt.

The suggested State Constitutional Amendment on Public Debt Limitation brings together in a single proposal a wide variety of fiscal restraints which seem to work well in various states.

Section A prohibits state agencies from maintaining separate accounts outside the state treasury for their self-generated funds and requires that all funds belonging to the state immediately be transmitted to the state treasurer and deposited in the state treasury. Such requirements are essential to any comprehensive system of managing and investing state funds and are necessary if the legislature is to oversee the spending of all state funds.

Section B prohibits the appropriation of funds from the state treasury except for a specific purpose. This is intended to prevent a state agency or public official from establishing a "slush fund" made up of moneys not dedicated statutorily for any particular purpose.

Section B also limits the duration of appropriations to one year so that a state agency may not carry over surplus funds from year to year. This requirement mandates the return of all surplus revenues to the state treasury at the end of the fiscal year and allows the legislature to determine the actual financial status of the state on an annual basis.

Section C prohibits the appropriation of money from the state treasury by order of the governor, a state agency or a legislative committee and provides that appropriations must be made by passage of a bill through the legislature. It also requires that appropriation bills, concurrence in amendments thereto, and conference committee reports on appropriation bills all be approved by a majority vote of the *total membership* of each house, rather than merely a majority of those *present and voting*. Some states require a majority vote of the elected members in both houses to pass appropriations bills initially but allow concurrence in amendments and adoption of conference committee reports by a majority of those present and voting. In such states, it is not uncommon for proposed amendments or conference committee reports to increase the size of appropriations substantially, since the vote required to pass amendments and reports is *less* than that required for passage of an original appropriation bill.

Section E provides that appropriation bills must be itemized, and Section F makes it clear that the governor may veto individual line items in an appropriation bill. Normally, the chief executive may veto entire bills but not portions of them.

The suggested State Constitutional Amendment on Public Debt Limitation provides three safeguards to insure a balanced state budget: 1) Section D forbids the legislature from passing appropriations which exceed anticipated state revenues for the year, 2) Section G requires the governor, under penalty of impeachment, to veto line items in appropriation bills, and 3) Section I prohibits the incurring of debt to pay state obligations if expenditures actually exceeded income.

Although Section I is recommended, legislators in states where public debt is permitted may find alternative Section I and the remaining alternative sections more applicable. These alternate provisions permit the incurring of public debt subject to numerous limitations.

Under alternate Section I, state debt may be incurred only with a two-thirds vote of the elected members of the legislature and then only for the specific purposes enumerated in Section J. The most important of these permitted purposes is for capital improvements.

However, Section K prohibits the incurring of debt even for capital improvements unless the improvements are included in the comprehensive capital outlay budget which may be adopted by the legislature. The purpose of requiring the inclusion of all proposed capital improvements in such a budget is to prevent the legislature from authorizing long-term public debt without proper planning and study or without considering the importance of the capital improvements in question in relation to the other capital needs of the state.

Over the years, numerous states have permitted the issuance of so-called "revenue" bonds which depend on some specific source of revenue, other than the state general fund, for their repayment. Frequently, these bonds have been authorized by the legislature with little debate an dissued without appropriate oversight. Yet, in cases where the expected revenue source has proven insufficient, legislatures have frequently turned to state general funds to meet the obligation, so as not to impair the credit of the state. The result is that revenue bonds have become, in effect, full faith and credit bonds which pay investors relatively high rates of interest.

In order to end this practice, Section L, in effect, prohibits the issuance of revenue bonds. The result would be that in theory, as well as in practice, all bonds would be full faith and credit bonds and would, hopefully, be treated by the legislature with appropriate seriousness.

Section L also eliminates the temptation of state legislatures to pay the debts of political subdivisions, as occurred in the case of New York City, by prohibiting this practice altogether.

Section M establishes a State Bond Commission with responsibility for approving all bonds of the state and political subdivisions prior to their issuance. This commission is designed to control the overall debt policy of the state and local governments and would have the power to limit the size and timing of bond issues so as to gain the best advantage in the bond markets.

In theory, there is virtually no limit to the number of worthwhile projects which can be constructed by state government. But, in fact, there is a very real limit which is exceeded when state taxes are so high and state credit so strained that further expenditures are demonstrably harmful. In order to prevent such an undesirable occurrence, Section N sets a permanent overall ceiling on the level of state debt. This ceiling is tied to a percentage of overall state revenues, excluding federal funds.

Obviously, bonds which have already been issued affect the amount of credit available to the state and the cost of such credit. But so do bonds which have been authorized and not yet issued. Some states have hundreds of millions of dollars in bond authorizations which have been "on the books" for years. Although many of these will never be issued, the mere possibility that they will can impair a state's financial standing.

In order to minimize this problem, Section O limits the duration of bond authorizations to three years. If the bond in question has not been issued in that period, a new act must be passed to re-authorize it.

Finally, Section P restricts the loan or donation of public funds, except for certain enumerated purposes.

As the problems of state governments multiply, the adoption of a comprehensive program of fiscal management can be a first step toward bringing state spending under control.

Suggested Legislation (Title, etc.)

Section 1. [*Text of proposed amendment.*] Be it resolved by the Legislature of the State of [name of state], two-thirds of the members of each house concurring, that there shall be submitted to the electors of the State of [name of state], for their approval or rejection in the manner provided by law, a proposal to amend Article [cite appropriate number] of the Constitution of the State of [name of state] by adding thereto a new section to read as follows:

§ [Cite appropriate number] *Prohibition of state debt; procedures*

A. Deposit in state treasury. All money received by the state or by any state board, agency or commission shall be deposited immediately upon receipt in the state treasury.

B. Expenditure by specific appropriation. No money shall be withdrawn from the state treasury except through a specific appropriation, and no appropriation shall be made under the heading of contingencies or for longer than one year.

C. Origin in House of Representatives. All appropriations shall originate in the form of a bill in the House of Representatives, but the Senate may propose amendments, as in other bills. No appropriation shall be passed in either house nor shall amendments be concurred in nor shall a conference committee report be adopted except by a favorable vote of a majority of the elected members of each house.

D. Balanced Budget. Total appropriations by the legislature shall not exceed anticipated state revenues for the fiscal year.

E. General Appropriations bill. The general appropriations bill shall be itemized and shall contain only appropriations for the ordinary operating expenses of government. All other bills for appropriating money shall be for a specific purpose and amount.

F. Item veto. The governor may veto any line item in an appropriation bill. Any item vetoed shall be void unless the veto is overriden as prescribed for the passage of a bill over a veto.

G. Reduction by veto. The governor shall veto line items or use means provided in an appropriation bill so that total appropriations for the year shall not exceed anticipated revenues for that year.

H. Grounds for impeachment. Failure of the governor to veto appropriation measures sufficient to insure that total appropriations for the year shall not exceed anticipated revenues for that year shall be grounds for impeachment.

I. Prohibition on incurring debt. The state shall have no power, directly or indirectly, or through any state board; agency, commission, officer, or otherwise, to incur public debt or issue or authorize the issuance of bonds. If any person attempts to incur public debt or issue or authorize the issuance of bonds on behalf of the state, such debt and bonds shall be void and have no effect. Any person who attempts to incur any debt or issue or authorize the issuance of bonds shall be subject to impeachment, if he holds any public office or employment.

Or, if it is felt the state should incur public debt, substitute a new Subsection I and the following:

I. Limitation on debt. The state shall have no power, directly or indirectly, or through any state board, agency, commission, officer, or otherwise, to incur debt or issue or authorize the issuance of bonds except by law enacted by two-thirds of the elected members of each house of the legislature.

J. Purposes of debt. The debt may be incurred or the bonds issued only if the funds are to be used to repel invasion; suppress insurrection; provide relief from natural catastrophies; refund outstanding indebtedness at the same or lower effective interest rate; or make capital improvements, but only in accordance with a comprehensive capital budget, which the legislature shall adopt.

K. Capital improvements. If the purpose is to make capital improvements, the nature and location and, if more than one project, the amount allocated to each and the order of priority shall be stated in the comprehensive capital outlay budget which the legislature shall adopt by bill each year by majority vote of the elected members of each house. No funds shall be expended on any project during a fiscal year unless the authorization for the project and the appropriation therefor have been included in the comprehensive capital outlay budget adopted by the legislature for that year.

L. Full faith and credit. The full faith and credit of the state shall be pledged to the repayment of all bonds or other evidences of indebtedness issued by the state directly or through any state board, agency or commission. No state funds shall ever be used, directly or indirectly, to repay any debt or bond authorized or issued by any political subdivision of the state or by any local public agency.

M. State Bond Commission. No bonds, notes, certificates, or other evidences of indebtedness or obligations of any manner shall be issued or sold by the state, directly or through any state board, agency, or commission, or by any political subdivision of the state, unless prior written approval of the State Bond Commission has been obtained in accordance with law. The State Bond Commission shall consist of the governor, or his designee, the secretary of state, the state treasurer, the chairman of the House Appropriations Committee, or its successor, and the chairman of the Senate Finance Committee, or its successor.

N. Ceiling on debt. The legislature shall not authorize the incurring of debt or the issuance of bonds if the amount of such debt and bonds, when combined with all debt and bonds outstanding exceeds twenty [or other appropriate percentage] per cent of the average annual revenues of the state for the last three fiscal years completed prior to such authorization. Revenues include the sum of all taxes, fees and royalties collected by the state during the fiscal year, as defined by law. It does not include federal funds or transfers between state agencies, boards or commissions. The state treasurer shall notify each member of the legislature of the current ceiling on debt at least thirty days prior to the beginning of each regular session of the legislature.

O. Duration of bond authorizations. The authority of the State Bond Commission to issue or sell bonds, notes, certificates, or other evidences of indebtedness or obligations of any manner shall terminate as to those not yet issued or sold within three years after the effective date of the act authorizing their issuance or sale.

P. Donation, loan or obligation of public credit. The funds, credit, property or things of value of the state or of any political subdivision shall not be donated, loaned or obligated to or for any person, association or corporation, public or private. However, this shall not prohibit (1) the use of public funds for programs for the aid and support of the needy, (2) contributions of public funds to pension and insurance programs for the benefit of public employees, or (3) the obligation of public funds, credit, property or things of value for public purposes with respect to the issuance of bonds or other evidences of indebtedness to meet public obligations as provided herein. Neither the state nor a political subdivision shall subscribe to or purchase the stock of a corporation or association or for any private enterprise.

Section 2. [*Date of election.*] This proposed amendment shall be submitted to the electors of the State of [name of state] at the next general election on [a certain date].

Section 3. [*Text of official ballot.*] On the official ballot to be used at said election, there shall be printed the following description of the proposed amendment:

FOR the proposed amendment to Article [cite appropriate number] of the Constitution of the State of [name of state] to add a new Section [cite appropriate number] to limit the state's authority to incur public debt.

AGAINST the proposed amendment to Article [cite appropriate number] of the Constitution of the State of [name of state] to add a new Section [cite appropriate number] to limit the state's authority to incur public debt.

Section 4. [*Procedure for voting.*] Each elector voting on this proposition for amending the Constitution shall indicate his vote relative thereto in the manner provided by the election laws of the State of [name of state].

3. ZERO-BASED BUDGET AND SUNSET ACT

The process recommended in the suggested Zero-Based Budget and Sunset Act has two principal elements. The first requires that all state government programs and all tax expenditures undergo a zero-base review by the appropriate legislative committees, with the assistance of executive branch departments or agencies and legislative support agencies, before they are re-authorized or re-enacted.

The second element requires that all authorizations of state programs and all tax expenditures terminate over a three-year period, unless they are re-enacted.

The zero-based budget element in the first part of the suggested act would also be phased in over a three-year period, with 10 per cent of all executive department agencies being phased in the first year after enactment.

The "sunset" element in the second part of the suggested act starts a review of all executive branch operations on an agency-by-agency basis, provides for termination of each statutory entity starting with one-fourth of all statutory entities in 1980 (or three years from the time that the bill is enacted), and establishes a procedure for immediately recreating all agencies and activities whose further existence is justified by the legislative review.

Zero-based budgeting is a successful management technique developed about eight years ago by Texas Instrumennts Inc., and carried from private industry to state government. It is a procedure for examining the entire budget, not just funds requested each year above the current level of spending.

Zero-based budgeting thus differs from traditional incremental budgeting, in which review is concentrated on proposed budget increases while the base is given little attention. The assumption underlying traditional incremental budgeting is that a program or activity deserves to be continued with the same or increased funding one year simply because it was funded the previous year.

The essence of zero-based review is the assumption that previous activities and expenditures of an agency should not be continued automatically—that all programs must be justified from a "zero-base" each time they are funded. It is that assumption that the suggested Zero-Based Budget and Sunset Act seeks to establish as the framework for the entire state appropriation process.

Suggested Legislation (Title, enacting clause, etc.)

Comment: Dates contemplate passage of this act during 1977. If passed in a subsequent year, the act should be amended to add one year to each date for the number of years after 1977 that the act is passed. The act also contemplates a fiscal year which begins on July 1.

Section 1. [*Short title.*] This act may be cited as the Zero-Based Budget and Sunset Act.

Part I. Zero-Based Budget

Section 2. [*Contents of executive budget.*] A. Beginning with the executive budget to be presented for the 1978–1979 fiscal year, as more specifically provided in Subsection C of this section, the executive budget shall present a complete financial plan for the ensuing year. It shall include:

(1) A budget message signed by the governor, providing a summary of his estimate of revenue, the names of the budget units for which a complete zero-based review was accomplished, the savings, reductions in personnel and consolidation of functions to be accomplished as a result of such review, and a statement of the new programs and functions he proposes for the ensuing year.

(2) For each budget unit, detailed statements identifying all substantial aspects of agency operations, priorities, and activities, to specifically include:

(a) a description of the objective or objectives of each program;

(b) a description of the activity or activities which are intended to accomplish each objective;

(c) indicators of quantity and quality of performance of these activities;

(d) a ranking of these activities by priority;

(e) the level of effort required to accomplish each activity in terms of funds and personnel; and

(f) a statement of the effect of funding each activity at seventy percent of its current level.

(3) A summary statement incorporating the information in Paragraph 2 above for the current and three prior fiscal years for each budget unit and detailed statements of the sources of funding for all fiscal years presented.

(4) A presentation of the actual measurements used to determine standards of performance and effectiveness of functions for each activity of each program of each budget unit for which an appropriation is made in the current year. An accompanying statement shall be provided demonstrating the validity of such measurements in assessing the performance and effectiveness of such activities.

(5) A statement for each activity which separately states the cost of administering each activity and the cost of providing the services or benefits of engaging in such activity. This shall be done for the request year only. For the current and prior years a comparison of the actual and estimated administrative costs shall be provided.

(6) A statement of the cash and accrued liabilities of the general fund and each special fund from which appropriations have been or are proposed to be made.

(7) A statement of the total authorized bonded debt of the state, the outstanding bonded indebtedness of the state and the annual cost of the debt service on such bonds.

B. Each budget unit shall receive a separate appropriation. The format of the general appropriations bill shall reflect the change to a zero-based budget format. The bill shall reflect separate expenditure categories for each budget unit.

C. In order to provide for the orderly implementation of zero-based budgeting in this state during the 1978–1979 fiscal year, ten per cent of the budget units included in the executive budget shall be prepared and submitted on a zero base as provided in this section. The executive budget office shall determine which agencies shall so prepare and submit their budget requests, and the executive budget shall present the budgets of such agencies on a zero base as provided herein. In selecting such agencies, the executive budget office shall include at least one agency in each of the following categories: 1) constitutional agencies; 2) agencies with multiple means of financing; and 3) agencies with a complex program structure. The executive budget for the 1978–1979 fiscal year shall be modified to reflect the changes to a zero-based budget to the extent provided in this subsection. For the 1979–1980 fiscal year the executive budget shall be prepared and submitted for at least fifty percent of the budget units in accordance with this section and format, and for all fiscal years thereafter the executive budget shall be prepared and submitted in accordance with the format outlined in this act.

D. The governor shall submit the executive budget to the Legislative Budget Committee and to each member of the legislature not later than the first day of March of each year.

Section 3. [*Forms for budget estimates.*] A. Beginning with the forms for budget estimates for the budget for the 1978–1979 fiscal year, the executive budget office shall prescribe the forms to be used by each budget unit to present a zero-based budget. Prior to preparing and modifying such forms, the executive budget office shall consult with the chairman of the Legislative Budget Committee as to the format and contents of such forms and shall consider any suggstions of the committee relative thereto.

B. On or before the fifteenth day of October of each year the executive budget office shall transmit to each budget unit a complete set of forms to be used by the budget unit to present a zero-based budget. The executive budget office shall include instructions on the proper method of completing the forms and shall provide consultation as requested by any budget unit on the establishment of measurements used to determine standards of performance and effectiveness of functions for each agency activity.

C. In order to provide for the orderly implementatin of zero-based budgeting in [name of state], the forms for budget estimates for the budget for the 1978–1979 and 1979–1980 fiscal years for the agencies selected in accordance with Section 2(C), shall be preapred and submitted to such agencies as provided in this section and those for all other agencies shall be prepared and submitted as provided by [cite previous state law on budget formats].

Section 4. [*Budget statements; forms; time of submission.*] A. The head of each budget unit and of each spending agency of the state shall at a date set by the budget office, but not later than the fifteenth day of December in each year, submit to the governor estimates of the financial requirements and of the receipts of the budget unit for the year, on the forms and in the manner prescribed and accompanied by such other data as may be required, together with such additional information as the governor may request.

B. If any budget unit shall fail to submit its budget statement on or before the fifteenth day of December in any year, the commissioner of administration [or other appropriate executive branch officer] shall prepare a budget statement for the delinquent budget unit and in no instance shall the budget request included in such a budget statement prepared by the commissioner of administration [or other appropriate executive branch agency] exceed the amount of the appropriation of the said budget for the previous year.

C. Not later than the first of January of each year, the executive budget officer shall submit to the president of the Senate and the speaker of the House of Representatives a copy of the budget statement prepared by each budget unit. The presiding officers shall immediately refer the budget statement to the standing committees having jurisdiction over the respective budget units. The standing committees of each house to which the budget statements of a given budget unit are referred shall then meet jointly to review the proposed budget. Not later than the fifteenth day of February, the joint committee shall submit its recommendations to the Legislative Budget Committee.

D. The provisions of this sectin shall be applicable to all budget units in the state on the effective date of this act.

Section 5. [*Legislative oversight of implementation of zero-based budgeting.*] A. In order to provide for legislative oversight of the budget process and to assist the legislature in obtaining information necessary to the legislative appropriation process, the legislature hereby establishes procedures for legislative oversight of zero-based budgeting.

B. The Legislative Budget Committee shall be resonsible for ensuring implementation of zero-based budgeting by all budget units of the state. The committee shall review the proposals of the executive budget office and of the Division of Administration [or other appropriate executive branch agency] for implementing zero-based budgeting and shall hold hearings with budget units on the develoment and implementation of zero-based budgeting.

C. The executive budget office and the Division of Administration[or other appropriate executive branch agency] shall cooperate fully with the committee to assist it in carrying out the responsiblity imposed upon it by this section and shall provide the committee with such information as it may request concerning the development and implementation of zero-based budgeting.

D. In carrying out its responsibility for ensuring the implementation of zero-based budgeting, the committee shall utilize the legislative fiscal officer and the staff of the legislative fiscal office as the staff of the committee.

Part II. Sunset Rewiew and Termination of Agencies

Section 6. [*Definitions.*] For the purposes of this act,

(1) "Statutory entity" means any department, administrative office, agency, commission, board, or other instrumentality of state government created and continued in existence by statute or legislative resolution, whether or not funds are appropriated to it.

(2) "Applicable termination data" means the date provided for termination of legislative authority for the existence of a particular entity, as provided in Section 7 of this act.

(3) "Sunset review and evaluation" means with respect to a statutory entity, a comprehensive evaluation to determine if the merits of the activities of the entity support its continuation, based upon a a justification by that entity of its budget from a zero base.

Section 7. [*Termination of statutory entities.*] All legislative authority for the existence of any statutory entity shall cease as of the date indicated in the following table:

A. July 1, 1980:

(1) The Department of Commerce, as established by [cite appropriate statute].
(2) The State Board of Opticians, as established by [cite appropriate statute].

Comment: At this point approximately one-fourth of all statutory entities should be listed.

B. July 1, 1981:

(1) The State Fire Ant Control Board, as established by [cite appropriate statute].
(2) The State Television Repairmen's Licensing Board, as established by [cite appropriate statute].

Comment: At this point, list another one-fourth of all statutory entities.
C. July 1, 1982:

(1) The Department of Revenue and Taxation, as established by [cite appropriate statute].
(2) The Occupational Health and Safety Administration, as established by [cite appropriate statute].

Comment: At this point, list another one-fourth of all statutory entities.
D. July 1, 1983:

(1) The XYZ Lake Commission, as established by [cite appropriate statutes].
(2) The Sweet Potato Commission, as established by [cite appropriate statute].

Comment: At this point, list all remaining statutory entities and the general provision: "Any other statutory entity not previously terminated by this act."
E. The commissioner of administration [or other appropriate officer] shall by July 1, 1978, file with the legislature a complete list of all state governmental entities which are affected by this act.

Section 8. [*Re-creation of statutory entity.*] Any statutory entity to be terminated by the provisions of Section 7 may be re-created only in accordance with the procedure established in Section 9 of this act.

Section 9. [*Procedure for re-creation.*] The procedure for re-creation of any entity to be terminated under the provisions of this act shall be as follows:
A. Two years prior to the year in which the applicable termination date occurs, the standing committees having jurisdiction over the matter in accordance with the rules of the House of Representatives and of the Senate shall meet as a joint committee to conduct the sunset review and evaluation of the statutory entity to be terminated. This sunset review and evaluation shall have as its objectives:

(1) The elimination of inactive entities;
(2) The elimination of entities which duplicate other entities or other governmental programs and activities, or an appropriate consolidation of them; and
(3) The elimination of inefficient, ineffective, unnecessary, or undesirable entities.

B. Upon completion of the sunset review and evaluation, the reviewing committee shall submit a report of its findings to both houses of the legislature. Such report shall include, but not be limited to:

(1) An identification of other entities, or other programs or activities of state government having the same or similar objectives, along with a comparison of the cost and effectiveness of such entities, programs or activities and any duplication of the entity under review;
(2) An examination of the extent to which the objectives of the entity under review have been achieved when compared to the objectives initially set forth for the entity under review and an analysis of any significant variance between projected and actual performance; and

(3) A statement of the objectives of the entity for the coming four years with the establishment of measurements of performance where feasible.

C. In the regular legislative session in the year prior to the year in which the applicable termination date occurs, a bill authorizing the recreation of the entity in question may be introduced and shall be referred to the standing committees which composed the reviewing committee. Such bill shall contain a termination date for the entity which is being re-created, no more than four years from the effective date of its re-creation. No such bill may contain re-creation authority for more than one entity.

D. Upon receipt of the bill, the committees may conduct such further hearings to evaluate the entity in question as may be necessary.

E. In all hearings required by this act, the entity shall have the burden of proving a public need for its re-creation.

F. If the bill authorizing re-creation of the entity becomes law, the reviewing committee shall hold hearings to determine a recommended level of funding for the next fiscal year. Its recommendations shall be presented to the Legislative Budget Committee not later than the fifteenth day of February prior to the beginning of the next fiscal year.

G. If the bill authorizing re-creation of the entity does not become law, the statutes creating and continuing such entity shall be construed as repealed on the applicable termination date fixed in Section 7 of this act.

H. No funds shall be appropriated or otherwise be made available from any source whatsoever to any entity after the applicable termination date of such entity unless it has been re-created in accordance with the procedure set forth in this act.

Section 10. [*Re-creation not permitted.*] After the effective date of this act, neither the House of Representatives nor the Senate may consider for final passage any bill or resolution, or amendment thereto, which creates or re-creates any statutory entity unless the report required by Section 9 of this act has been submitted to the House of Representatives or the Senate, as the case may be.

Section 11. [*Continuation of claims and rights.*] Nothing in this act shall be construed to effect the termination or dismissal of any claim or right of a citizen against an entity terminated by its provisions, nor to effect the termination or dismissal of any claim or right of the entity. Such obligations, claims, and rights shall be assumed by the state.

Section 12. [*Earlier termination possible.*] Nothing in this act shall be construed to prohibit the legislature from terminating an entity covered by its provisions at a date earlier than that provided herein, nor to prohibit the legislature from considering any other legislation relative to such an entity.

Section 13. [*Retirement systems excluded.*] The provisions of this act do not apply to state retirement systems.

Section 14. [*Severability clause.*]

Section 15. [*Repealer clause.*]

Section 16. [*Effective date.*]

APPENDIX G

THE "MAGIC" PROP 13 MAILING PIECE

Text from the single mailing piece credited with putting "Prop 13" over the top. It is a mock property tax bill that, in the final weeks before the initiative, was mailed out to all property owners in the state. It was computer-generated from a master tape of all property owners in the state. In that way, it graphically set out for the property owner exactly how much he personally would save by voting in favor of the amendment. In addition, its appeal for funds brought in additional money that was badly needed for last-minute television spots.

Note the carefully worded mailing envelope. Simple—but designed to get the home-owner to open and read it.

The Despain Family
218 S. Garnsey Avenue
Bakersfield, California 93309

Dear Despain Family:

The average homeowner pays property taxes equal to 3% of the value of his or her property.

Proposition 13, the Jarvis-Gann Amendment would permanently reduce this unreasonable tax rate to 1% of the market value of your property.

Don't think that it will be easy to pass Proposition 13. Powerful public employee unions and other tax spending special interests plan to spend 3 million dollars on a sophisticated propaganda campaign to defeat Prop. 13.

To win, we taxpayers must spend at least ⅓ as much as our opponents. That's ONE MILLION DOLLARS. You can help by sending your maximum contribution to YES on 13.

If you want to reduce the tax on your home on Garnsey Avenue by ⅔rds, try to send $25 to YES on 13. I hope you are concerned enough to send $50, $100, $500 or even $1,000 if you can.

Believe me, this is our last chance to permanently reduce property taxes. Your maximum contribution to YES on 13 is needed today!

Sincerely,

Howard Jarvis, Chairman, YES on 13 Committee

P.S. The 1978 property tax bill at the bottom of the page is a reminder of the amount of money you will lose EACH YEAR if Proposition 13 is defeated.

If you don't care about property tax reform, keep the bill. If you want property tax reform, return it together with your maximum donation today.

YES ON 13 COMMITTEE
9454 WILSHIRE BLVD., SUITE 209 • BEVERLY HILLS CA 90212

Pay this amount in additional 1978 Property Taxes if Prop. 13 is defeated <u>$1,000*</u> Dollars

IMPORTANT
Political Contributions of $200 are tax de-
ductible on a joint return. $100 is deduct-
ible on a single return. All corporate, part-
nership and personal contributions are
acceptable.

( ) YES:
I want to reduce my annual property taxes
by as much as 67%. Enclosed is my maxi-
mum donation to YES on 13 of (circle one):
$1000 $500 $100 $50 $25 $_____

TAXPAYER:
RZ7486160
The Despain Family
218 S. Garnsey Avenue
Bakersfield, California 93309

SIGN HERE _____
*Based on average statewide tax on a home worth $50,000

On envelope:
Your 1978 Property
Tax Increase Statement
Enclosed
RESPONSE REQUIRED

A MAILING PIECE USED SUCCESSFULLY IN TENNESSEE

Text from a mailing piece sent out in Tennessee that is credited with gaining public support for the tax-limitation amendment as the state legislature was debating the measure.

YES, ONLY YOU CAN . . . LIMIT GOVERNMENT SPENDING

. . . ONLY YOUR DELEGATE TO THE 1977 CONSTITUTIONAL CONVENTION CAN LET YOU VOTE IN 1978 TO DO SO.

• In 15 years (1960–1975) Tennessee Personal Income grew 208%—but taxes increased 302%.

• In 1969 Tennessee's budget was less than 1 Billion dollars. . . . in May 1977 it increased to 2.8 Billion dollars.

• In 10 years the average tax bill rose 65%, but the Cost of Living increased by only 44%.

YES on 13 • HOWARD JARVIS, JR.
9454 WILSHIRE BLVD., SUITE 209
BEVERLY HILLS, CALIFORNIA 90212

STOP THE SPENDTHRIFT POLITICIANS

Every year the politicians promise property tax reform. This year they have failed to keep their promises once again. Instead of giving us property tax relief and reform, the politicians have increased California government spending to a total of 50 billion dollars a year.

Proposition 13 is the people's answer to the spendthrift politicians. It is your last chance for property tax reform.

Proposition 13 will reduce your property taxes by as much as 75% and force the politicians to cut bloated government budgets by at least 9%.

STOP THE SPECIAL INTERESTS

Powerful public employee unions and other tax spending special interests have declared total war on Proposition 13.

These greedy special interests have launched a massive scare campaign to make you believe that Proposition 13 would deprive you of vital government services or raise new taxes.

According to respected U.C.L.A. economist Dr. Neil Jacoby, and other tax experts, Proposition 13 will leave more than enough property tax revenue to pay for property related services such as police and fire protection without raising new taxes.

Reject special interest scare tactics. Support YES on 13, your last chance for property tax reform.

SUPPORT
Yes on 13

THE FACTS SAY . . . "YES on 13"

Proposition 13 will:
$ Reduce your yearly property tax to 1% of the value of your property (see chart).
$ Limit future assessment increases on your property to 2% per year.
$ Make rent reductions possible.
$ Reduce monthly mortgage impound tax payments for home buyers.
$ Require a ⅔ vote of the legislature to raise any other taxes.

Proposition 13 will not:
$ Reduce tax money for police, fire protection, schools or any vital services.
$ Raise sales taxes, income taxes, or any other taxes.
$ Tax business property at a lower rate than residential property.
$ Remove or reduce tax exemptions for churches and charities.
$ Affect veterans benefits or tax exemptions for senior citizens.

THE FIGURES SAY . . . "YES on 13"

If Your Home is worth	Your 1977 Property tax was	Proposition 13 will reduce your Taxes to	Each Year you will save
45,000	1,350	450	900
55,000	1,650	550	1,100
65,000	1,950	650	1,300
75,000	2,250	750	1,500
85,000	2,550	850	1,700
95,000	2,850	950	1,900
105,000	3,150	1,050	2,100
150,000	4,500	1,500	3,000

*Based on current average property taxes of 3% of market value. Tax rates in some counties are over 7%.

A SUCCESSFUL HANDOUT-MAILER USED IN MICHIGAN

Text from the key handout-mailer used in Michigan by Taxpayers United:

Q   What is meant by tax limitation?

A   By an amendment to the Michigan Constitution, a limit will be placed upon the ability of the legislature to increase state taxes beyond their current share of the Michigan economic pie. Future tax revenues would be tied directly to the total personal income of the people. As the economy expands and personal income grows, the legislature would have more money to work with, but state government could not enlarge its slice of the economic pie without voter approval.

Q   Why is tax limitation needed?

A   Government is out of control. The number of state government employees grew in the past ten years by 50.3 percent while the state population during the same ten years increased by only 6.7 percent. Most taxpayers have not received that kind of increased service, and have certainly not voted for it.

In the past ten years, state spending increased by 235 percent, almost double the growth in the overall personal income of the people of Michigan. For every dollar of your money that state spent in 1968, it is now spending $3.50.

Government is spending more and more, and the taxpayer is left with less and less. At the present time, the taxpayer has no direct control.

Q   What will be the main effect of tax limitationP

A   Tax limitation will stabilize the size of state government in relation to the overall state economy, permitting expansion only with the taxpayers' approval (expressed through their vote) or economic growth to pay for the expansion.

Q   Why shouldn't state government continue to increase its share of the economy?

A   The economic pie is only so big! To permit growth other than through an expanded economy places undue hardship on the individual taxpayer's family budget. The individual, after all, pays all the taxes. Businesses, utilities, banks and others who pay "business taxes" simply build those taxes into their prices and collect them from their customers, and pass the revenues on to the government. *Ultimately, the individual pays for everything.* Continuous enlargement of the government's share of personal income forces families to cut back further in their budgets for food, clothing, shelter, utilities, medical care, transportation and other personal spending (if any is possible). If the government keeps enlarging its share, it leaves the taxpayer less and less.

Q How would tax limitation stop continuous property tax increases?

A If your home has an assessed value of $20,000 and the voters have approved a tax levy of 30 mils, your property taxes are currently $600. If the assessed value of your home is raised to $30,000 (through state equalized valuation), raising your taxes to $900 (30 mils × $30,000) the approved tax millage would be *ROLLED BACK* to 20 mils, to yield the same $600 as before. A small additional millage is authorized to meet the costs of inflation as reflected by the consumer price index of the U.S. Department of Labor.

Q How would tax limitation work for you?

A By constitutional amendment, the legislature and the various local taxing bodies would be required to hold revenues to current levels, in relation to personal income, unless an emergency should arise requiring special consideration or the people themselves agree to an increase in the tax rates.

Q Is there any other way to keep your taxes from rising faster and faster?

A Apparently not. Legislators and governors have been promising for years to control taxes, yet taxes go up higher and higher. Many legislators have indicated that the tax limitation amendment would help them do their job better. It would require them to set priorities and would help them to resist demands for an endless list of new programs.

Q Would tax limitation strangle progressive government?

A No. Progressive government should mean efficiency, economy and establishing proper priorities. A limit on tax revenues will improve government by requiring careful study and evaluation of each proposed dollar of state spending.

Q How about emergencies? Legitimate new needs?

A It will provide for emergencies being met by establishing conditions when the limit may be exceeded. Should a *real* emergency arise which cannot be met with current revenues or rainy day funds, upon recommendation of the governor and approval of two-thirds of the legislature the limit may be exceeded for that fiscal year for the express purpose of the identified emergency.

Q Couldn't the state government just shift the tax burden to local government by requiring the local government to provide more services?

A No! The amendment provides that the proportion of state revenues paid to all units of local government and authorities created by the state, as a group, could not be reduced below that in effect at the present time. The amendment also prevents the state government from mandating new or expanded programs to local governments without providing state appropriations to completely finance those new or expanded programs.

Q Will tax limitation bring the same requirement for fiscal good housekeeping to local governments? Yes. It will require voter approval for any increase in local government taxes beyond currently authorized levels.

Q What if our local school district, local fire department, etc., needs more money to provide services we want?

A The amendment provides that local voters may approve any local tax they wish, however, local bodies of government could not increase taxes or levy any new taxes above currently authorized limits without voter approval.

Q Doesn't the constitution now provide for local tax limitation?

A Up to a point. There is one major loophole in the constitution. Local government may issue bonds *without a vote of the people* and then levy taxes (again without a vote) to pay off the bonds. This constitutional amendment closes that obvious loophole.

Q Will property tax credits for senior citizens or farmers be threatened if the tax limitation proposal passes?

A No. Tax credits such as these are specifically protected by this amendment.

Q What is Taxpayers United doing to bring about tax limitation in Michigan?

A Taxpayers United is staging a campaign to amend the Michigan Constitution, by obtaining 350,000 signatures of qualified voters to get the amendment on the November, 1978, ballot and then campaigning for its adoption.

Q Who is behind this drive for tax limitation?

A Retirees, housewives, farmers, factory workers, professionals, a broad spectrum of men and women. Many members of the Michigan Legislature endorse this campaign. Democrats, Republicans, and Independents support this effort.

Q Who is financing this campaign?

A Taxpayers United receives contributions from all walks of life, from just a few dollars to many hundreds of dollars. We are seeking 100,000 concerned taxpayers to contribute a minimum of $5 each. You can help! Send a check to **Taxpayers United for Tax Limitation.**

Q What can I do to help?

A Get involved, by signing or helping to circulate petitions in your neighborhood. Sign the tax limitation petition even if you already have signed other petitions associated with the November, 1978, election. Become familiar with the issues involved and let your friends and neighbors know what's really at stake: their right to have a strong voice in the setting of tax rates in Michigan. Above all, in November, vote YES to the tax limitation proposal.

Paid for by:
Taxpayers United for Tax Limitation
P.O. Box 5060
Southfield, MI 48037
Phone (313) 358-1978

Co-Chairpersons:
Jeffrey M. Leib, Thomas H. Ritter,
Mrs. Vickie St. Louis, Jay VanAndel;
Treasurer: James Barrett.

Sponsored by:
Taxpayers United, Inc.
Richard H. Headlee, Chairman
William Hanson, Executive Director

MILTON FRIEDMAN ON TAX LIMITATION

The Limitations of Tax Limitation
by Dr. Milton Friedman
Senior Research Fellow, Hoover Institution, Stanford University; Professor Emeritus, University of Chicago.
(This article appeared in the Summer 1978 issue of *Policy Review,* and is reprinted with the permission of the Heritage Foundation.)

Two down, 48 to go.

The approval on June 6, 1978, by the people of our largest state of Proposition 13 —a tax limitation amendment to the California Constitution—has given great impetus to the grassroot movement that Governor Ronald Reagan began in that state five years ago when he sponsored Proposition 1.[1]

The first victory for those who believe that government does not have an open-ended claim on the incomes of Americans came in Tennessee three months ago (March 7, 1978) when the people of that state, by a two-to-one majority, approved an amendment to limit the "rate of growth" of state spending to the "estimated rate of growth of the state's economy."

Similar amendments will be on the ballot in a number of other states this fall, and the prospects now look very good for their adoption.

The Jarvis-Gann amendment, Proposition 13, will limit property taxes in California to one percent of assessed valuation. It will restrict increases in assessed valuation to a maximum of 2 percent a year except when property changes hands. In addition, it will require a two-thirds vote of the legislature to raise other taxes. It is estimated that this amendment will cut property taxes by more than half—or by some $7 billion.

Jarvis-Gann, it must be said, has many defects. It is loosely drawn. It cuts only the property tax, which is by no means the worst tax. It does nothing to halt the unlegislated rise in taxes produced by inflation. Proposition 1 was a far better measure and a revised version will be needed even though Jarvis-Gann has passed. Yet

---

[1]That proposal was preferable to the one adopted yesterday. It would have limited spending by the state government to a specified and slowly declining fraction of the personal income of the people of California. That amendment was narrowly defeated, as were similar amendments in two other states in recent years.

I strongly supported Jarvis-Gann. It does cut taxes. It does raise obstacles to further increases in government spending. Those in favor of more government spending mounted an expensive fear campaign financed in large part by big business (which apparently allowed its own fear of the politicians in Sacramento to trigger its unerring instinct for self-destruction). In this media blitz, the state employees' union leaders (naturally the core of the opposition) predicted that state services would be drastically cut, that thousands of policemen and firemen would be dismissed, and so forth and so on.[2]

In fact Jarvis-Gann will not have the dire effects its opponents threatened. The California government has a surplus of some $3 billion to offset the $7 billion revenue reduction. The remaining $4 billion is roughly 10 percent of the state and local spending now projected for the next fiscal year. Is there a taxpayer in California (even if he is a government employee) who can maintain with a straight face that there is not 10 percent fat that can be cut from government spending without reducing essential services? Of course, the reallocation of revenues to finance the most essential services will not be an easy or pleasant task but that, after all, is just what we pay our elected representatives for.[3]

Which brings us to an important point of political philosophy. It is my view that it is desirable for the people to limit their government's budget, to decide how much in total they are willing to pay for their government. Having done this, it is desirable for them to delegate to their elected representatives the difficult task of dividing that budget among competing good proposals. The opponents of tax limitation laws charge that we are being undemocratic in proposing to tie the hands of government. After all, they say, don't we elect our state representatives and our congressional representatives in Washington to handle the affairs of government? I believe that if we are going to be effective in passing tax limitation laws, we must understand and make other people understand that these referenda are far from being undemocratic. I believe that the real situation is precisely the opposite.

The problem we face is that there is a fundamental defect in our political and constitutional structure. The fundamental defect is that we have no means whereby the public at large ever gets to vote on the total budget of the government.

Our system is one in which each particular spending measure is treated separately. For any single spending measure, therefore, there is always a small group that has a very strong interest in that measure. All of us are parts of such small groups. We are not talking about somebody else. As Pogo used to say, "We have met the enemy and they are us."

The vested interests are not some big bad people sitting on money bags; the vested interests are you and me. Each of us is strongly in favor of small measures that will

[2]In their column for *The Washington Post* on June 1, 1978, Rowland Evans and Robert Novak reported from Los Angeles that some politicians were claiming that the referendum was "a fight between the haves and the have-nots." Evans and Novak concluded that this view was "almost surely wrong." They explained that "On the contrary, the establishment—business, labor, the big newspapers, the academic community, civic groups and practically every important elected official —vigorously opposes the Jarvis amendment."

They went on to point out that "in contrast, the amendment's hardcore support comes from lower income homeowners who are going under because of oppressive taxes. Their ranks, oddly, are swelled by substantial numbers of school teachers and other government workers who are first and foremost taxpayers . . . State Senator Bill Greene, a black Los Angeles legislator, told us he is astounded how many of his constituents are voting for the measure."
[3]It is not without interest that California has the highest paid state legislators in the nation.

benefit us and each of us is not too strongly opposed to any one small measure that will benefit someone else. We are not going to vote anybody out of office because he imposes a $3 a year burden on us. Consequently, when each measure is considered separately, there is considerable pressure to pass it. The proposers have greater force than the opponents (who are often called "negative" or "obstructionists") and the total cost is never added up.

The purpose of tax limitation is to remedy that defect. It will enable us to say to the legislature, "We assign you a budget. Now it's your job to spend that in the most effective way." The effect of removing this defect is to enable special interests to work for the general interest instead of against it. This is because with a given total budget, a special group that wants a special measure has to point out the other budget items that can and should be reduced. Each item that people want is a good item. There is no pressure on Congress or on the legislature, or very little, to enact bad legislation. The problem is that there is an infinite number of good and desirable proposals and you have to have some device to limit the appetite and that's the function of tax limitation.

The next time somebody says that tax limitation is undemocratic, we should ask him whether that means he is against the First Amendment of the Constitution. Because, after all, the First Amendment of the Constitution limits very clearly what Congress can do. The First Amendment says Congress shall make no laws interfering with the freedom of speech or the free exercise of religion. Consider what would happen if we didn't have that amendment. For any single measure restricting freedom of speech you might very well obtain a majority. I am sure there would be a majority to prevent the Nazis from speaking on the street corner. There might be a majority to prevent the Seven Day Adventists or vegetarians from speaking—or any other little group you could name. But our Founding Fathers had the wisdom to roll it up into one and say we are not going to let each individual issue be decided separately by a majority vote. They said that we are going to adopt the general principle that it is not the federal government's business to restrict freedom of speech.[4] In the same way, what is being proposed today is the enactment of a principle that a government shall have a budget determined by the voters and that it will have to stay within that budget.

Right now total government spending—state, federal and local—amounts to 40 percent of the national income. That means that out of every dollar anybody makes or gets, forty cents is being spent for him by the bureaucrats whom he has, through his voting behavior, put into office. There is upward pressure on that percentage. The screws will be put on. The real problem for the future is to stop that growth in government spending. Those who are really concerned, who really are fiscal conservatives, should forget about the deficit and pay all their attention to total government spending. As we have seen, California and Tennessee have recently led the way toward the goal of a limit on government spending.

On the federal level, there have been moves to try to get a federal Constitutional amendment providing for a balanced budget. I think, however, that is a serious mistake. It spends the energies of the right people in the wrong direction. Almost all states have a balanced budget provision, but that hasn't kept spending and taxes from going up. What we need on the federal level, as we need it on the state and local level, is not a budget-balancing amendment, but an amendment *to limit gov-*

---

[4]It was left to the states to deal with such problems as an immediate danger of violence, and so on.

ernment spending as a fraction of income. Recently a task force of the Southern Governors' Conference, which was headed by Governor James Edwards of South Carolina, has worked extensively to produce a government spending limitation amendment for the federal government.

Congressman Jack Kemp has been pushing for several years now a so-called tax reduction bill (the Kemp-Roth Bill). I support this bill since I believe that any form of tax reduction under any circumstances must eventually bring pressure to bear to cut spending. Moreover, I believe some taxes do more harm than others. There is no doubt that the method by which we collect taxes could be rearranged so as to have a less adverse effect on incentives and production. And, from this point of view, the Kemp-Roth Bill is certainly desirable. We should be clear, however, that it is in reality not a tax reduction bill; it is a proposal to change the form of taxes. As long as high government spending remains, we shall have the hidden tax of inflation. The only true tax cutting proposal would be a proposal to cut government spending. To my knowledge, no one in Washington has yet proposed a genuine tax cutting bill, not President Carter, not the Democrats in Congress, not the Republicans. Every single so-called "tax cut plan" still envisions a higher level of government spending next year and consequently a higher level of taxes, both overt and covert.

There is an important point that needs to be stressed to those who regard themselves as fiscal conservatives. By concentrating on the wrong thing, the deficit, instead of the right thing, total government spending, fiscal conservatives have been the unwitting handmaidens of the big spenders. The typical historical process is that the spenders put through laws which increase government spending. A deficit emerges. The fiscal conservatives scratch their heads and say, "My God, that's terrible, we have got to do something about that deficit." So they cooperate with the big spenders in getting taxes imposed. As soon as the new taxes are imposed and passed, the big spenders are off again, and then there is another burst in government spending and another deficit.

The true cost of government to the public is not measured by explicit taxes but by government spending. If government spends $500 billion, and takes in through taxes $440 billion, which are the approximate figures of President Carter's estimated budget, who pays the difference? Not Santa Claus, but the U.S. citizen. The deficit must be financed by creating money or by borrowing from the public. If it's financed by printing money, that imposes the hidden tax of inflation in addition to the explicit tax. If it's financed by borrowing, then the government gets those resources instead of the private sector. In addition, there will have to be a higher level of taxes in the future to pay the interest or to pay back that debt. Essentially every current piece of wealth in the United States has a hidden tax imposed on it because of the future obligation to pay those extra taxes. In effect, what you have are two kinds of taxes: the open, explicit taxes and the hidden taxes. And what's called a deficit is a hidden tax.

I would far rather have total federal spending at $200 billion with a deficit of $100 billion than a balanced budget at $500 billion. The thing we must keep our eye on is what govenrment spends. That's the measure of the amount of the resources of the nation that people cannot individually and separately decide about. It's a measure of the amount we turn over to the bureaucrats to spend on our behalf. I believe along with Parkinson that government will spend whatever the tax system will raise plus a good deal more. Every step we take to strengthen the tax system, whether by getting people to accept payroll taxes they otherwise would not accept, or by cooperating in enacting higher income taxes and excise taxes or whatnot, fosters a higher level of government spending. That's why I am in favor of cutting taxes under any circumstances, for whatever excuse, for whatever reason.

We have to bear in mind that tax limitation laws are not cure-alls; they are temporary stop-gaps. They are a way of trying to hold back the tide, until public opinion moves in the direction that those of us who believe in limited govenrment hold to be desirable. Without the support of public opinion all the written laws or constitutions you can think of are fundamentally worthless. One has only to look at the results of trying to transplant versions of the American and British constitutions to other nations around the world. I believe, however, that there is a definite movement in public opinion toward greater skepticism of large-scale government programs. People are aware that they are not getting their money's worth through government spending. Among intellectuals, more and more scholars are coming to the conclusion that many government programs have not had the results intended by their supporters. In journals read by opinion-leaders (for instance, *Commentary, Encounter, Harper's, The Public Interest, The Washington Monthly*), this view is becoming more and more commonly expressed. However, it takes time for such ideas to be accepted by the politicians who, after all, are mostly followers and not leaders of public opinion.

Let me give an example of what I mean. For about 150 years since the birth of our government (until about the late 1920s) there was no general tendency for government spending to get out of hand. Despite the fact that the same pressures inherent in representative democracy were present through this period, state, local and federal spending was still about 10 percent of national income. For the past 40 years, however, there has been a considerable change in these percentages, to say the least. Except for the Income Tax Amendment, the Constitutional provisions relating to the financing of government were essentially the same as they were in 1789 (and the income tax rate was quite low during this period). The essential difference was that before 1930 or so there was a widespread belief on the part of the public that government should be limited and that danger arose from the growth of government. President Grover Cleveland maintained, for instance, that while the people should support their government, the government should not support the people. President Woodrow Wilson remarked that the history of liberalism was the history of restraints on government power. Almost everyone then agreed that the role of government was to act as a referee and umpire and not as a Big Brother. Once this fundamental attitude of the public changed, however, constitutional restrictions became very much less effective against the growth of government. As we all know, the Supreme Court does follow the election returns (sometimes tardily) and most of the New Deal measures which were ruled unconstitutional by the Court in President Roosevelt's first administration were ruled to be constitutional in the second administration.

The interstate commerce clause as an excuse for federal action is a good case in point. At one time in our history there were transactions which were regarded by the Court and Congress as *intrastate* commerce, but it would take a very ingenious man today to find any transaction whatsoever that the Supreme Court would not declare to be part of *interstate* commerce. The federal government, basically as a result of this change in public opinion, is now allowed to take all sorts of actions that would have been held *by the public* to be unconstitutional sixty or a hundred years ago.

In the same way, I believe that the effectiveness of tax limitation laws will depend upon their acceptance by the great bulk of the public as part of our constitutional tradition.[5] My own view is that we are seeing a genuine trend in support of the basic philosophy that there should be definite limits on government spending; however, I also believe that such trends take time to solidify and in the meantime I regard tax limitation amendments as a stop-gap measure to hold back the tide.

---

[5] In addition, they will not by themselves prevent all further government intervention. Many of the worst kinds of government intervention do not involve much spending. Some examples are tariffs, or regulation of industry (ICC, FCC, FPC) or the controls on the price of natural gas which have done such tremendous harm in the energy area. All of those involve government intervention into the economy in which the spending element is very small.